THE
FANTASY TRADITION
IN
AMERICAN LITERATURE

THE
FANTASY TRADITION
IN
AMERICAN LITERATURE

From Irving to Le Guin

BRIAN ATTEBERY

Indiana University Press
Bloomington

Manufactured in the United States of America

Library of Congress Cataloging in Publication Data

Attebery, Brian, 1951-
The fantasy tradition in American literature.

Bibliography: p.
1. Fantastic fiction, American—History and
criticism.   I. Title.
PS374.F27A86   813'.0876   80-7670
ISBN 0-253-35665-2   1 2 3 4 5 84 83 82 81 80

Contents

PREFACE

Fantasy in America, the country where pragmatism became a philosophy and "normalcy" a point of faith? Surely there is nothing so eccentric and impractical to be found here. One might as well try to study American opera. The English write fantasy; Americans write Westerns, detective stories, and lurid novels about Hollywood.

When I began this study, I expected to unearth a few isolated writers working against the mainstream of American literature. There was at least L. Frank Baum's Oz—perhaps enough other oddities could be found to make some point about the American imagination, on the rare occasions when it was really let loose. What I found, instead, is a tradition, although it is a tradition that runs counter to the main force of American belief as evidenced by the bulk of our folklore and literature up to the turn of the last century. One might think of it as a resistance movement, working to undermine the national faith in things-as-they-are. It even went underground, hiding out in the nursery and periodically venturing out disguised as romance or satire or science fiction.

One mark of a true tradition is that its authors are aware of one another. I found this to be true to a surprising degree in American fantasy. My authors read each other, lunched together, even illustrated one another's work. But perhaps I should not have been surprised. If stories of the marvelous are few, it is all the more likely that those with a taste for them will seek out every available example.

Another sign of a tradition is that by becoming aware of it, one's response to any of its members is enriched. One can see, for instance, that American fantasists share certain inescapable problems: in particular, a fundamental bias against fantasy in the folklore of this country. This bias leaves the fantasist cut off from the stock of magical images and events that abound in European tales and legends, from which the British fantasists have drawn so much of the raw material for their stories. The American writer must find some way of reentering the ancient storytelling guild: he must validate his claim to the archetypes that are the tools of the trade. To do so, he must find an archetypal analog for his own land—an American fairyland—to which those old world magical motifs may be drawn.

The American tradition of fantasy can be considered a long-range attempt at that one task: creating an American fairyland. The process has been a slow, fitful one involving repeated borrowings from other literatures, reconstructions of any supernatural lore that has survived in fragmentary or rationalized form, and eventually the elevation of wordplay and symbolism into mythlike narratives.

My approach to the study of fantasy is not a rigorously formalistic one. I have tried not to put myself in the position of dictating to authors long dead and then blaming them for not following instructions. Each work responds to a different blend of approaches: structural analysis, comparison of motifs, reference to social or biographical context, myth reading. As a general guide I have kept in mind the following question: How did the author move his story out of the everyday world into the realm of the marvelous?

Some of the books I discuss are widely read today; some had their moment of popularity and have since retired to special collections and used bookstores. A few have never been anything but obscure. For every book in the last category that I managed to locate, there are probably half a dozen I did not. I can only hope that the reader whose childhood favorite was missed will try out my methods and conclusions himself to see if they apply.

There are categories omitted intentionally. For example, fantastic themes play an important part in American painting from Benjamin West to Frank Frazetta, but neither the problems nor the techniques involved correspond closely to those of narrative. The independence of the two modes can be shown by considering the animated cartoons of Walt Disney—visually bold and evocative, but unoriginal and gimmicky in the stories they tell. For the same reason I have not attempted to deal with picture books for young children (though many of these, books by Wanda Gag, Theodore Seuss Geisel, or Maurice Sendak, are remarkable fusions of story and image) nor with live-action films like *I Married a Witch* or *Death Takes a Holiday*.

I do not talk about ghost stories, which are rather an important subgenre of supernatural narrative in America, because they never, so far as I can see, lead to any conception of an enchanted Other World. The typical ghost story becomes, instead, a study of guilt or repression on the part of the observer of the ghost: the apparitions themselves give no impression of having any independent existence. Neither do I attempt to explain those curious works which purport to give us a vision of the afterlife, the Atlantean past, or astral journeyings. These books rarely involve any interesting or comprehensible story line, and their claims to nonmetaphoric truth put them in the category of delusion or hoax, rather than fantasy. They could, however, provide a writer with the bare base for an interesting fantasy.

With these exceptions, I have tried at least to mention every American work or class of works to date that is devoted wholly or in major part to portraying the marvelous. This is a history of American Fantasy: it is arranged more or less chronologically, and the works are grouped to reveal what I believe are important trends. I have been greatly aided, in tracking down elusive works and in finding fruitful approaches to them, by Barton St. Armand and Robert Scholes. Bruce Rosenberg and my wife, Jennifer Eastman Attebery, helped keep my folklore scholarship honest. The staff at the John Hay Library of Brown University was helpful in locating volumes gathered by the late S. Foster Damon, many years curator of the Harris Collection of American Plays and Poetry. He once considered doing a study along these lines, and the collection of "American Tales of Imagination" that he bequeathed to the library has made my own project possible and suggested the title of this book.

THE
FANTASY TRADITION
IN
AMERICAN LITERATURE

ONE

Locating Fantasy

WHAT IS FANTASY? Is it a genre, a structure, a state of mind, a technique? How can the word be precisely and usefully defined without falling into the vague, the arbitrary, or the ponderous? Perhaps the most satisfying way would be to line up a shelf of books and say, "There. That is what I mean by fantasy." My own shelf would include Tolkien's *The Lord of the Rings*, Lewis' Narnia and Perelandra books, *The Wind in the Willows*, the Alice books, *The Princess and the Goblin* and all of George MacDonald's other magical stories, some of Saki's tales, *Titus Groane* and its successors, E. Nesbit's magic adventures, E. R. Eddison's private epics, and Lord Dunsany's wonder stories. I could name enough lesser works to fill several shelves more. With these works as a standard, we could go on and decide together whether or not to include Gothicism, the grotesque, existential absurdism, science fiction, utopia, and all sorts of writing that seem to share characteristics with fantasy. Sooner or later, though, we would have to decide just what characteristics were the essential, the defining ones.

W. R. Irwin has pointed out that the primary feature, without which a work simply cannot be fantasy, is "an overt violation of what is generally accepted as possibility."[1] He goes on to expand his description: "Whatever the material, extravagant or seemingly commonplace, a narrative is a fantasy if it presents the persuasive establishment and development of an impossibility, an arbitrary construct of the mind with all under the control of logic and rhetoric" (p. 9). Fantasy, then, presupposes a view of exterior reality which it goes on to contradict. It is, as J. R. R. Tolkien said, "founded upon the hard recognition that things are so in the world as it appears under the sun; on a recognition of fact but not a slavery to it."[2]

1

Any narrative which includes as a significant part of its make-up some violation of what the author clearly believes to be natural law—that is fantasy. There are various ways a story can proclaim its fantastic nature. It can involve beings whose existence we know to be impossible, like dragons, flying horses, or shape-shifting men. It can revolve around magical objects: rings, hats, or castles possessing wills, voices, mobility, and other attributes inanimate objects do not, in our experience, possess. It can proceed through events—two people painlessly exchanging heads, a tree reaching out to grab passers-by—that violate fundamental assumptions about matter and life. And fantasy treats these impossibilities without hesitation, without doubt, without any attempt to reconcile them with our intellectual understanding of the workings of the world or to make us believe that such things could under any circumstances come true.

By demanding a straightforward treatment of impossible characters, objects, or events, we can distinguish between fantasy and related genres. Science fiction spends much of its time convincing the reader that its seeming impossibilities are in fact explainable if we extrapolate from the world and the science that we know. Most escape fiction, as C. S. Lewis points out, utilizes unconvincing characters and unlikely events, but it makes every effort to place them in a mundane, nonfantastic world.[3] Lyric poetry often deals with impossibilities, but it generally does so not by asserting their existence in a fictional universe but by treating them as temporary manifestations of states of mind. Emily Dickinson speaks of a carriage ride with Death to a place beyond the sun, but she does not require us to start imagining the ground rules of a world where such a ride is possible. Unlike the fantasist she can, if she wishes, drop that image and propose another to further her theme. Narrative poetry often approaches the fantastic, but narrative verse seems to have been all but phased out by less restricted lyric forms. Surreal fiction has the same freedom: it can flash a succession of worlds before the reader or suddenly drop all pretense and begin speaking discursively. Fantasy, though, needs consistency. Reader and writer are committed to maintaining the illusion for the entire course of the fiction. Tolkien refers to this commitment as "secondary belief";[4] E. M. Forster speaks of the reader of fantasy as being asked to "pay something extra,"[5] to accept not only the conventions of fiction but also implausibilities within those conventions. Fantasy is a game of sorts, and it demands that one play whole-heartedly, accepting for the moment all rules and turns of the game. The reward for this extra payment is an occasional sense of unexpected beauty and strangeness, a quality which C. N. Manlove, among others, calls "wonder."[6]

I do not believe that it is useful to take the definition of fantasy any further than this. The single condition, that a story treat an impossibility as if it were true, marks off a large body of literature for us; we can then seek to determine the characteristics of that body as a whole and of the various subdivisions we may wish to make within it. Several lines of division suggest themselves: the preponderance of the marvelous within the story, the orientation of the tale toward wonder or its obverse, horror, the location of the supernatural in another world or in this, the presence of allegory and symbolism, the story's moral weight, and the types of supernatural machinery involved. The simpler the definition, the more room it leaves for subclassification and evaluation. Some critics have, I believe, limited their studies by over-exact definition, giving the name fantasy to what is only a minor subtype of fantasy. Tzvetan Todorov, for example, classes under the heading "the fantastic" only "that hesitation experienced by a person who knows only the laws of nature, confronting an apparently supernatural event."[7] His analysis is appropriate to such vacillating tales as Henry James's ghost stories, but he has nothing to say about the broader class that he calls "the marvelous," in which characters are confronted with unquestionably supernatural happenings.

Eric Rabkin explores an equally limited subgroup: fantasies which contradict, not our accepted model of the world, but rather the model generated within the story itself. That is, his fantasy is what is more generally termed *nonsense* or *absurdity*; it involves periodic overturning of the ground rules of the fiction. For Rabkin, "true Fantasy" is represented by *Alice in Wonderland*, and the internally consistent mode favored by MacDonald or Tolkien is classed, without further examination, as "fairytale."[8]

Utilizing Irwin's definitions, then, we can pare away extraneous areas of literature—poetry, discourse, realistic fiction, science fiction—and begin to take a closer look at what we have left. What do the works we group as fantasy have in common, besides the fundamental alteration of reality? How do they engage our attention? What is their origin?

The most important thing they share is the sense of wonder mentioned above. Fantasy invokes wonder by making the impossible seem familiar and the familiar seem new and strange. When you put a unicorn in a garden, the unicorn gains solidity and the garden takes on enchantment. As to engaging attention, fantasy does so in many of the ways any fiction does: by generating suspense, by presenting characters whose fates we are interested in, by appealing to our senses, by calling forth human longings and fears. However, it can, in addition, take advantage of our curiosity. When we read fantasy we explore the unknown, and that interest alone can carry an otherwise undistinguished work. A better work of fantasy can also engage us intellectually and morally by presenting the clash of ideas and issues in simple and concrete form. More than realistic fiction, it can clarify philosophical and moral conflicts, embodying them in story lines that may not be directly applicable to our own complex and muddied lives but which can please or inspire because of their open and evident design. That is one of the most important accomplishments at which fantasy can aim, to give comprehensible form to life, death, good, and evil; this has always been the primary aim of the earliest kind of fantasy, the folktale.

The folktale was one of the early genres of folklore to be recognized and studied. The type of folktale known as fairy tale, wonder tale, or, among most folklorists, *Märchen* was collected, edited, and published in the early nineteenth century by the Grimm brothers, whose versions of many of the tales are still the best known. European folktales are stories, usually of peasant origin, told not as fact but as entertainment.[9] True *Märchen* are full of magic and supernatural beings. They are tales of witches, dragons, soldiers, and princesses, pitting tailor against king, god-mother against stepmother, Jack against giant. Their origins are obscure, but they seem to be akin to epic and myth, deriving from them or evolving alongside.[10] The story of Cupid and Psyche is a version of one familiar *Märchen*, sometimes called "East of the Sun and West of the Moon," and Perseus stands at the head of a long line of fairy tale dragon slayers. Linda Dégh, who has studied a group of modern *Märchen* narrators in a small village in Hungary, finds that *Märchen* are an important element in the lives of the peasants, for whom they are a primary means of self-expression: "the story is not just entertainment or recreation for the folk community, but more than that—contentment, an outlet for protesting social injustice and fulfillment of the hopes and wishes of man generally, especially of the poor man in backward, rural communities."[11]

The peasant who recounts folktales and the peasants who listen to them recognize their essentially imaginary character; nevertheless, they find *Märchen* neither idle nor foolish. The wonderful adventures of the folktale hero provide a counterbalance to the lives of the peasant hearers: in the tales authority and property are challenged by benevolent forces of nature, ancient wisdom, and the hero's own boldness. *Märchen* are disrup-tive and democratic: the weak overthrow the strong, the old give way to the young, and the villager becomes king. Perhaps it is for this reason that a higher standard of living can dull the taste for *Märchen*: "the well-to-do peasants in the village have little respect for the folktale. They will tell anecdotes during their get-togethers but only laugh at the long magic tale. The respectable person wants to hear something 'true,' a historical event; he reads newspapers and no longer listens to 'lies.' "[12]

Dégh's view of *Märchen* as the product and shaper of the social environment provides a necessary corrective to the common notion of "nursery-tales," told by grandmothers and nurses to put their charges to sleep and abandoned along with dolls and toy soldiers. There is enough wonder in the old tales for all members of the family. Nonetheless, there are special values for the young in the folktale. A noted child psychologist, Bruno Bettelheim, finds that "each fairy tale is a magic mirror which reflects some aspects of our inner world, and of the steps required by our evolution from immaturity to maturity."[13] The traditional tales helped lead peasant children into adult society, and it was probably the peasant granny or nanny who most aided those tales in their transformation into written form by exposing children of the upper classes to the splendors of magical adventure.

The brothers Grimm not only collected tales from peasant narrators; they popularized them, couching them in acceptable written form and distributing them among the literate of Europe, many of whom, lacking nannies, had never come in contact with folktales in their oral form. Perrault, in France, had done much the same thing, and Andrew Lang was to make wonder tales available to the English-speaking world with his rainbow-colored fairy books. These transcribed and edited *Märchen* are formally indistinguishable from fantasy: prose narratives evoking wonder through the consistent treatment of the impossible as though it were possible. They were generally, however, better suited to oral than to written delivery, with their simple and standardized characterization and description. Readers of novels had come to expect the fuller documentation that gives weight to fiction, and they had grown accustomed to more sharply individualized heroes than the young Everyman who is the prince or princess of the fairy tale. In addition, there were limited numbers of *Märchen* and narrators of *Märchen* available. It is not surprising that writers who loved and understood the folktale should seek to create their own imitations of it; nor, considering the difference between oral composition and written creation, that the new tales should be distinctly different from their models.

The literary fairy tale, like the literary ballad or epic, proved to have its own strengths as a written genre. The first to explore its possibilities were the early German Romantics—Tieck, Novalis, Brentano, Hoffmann—described in Marianne Thalmann's *The Romantic Fairytale*.[14] A good example of the literary fairy tale in English is John Ruskin's *The King of the Golden River* (1851). This story takes a familiar folktale setting, a half-wild countryside; a conventional hero, the youngest and kindest of three brothers; and a story structure derived from many traditional tales, the testing and subsequent reward or punishment of the hero and his brothers by a supernatural agency. But the style of the story is more highly polished than that of most oral narrators, the setting is given a richer development and becomes an integral part of the story, and the action is made to take on an ideological slant that is Ruskin's own and not the product of peasant life and its pressures. The hero becomes the rescuer of his home valley from the greed and squalor of industrial development, as represented by the two evil brothers. Ruskin does not impose his message as a moral, as he might be forced to in a more naturalistic framework; the entire story is steeped in his values and indeed cannot be imagined without them. Ever since Ruskin's time, writers have found that the fairy tale form seems most compatible with a certain bent, whether conservative or radical it is difficult to say, that rejects the modern world for the small, quiet, green one that the peasants knew. Ruskin set his tale in Alpine Styria, but his message concerned the beloved and threatened countryside of England and Scotland.

Important developments were made in the literary fairy tale by two men, one a contemporary, the other a disciple of Ruskin. George MacDonald and after him William Morris infused the *Märchen* form with greater narrative sweep and significance than Ruskin had attempted.

MacDonald was a well-known minister and a novelist of the Scottish countryside, but his most lasting achievements are what he himself called his fairy tales. Some of these, especially the early ones, are modeled closely on traditional tales: "The Giant's Heart," for example, is even closer to traditional sources than Ruskin's story; it is a retelling of a tale type known throughout Europe: the defeating, with the aid of his wife/daughter, of a giant/magician who has stored his heart/soul in a seemingly inaccessible place. But MacDonald found other sources for his fantasy besides the simple wonder tale. In "The Golden Key" and "Little Daylight" he wove into his *Märchen* frameworks flexible and engaging allegory; *Lilith* is linked to the legends of the *Apocrypha; Phantastes* is infused with the Romantic imagery and sentiment of the German Novalis; *At the Back of the North Wind* is a double story, both wonder tale and novel of London life; and MacDonald's finest works, *The Princess and the Goblin* and *The Princess and Curdie*, call upon the rich body of Celtic belief and legend to lend complexity to the plot and immediacy to the effect.

Legend, in European folklore, is distinct from *Märchen* in that it is told as truth, usually having a localized setting and often utilizing a historical figure as protagonist. Though it may share many motifs with the fairy tale, it tends to be fragmentary, rather than a fully developed narrative, and inclines toward the uncanny and disturbing.[15] MacDonald uses some of the same elements of Scottish legendry that another clergyman, Robert Kirk, described in his seventeenth-century treatise on *The Secret Common-Wealth*. His goblins, for instance, are the underground members of the fairy tribe, which, according to Kirk, "grovell in different shapes, and enter in anie Cranie or cleft of the Earth (where air enters) to their ordinary dwellings: The Earth being full of Cavities and cells, and their being no place or creature but is supposed to have other Animals (greater or lesser) living in, or upon it, as Inhabitants; and no such thing as a pure wilderness in the whol Universe."[16] These goblins are grotesque and malicious, comical and fearful, and they possess, in the books and in the original legends, a sense of independent reality not found in the supernatural helpers and antagonists of *Märchen*.

True fairies are born of a sense of the danger and unknowableness of the world around us: those who believe in them give offerings to placate them and carry iron and other charms to ward them off, but they do not tell fanciful tales about them.[17] "Fairy tales," or *Märchen*, are entertaining, but fairy legends are serious business. MacDonald conveys some of that seriousness within his fantasies. His heroine and hero pass through real danger, and, more importantly, are presented with real dilemmas: whereas a fairy tale hero can do no wrong, Irene and Curdie make mistakes and must suffer for them. They have no elder brothers or sisters to act as foils for them, to display all the foolishness and greed and reap all the punishment. The danger Princess Irene faces, being stolen by the goblins as a bride for their prince, is a legend motif: Kirk notes that the fairies are often guilty of "stealing of Nurses to their children, and that other sort of Plaginism in catching our Children away (may seem to Heir some Estate in those invisible dominions) which never return" (p. 62).

Fairy legends often end tragically, with disrupted lives, broken marriages, or deaths. MacDonald uses the potential tragedy of his legendary material to heighten the relief of his *Märchen*-based happy ending. To his supernatural helpers, as well as to his adversaries, he lends some of the force of legend. The beautiful young-old lady spinning in the tower, Irene's elusive great-great-grandmother, with her doves and her moon-lamp, who is the primary mover for good in both stories, also fits into the mold of the fairy legend. Kirk says of the fairies that "their women are said to spin, verie fine, to dye, to tissue and embroyder: but whither it be as manual operatione of substantial refin'd stuffs with apt and solid instruments, or only curious cob-webs, impalpable rainbows, and a phantastic imitatione of the actiones of more terrestrial mortals, since it transcended all the senses of the seer to discern whither, I leave to conjecture as I found it" (p. 55). The grandmother also resembles the heroine of another body of traditional legends, the Virgin Mary. Essentially MacDonald has drawn together two separate but related narrative types, tale and legend, to create a more potent written form.

MacDonald noticed that an essential part of the traditional fairy tale is its absolute self-consistency. He could be describing a well-told *Märchen* or his own best work when he says that "the natural world has its laws, and no man must interfere with them in the way of presentment any more than in the way of use; but they themselves may suggest laws of other kinds, and man may, if he pleases, invent a little world of his own, with its own laws; for there is that in him which delights in calling up new forms—which is the nearest, perhaps, he can come to creation."[18] One great virtue of his stories is the way in which he makes his legendary materials conform to the more highly ordered structure—the laws—of the fairy tale. His view of fairy tale form approaches that of a modern structuralist: "It cannot help having some meaning; if it have proportion and harmony it has vitality, and vitality is truth" (p. 25). MacDonald opened the way for later fantasists by asserting and demonstrating that truth can reside in the very shape of a story, as well as in its pictures of nature or society.

William Morris found other traditions of oral literature to fuse with the wonder tale. Like MacDonald and Ruskin he was of Celtic ancestry, but his forefathers were Welsh rather than Scottish, and the stories that first attracted him were those of the Arthurian cycle, passed from Welsh and Breton storytellers to courtly France and thence back to England. As a schoolboy, Morris was known to wander alone, telling himself tales of knights and fairies.[19] As an adult he found Malory's stories preferable to Tennyson's pallid retellings of them, and, like his friends in the Pre-Raphaelite Brotherhood, sought to recapture in art and literature the freshness and vigor he saw in the Middle Ages, when the artist was on intimate terms with the traditional craftsman and the folk raconteur.

Morris' own stories gained in clarity and force as his understanding of medieval narrative deepened, and he achieved a stylistic breakthrough when he translated the Scandinavian epic of the Volsungs, the heroic and tragic sons of Odin. Though extant only in written form, the Volsung saga is made up of motifs and characters developed within an oral tradition. Morris' translation is stern and archaic and well suited to the saga's rich mixture of the noble and the barbaric.

The first of Morris' own major fantasies, *The House of the Wolfings*, carries on the Nordic mood of desperate courage, and in his successive works, *The Well at the World's End, The Wood Beyond The World*, and so on, he worked the fairy tale form into something close to heroic myth. Just as importantly, Morris invented a storytelling language to match his imaginary worlds: grand, but severe sometimes to the point of stiffness. Both the grandeur and the severity are shown in the opening of *The House of the Wolfings*, with its generalized but lucid descriptions and its curious but compelling constructions: "The tale tells that in times long past there was a dwelling of men beside a great wood. Before it lay a plain, not very great, but which was, as it were, an isle in the sea of woodland, since even when you stood on the flat ground you could see trees everywhere in the offing, though as for hills, you could scarce say that there were any,—only swellings-up of the earth here and there, like the upheavings of the water that one sees at whiles going on amidst the eddies of a swift but deep stream."[20] Such a style gives his stories a distant quality, like faded tapestries, but they are lovely and often quite moving. Whereas MacDonald deepened the emotional scale—the danger and excitement—of the fairy tale, Morris discovered the linguistic tools by which to lend it some of the range and dignity of myth.

C.S. Lewis considered himself a "dinosaur." relic of an older world view and defender of a vanished literature.[21] Like Morris a medievalist, though a more thorough scholar, he devoted several books to recapturing what he termed "the discarded image." His important fictions are all fantasy: the Chronicles of Narnia, which follow an imaginary world from its creation in *The Magician's Nephew* to its end in *The Last Battle*; the Perelandra trilogy, set on a pre-lapsarian Mars, a Miltonic Venus, and an earth partly diabolical and partly Arthurian; and his version of the myth of Psyche, *Till We Have Faces*. The last is clearly built on a *Märchen* pattern (as mentioned above, Psyche's story is a well-known folktale) but the realization, the actual working-out of the story, relies on archeological reconstruction of ancient Mediterranean culture and on the application of Jungian psychology. The Perelandra books utilize a few science fiction techniques, but their primary movement is a fairy tale voyage through a neomedieval cosmology. The Narnia stories are reworkings in fairy tale form of the Biblical accounts of Creation, Fall, Redemption, and Apocalypse. Their Christian and moral emphasis is reminiscent of George MacDonald's, and Lewis credits MacDonald as an important influence, religious and literary: "I have never concealed the fact that I regarded him as my master; indeed I fancy I have never written a book in which I did not quote from him."[22]

Lewis is the first of our writers to write at length about his methods as a writer of fairy tale or fantasy. For him, the origin of every story was in a set of vivid images, not necessarily related, which came welling into his mind unbidden. He then had to determine a proper container or form for his "pictures"—usually, because of their nature, a fairy tale—and try to connect them into a narrative thread.[23] The stories bear out his account of their origin: their primary strength is a peculiar concreteness of detail, a sense of substance and texture, light and color, taste and smell, in the most remote places and amazing beings. Here is an example from his justly famous depiction of the floating islands of Venus:

> His first discovery was that he lay on a dry surface, which on examination turned out to consist of something very like heather, except for the colour which was coppery. Burrowing idly with his fingers he found something

friable like dry soil, but very little of it, for almost at once he came upon a base of tough interlocked fibres. Then he rolled round on his back, and in doing so discovered the extreme resilience of the surface on which he lay. It was something much more than the pliancy of the heather-like vegetation, and felt more as if the whole floating island beneath that vegetation were a kind of mattress. He turned and looked "inland"—if that is the right word—and for one instant what he saw looked very like a country. He was looking up a long lonely valley with a copper-coloured floor bordered on each side by gentle slopes clothed in a kind of many-coloured forest. But even as he took this in, it became a long copper-coloured ridge with the forest sloping *down* on each side of it.[24]

Lewis' reading gave him a strong sense of the marvelous, and of effective ways of presenting it, some of which he explains in his discussion of "realism of presentation" versus "realism of content" in his *Experiment in Criticism*.[25] He did not, however, have the infallible sense of story of an experienced traditional narrator. His stories are often weak in motivation and denouement: sometimes he seems to slash his way out of a story like a cat from a paper bag. He came to the fairy tale comparatively late in life and primarily through books—he refers in his essays to nearly every writer of modern fantasy and has written extensively on MacDonald, Morris, and his friend Tolkien—and his strengths and weaknesses as a fantasist are accordingly bookish. He pulled motifs from literary *Märchen*, medieval legend, poetry, and myth, and colored them wonderfully with his own sensuous experience, then marched them across the page in patterns all too often preset, derivative, and limiting to his imagination.

J. R. R. Tolkien's trilogy *The Lord of the Rings*, compared to others, is an achievement of such magnitude and assurance that it seems to reshape all definitions of fantasy to fit itself. Indeed, no important work of fantasy written After Tolkien is free of his influence, and many are merely halting imitations of his style and substance. Without Tolkien's work before us it might not seem worthwhile to isolate fantasy as a distinct form. If there were no *Scarlet Letter* or *Moby-Dick* the American romance might still be treated in terms of its deviation from the English social novel; likewise the forerunners of science fiction are significant only in light of *Frankenstein* and its descendants. *The Lord of the Rings* is a new kind of story, so much so that critics like Edmund Wilson and C. N. Manlove who condemn its departures from their canon of literary values seem in their discussions to be talking about some wholly other work.[26] It sets its own standards.

Even so, Tolkien's work is an extension of Ruskin's, MacDonald's, Morris', and Lewis'. It is still essentially fairy tale writ large. Unlike Lewis, who discussed fairy tales in terms of memorable detail, Tolkien was concerned with the movement of the tale, its progression toward the ultimate and all-important happy ending. In his essay "On Fairy-Stories," Tolkien wrote: "It is the mark of a good fairy-story, of the higher or more complete kind, that however wild its events, however fantastic or terrible the adventures, it can give to child or man that hears it, when the 'turn' comes, a catch of the breath, a beat and lifting of the heart, near to (or indeed accompanied by) tears, as keen as that given by any form of literary art, and having a peculiar quality."[27] This happy turn of events, or "eucatastrophe," is for Tolkien the essential feature of the fairy tale, just as the purgative death is the thing which marks tragedy; it is the crowning triumph of the wonders evoked in the tale.

In order to achieve an effective fairy tale turn, the teller or author must give his creation all possible solidity, keeping his viewpoint strictly within the confines of his imaginary world and developing its premises, as Mac-Donald pointed out earlier, with sober logic. He must also strive to touch patterns of truth which transcend the merely fanciful and approach the mythic. Tolkien's creation is rigorously consistent and clearly akin to myth. Among its many subplots and embedded plots are reworkings of Christian, classical, and especially Norse myths: the ring itself strongly suggests the ring of the Nibelungs, though Tolkien's treatment of it differs markedly from Wagner's. Wound around the fairy tale structure of quests and comings-of-age is a countermovement of withdrawal and ending reminiscent of the Scandinavian myth of Ragnarok, the twilight of the gods. Tolkien, much more than Lewis, works from originally oral sources: *Beowulf,* the Scandinavian *Eddas*, the Finnish *Kalevala*, the Celtic mythos which predates Arthurian romance. He felt the lack of a body of English myths and legends comparable to those of Ireland, Greece, or the North, and first the *Silmarillion* and then *The Lord of the Rings* were intended in part to counter this lack.[28] His work introduces demigods and heroes from other lands into a thoroughly English landscape, much as the Romans enriched their pantheon with generous borrowings from Greece and the Near East, though, as a Christian and an heir of the Enlightenment, he could only do so within the bounds of imaginative literature.

Like Morris, whose *House of the Wolfings* was an important early influence (Carpenter, p. 70), he developed a lofty style for presenting heroic materials, though Tolkien's benefits from a counterbalancing style, comic and familiar, used primarily for hobbit doings. The wizard Gandalf is introduced with folktale simplicity: "At the end of the second week in September a cart came in through Bywater from the direction of Brandywine Bridge in broad daylight. An old man was driving it all alone. He wore a tall pointed blue hat, a long grey cloak, and a silver scarf. He had a long white beard and bushy eyebrows that stuck out beyond the brim of his hat."[29] A much different language is used for Gandalf at the height of his power: "But Gandalf sprang up the steps, and the men fell back from him and covered their eyes; for his coming was like the incoming of a white light into a dark place, and he came with great anger. He lifted up his hand, and in the very stroke, the sword of Denethor flew up and left his grasp and fell behind him in the shadows of the house; and Denethor stepped backward before Gandalf as one amazed" (3:128). High and low, myth and *Märchen* blend to produce a uniquely moving story.

The five writers I have considered, Ruskin, MacDonald, Morris, Lewis, and Tolkien, outline a natural progression in the development of literary fantasy from recounted folktale. Each drew on oral tradition and on the achievements of his predecessors to create increasingly complex stories of wonder. The limited fantasy tradition that they represent—some refer to it as "high fantasy"—can be described more fully than can the field of fantasy as a whole. The works discussed above show an important consistency in five particulars. Since these five characteristics are so important to the school of high fantasy, I will be bringing them in again from time to time as a scale of comparison. They are setting, structural framework, role and character of the protagonist, types of secondary characters, and ways of tying events to values and ideas.

The realm of the impossible—an abstract concept or mere figure of speech—is given a definite location by the fantasist. Nearly all fantasy takes place in or postulates another world, in which the fantastic or magical becomes the expected and normal. This Other World is not accessible by ordinary means: it does not exist on the same plane or in the same time as our own. The notion of a magical Other World is present in oral *Märchen*, with their opening formulas: "Once upon a time" and "Once there was, One day there will be."[30] Fairy tales, like myths, are always and never, long past and yet still taking place. The same close but inaccessible realm appears in fairy legendry as the Kingdom Under the Hill, the Hidden World, Alfheim, or Faerie. It can be visited only by special dispensation from the inhabitants.

Some form of Other World seems to be well-nigh universal, an archetype. The fairy world is neither so perfect as heaven nor so fearful as hell, but strikes one rather as if our own world were made fresher, grander, more alive, and more dangerous. Like the so-called Green World of certain of Shakespeare's plays, it is a place free of crowds, noise, and daily business, where elemental passions and eternal conflicts take the foreground. The best fantasies perform the trick of investing the familiar with enough touches of the unreal—heightened color, heroic action, unexpected transformations, and dislocations in time—to evoke an acute sense of longing in the reader, a nostalgia for the never-was.

The structural organization of high fantasy is the same as that of its ancestor, the fairy tale. The clearest analysis of that structure is the scheme proposed by Vladimir Propp in 1928. Propp analyzed selections from Aleksandr Afanas'ev's collection of Russian fairy tales to produce a "morphology" consisting of a series of events, or "functions," beginning with an opening problem—"one of the members of a family absents himself from home"—and proceeding through interdiction, violation of interdiction, lack, testing of the hero, receipt of a Magical Agent, and so on, to liquidation of the lack, punishment of the villain, and the hero's marriage and ascent to the throne.[31] In a fairy tale these functions (of which I have omitted a great many) are arranged in a fixed sequence; however, a given tale may begin at any of several points along the way, skip functions or groups of functions, and end at one of the partial resolutions short of the ultimate marriage and coronation.

This fairy tale structure may underlie other, nonfantastic forms of narrative: Horatio Alger stories, for example, or romances of the *Jane Eyre* type. Indeed, there seem to be few more satisfying routes to a happy ending. But true fantasy begins when the Proppian morphology operates within the realm of the manifest impossible.

The hero of a fairy tale embodies every reader's desire to come into his own. Extraordinary things happen to him, but he himself is ordinary: a maiden thwarting a witch, a fool outwitting the wise, a mere man slaying giants. The protagonist of a fantasy is likewise ordinary: lucky and clever, perhaps, but no more so than we imagine ourselves to be. It is important to have a limited hero in the unlimited realm of fantasy. He is our entry into the enchanted kingdom and our guide toward understanding the marvels therein. We come to know Lewis' Narnia through the eyes of children and Tolkien's Middle Earth from the perspective of hobbits.

Those around the hero, however, may be as extraordinary as imagination permits. It is difficult to conceive of a fantasy world with only men and women in it, and no elves, goblins, or talking beasts. The inhuman peoples of fantasy may be a little lower than man, like the fauns of Narnia, but not so low that they may not communicate with man. They may be higher, like the flamelike eldils of Perelandra, but not so high as to be above error and emotion. Much of the wonder in fantasy rests on the interaction between two-footed and four-footed folk, or between mortal and immortal.

Finally, high fantasy establishes a sphere of significance, in which the actions of hero and inhuman, helper and villain, reflect a coherent and extractable order. Characters are not merely individuals but the upholders of moral and intellectual standards. In most fantasies there is a strong polarization of good and evil, so that the hero's quest concerns not only his own coming of age but also the fate of the kingdom. Acts in a fantasy are always meaningful, because everything connects with, or signifies, everything else. The least detail may be an omen of the future, and the smallest action may bring that future to pass. Such a system of relationships is magical, whether the magic is openly displayed in spells and talismans or submerged in landscape or atmosphere or the very fabric of the created world.

These are the characteristics that most clearly indicate a work in the tradition of high fantasy. More difficult to point out, but equally characteristic, are certain feelings that seem to underlie the great fantasies. Among them are respect for the past, love of simple things and simple language, delight in the hills and forests of the English countryside, an unorthodox but profound religious sense, and a fascination with the impossible. Perhaps these are not so much characteristics of fantasy as prerequisites for the writing of it. The same feelings also pervade other works which, because they date from less rational times, may not hold the formal distinction between the impossible and the possible that marks modern fantasy: *A Midsummer's Night's Dream, The Tempest, The Fairy Queen, Le Morte D'Arthur, Sir Gawain and the Green Knight*, "The Wife of Bath's Tale," *Beowulf*. These works are usually grouped as "romance," and one of the aims of this book will be to examine some of the relationships between romance and fantasy. The tradition of wonder is an old and distinguished one in English literature, and the modern fantasists must be given credit for striving to maintain it.

That same tradition should operate in America. We share with England its language and literature; we should presumably have developed something comparable to its fantasy school, not a Tolkien or a Lewis perhaps, but something similar with an American flavor. Among the books listed at the beginning of the chapter not one has an American author. Who has been left out?

Before answering that question, I would like to speculate on what sorts of things an American fantasist would use to create an imaginary world. Most of the sources an English writer has available to him are equally available to an American: the works of Shakespeare and the other writers of romance, translations of classical and Norse epic, collections of European fairy tales, the Bible with all its fantastic and allegorical elements. There are American storytellers and ballad singers whose repertoires are largely adapted from British tradition. America has its own unique landscape, as worthy of devotion as the English. We have, in addition, a body of native lore which could easily have been acquired from the Indian along with his land. But because our culture evolved along its own lines, all of these things must be assimilated anew by a writer who wishes to create

American fantasy: the land and legends must enter into his unconscious, or into his blood.

A fantasy is generally only as good as its materials. Unlike the novelist, whose responsibility is to portray the society he finds around him, the fantasist must create a society, and an entire world, which is unlike his own and yet intimately connected with it, reflecting its beliefs, wishes, and fears. Unless he can create from nothing, not only weaving the cloth but also spinning the thread, the fantasist must find elements—magical implements, fabulous beasts, imaginary peoples—in the common imagination; they may then be recognized and responded to within his work. The materials of fantasy, the things that call forth feelings of wonder, the manifest impossibilities that mark a work as fairy tale, are partly individual invention and partly communal property. If the first is not evident, we at least have the skeleton of a traditional tale. If the second is lacking, we have something obscure like someone's imperfectly translated dream, or a transparent allegory, or, worst of all, an artificial contraption, grotesque or sentimental, or both, since it has neither objective observation nor traditional wisdom to chasten it. Pure invention plays no greater role in fantasy than in any other form of literary art.

I intend to use the English fantasists as a standard of comparison because their works, though not perfect, are nonetheless notably successful in their assimilation and use of traditional materials. Their elves, eldils, witches, and goblins are oftentimes more clearly imagined and more memorable than their counterparts in folklore, and they lend their magic easily and naturally to the English gardens, woods, and marshes where their creators place them. The American writers I will deal with are those who, in my opinion, have found on the American scene, or have successfully naturalized to that scene, figures, objects, and events which inform this land with the same kind of wonder the English have given their own land. The works I have chosen vary greatly in complexity and style, but none strikes me as entirely labored or hopelessly derivative. All are in some way or other distinctly American, and also distinctly un-American, for, as we will see, there is a strong distrust of the fantastic in our nation's make-up as expressed in lore and letters both.

TWO

❦

Fantasy and the Folk Tradition

JOHN GREENLEAF WHITTIER, in the collection of curiosities he called *The Supernaturalism of New England*, recounts the story of a family of Irish immigrants in New Hampshire, proprietors of a disastrously unsuccessful tavern. "The landlord," he says, "was a spiteful little man, whose sour, pinched look was a standing libel upon the state of his larder," and the wife was no better, being a scold, a slattern, and a tippler.[1] Nevertheless, their trade suddenly took a turn for the better when a company of Irish fairies took up residence and began holding conversation in the parlor. British fairies, as a rule, abhor both sloppiness and ungenerous dealings,[2] but these may have been lured by voices from home. At any rate, the inn prospered under their influence until the novelty wore off and the crowds once more deserted. Says Whittier: "Had the place been traversed by a ghost, or disturbed by a witch, they could have acquiesced in it very quietly, but this outlandish belief in fairies was altogether an overtask for Yankee credulity" (p. 61). The fairies, "unable to breathe in an atmosphere of doubt and suspicion" (p. 62), promptly departed for greener shores. Whittier himself stands firmly on the side of the unbelieving Yankees, suggesting that the whole incident was an ingenious fraud.

Fraud or not, this anecdote suggests a great deal about the nature of Anglo-American folklore. A general trend, since the landing of the Puritans, has been a paring away of the supernatural in those folk genres most amenable to its presence: ballads, tales, and legends. A writer who wishes to produce something both American and fantastic, and who would root his creation, as did the British fantasists, in his native lore, must move against the current, restoring what has been lost over the years or finding eddies of tradition that have resisted the general erosion of the marvelous.

16

Tristram Coffin, in his analysis of *The British Traditional Ballad in America*, refers to a process of "rationalization," which the ballad tends to undergo in transmission, especially from England to America.[3] A singer, consciously or unconsciously wishing to make the text of his song conform to his and his listeners' expectations, replaces an outlandish element with something more familiar and mundane. It is not surprising that such a transformation should take place: the same impulse changes European place names to those of nearby sites and ascribes ballad activities to local characters. When the supernatural is rationalized, though, the effect is all too often to obscure motivations, trivialize effects, and render entire groups of related ballads indistinguishable: another unfaithful lover, one more murdered girl.

The heyday of British ballad collection was represented in such anthologies as Thomas Percy's *Reliques of Ancient English Poetry* (1765) and Sir Walter Scott's *Minstrelsy of the Scottish Border* (1802-03), both important sources for the scholarly compilation done by Francis James Child (1882-98). A significant number of so-called Child ballads from these and other sources, and some of the most memorable, are built around supernatural episodes and characters, and the treatment given to the uncanny elements is as sober and concrete as that of serious fantasy. M. J. C. Hodgart describes the universe of the ballads as "peopled with animals and birds that speak, with fairies and with ghosts who return from the grave. There is no clear line of demarcation between such creatures and ordinary mortals. The supernatural is treated in a matter-of-fact and unsensational way, and to the ballad singer there seems to be no question of a suspension of disbelief. Fairies, for example, are not the minute creatures of modern whimsy, but are like human beings in size and in some of their ways of life."[4] So important to balladry were the elves and fairies that one of Scott's informants, Margaret Laidlaw, considered them the ballad muses and feared that Scott's writing her songs down would offend them.[5]

Of the English fantasists, Tolkien seems to have been most influenced by traditional ballads. His essay "On Fairy-Stories" makes use of a quotation from one of the most haunting fairy ballads, that of Thomas the Rhymer or "True Thomas" (Child no. 37). The passage which Tolkien cites to illustrate his conception of the enchanted world of Faerie is the Queen of Elfland's description of the three great roads to Heaven, Hell, and Fairyland. The first is the "path of Righteousness," narrow, thorny, and little used. The second is the "path of Wickedness," broad and lily strewn. The third is neither good nor wicked, merely Other:

And see ye not yon bonny road
That winds about yon fernie brae?

That is the road to fair Elfland,
Where thou and I this night maun gae.[6]

Much of the beauty and peril of Tolkien's world is comparable to that of the ballads, and indeed *The Lord of the Rings* is filled with the ballads of elves and men. The pivotal incident in *The Hobbit*, in which Bilbo Baggins trades riddles with Gollum at peril of his life, is closely akin to the traditional ballads known as "Riddles Wisely Expounded" and "The Fause Knight upon the Road" (Child nos. 1 and 3), both of which, in their early forms, tell of mortals saved from death or damnation by outwitting riddling fiends. The last answer in the former ballad not only solves the riddle but unmasks the questioner: "As sune as she the fiend did name,/ He flew awa in a blazing flame."[7]

There are in the ballads a great number of other supernatural motifs available to the writer of fantasy, already presented with the necessary vividness and solidity. Lowry Charles Wimberly devoted an entire volume to classifying the supernatural lore of the English and Scottish ballads. He found treatments of such promising themes as transmigration of souls, revenants from the grave, otherworld journeys, enchanted forests and caves, fairies, shapeshifters, witches, spells and enchantments of all varieties, and even a paganized heaven and hell.[8] Not even a work of the scope of *The Lord of the Rings* could possibly exhaust the available material.

What happens to a typical supernatural ballad when it comes to America? Some of them survive intact, or nearly so. The Frank C. Brown collection of North Carolina Folklore contains one text of "True Thomas" that is a close parallel to the Scottish version in Child. According to Coffin, however, this is the only recorded American version—not a very vigorous survival.[9] Other ballads, like that of "Tam Lin" and his rescue from Elfland, are not found in American tradition at all. Those that are actively transmitted in this country are generally altered, "rationalized," as Coffin says. An example is "The Marriage of Sir Gawain" (Child no. 31), derived from the medieval romance "The Wedding of Sir Gawen and Dame Ragnell." The version in Percy's *Reliques* is a graceful retelling of the old story (most familiar as Chaucer's "Wife of Bath's Tale") of a loathly lady transformed through her lover's acquiescence to a beautiful young maiden. The tone is serious, the atmosphere courtly. The magic in the story is accepted without question:

Shee witched me, being a faire young lady,
To the greene forrest to dwell,
And there I must walke in womans liknesse,
Most like a feend of hell. (Child 1:296)

The nearest American treatment of this theme is a comic ballad called "The Half Hitch." In it there is no magic at all: the transformation is the doing of the bride herself and involves nothing more than old clothes and chimney soot. There is material here for the humorist, but none for the writer of fantasy.

The British ballad "The Twa Magicians" (Child no. 44) tells the story of a coal-black smith and a lady, both skilled in magic, and their unconventional courtship. To escape the smith, the lady turns herself into a dove, an eel, a duck, a hare, a mare, a girdle, a ship, and a blanket, while the smith tops each transformation with one of his own: "And a' the ways she turnd hersell,/ The blacksmith was her make" (Child 1:403). He ends up as a coverlet over her blanket and the game is over: she's trapped in bed. The transformation motif is found in many old tales and myths, but the ballad treatment is notable for its pungency and wit. In American versions, the mysterious smith and his proud lady have both disappeared, and their contest shrinks into a series of boasts. The aura of magic in the original is replaced by broad humor:

> Young women they'll run like hares on the mountains,
> Young women they'll run like hares on the mountains,
> If I were but a young man I'd soon go a-hunting,
> To my right fol diddle dero, To my right fol diddle dee.[10]

The magic of the ballad has dwindled to a figure of speech, and it would take a magician of a writer to retrieve it.

In addition to the British ballad tradition in America, a body of native balladry exists. Whereas many motifs in the British ballads may be presumed to survive merely because of the essential conservativeness of oral tradition, and thus may only imperfectly represent the tastes and beliefs of their hearers, ballads which have arisen within American culture should mirror that culture quite directly. Malcolm Laws, in his study of *Native American Balladry*, proposed as his definition of a ballad "a narrative folksong which dramatizes a memorable event."[11] If we accept his definition, which is brief but fair, then we can take the ballad tradition as a guide to what kinds of events Americans, or at least folksinging Americans, consider memorable. The primary concerns of the British ballads are love, treachery, and dealings with the supernatural. Laws finds that none of these is of great prominence in American balladry:

The knights and ladies, the gold and silver, the magic transformations, and the evil stepmothers of Child balladry have no place in the native balladry of America. Even love, the most popular of all narrative and dramatic topics, is rarely treated by the American ballad maker. Crafty plottings, deep seated jealousies, seductions, disguises, strife within families, duels to the death—such topics are almost unheard of in our balladry. We hear, instead, of the difficulties and perils of various occupations, of sordid crimes committed by insignificant people, of fires and mine blasts and railroad wrecks, of struggles against the frontier, of death by snake bite or freezing, of trips on clipper ships and lake schooners, of death in dozens of different forms. (Laws, p. 13)

The interests of the American ballad composer are not like those of the fantasist but those of the local color writer, Bret Harte or Mary Hallock Foote, seeking to invest obscure corners of the nation with "human interest," or the naturalistic documenter, Jack London or Frank Norris, telling with glum satisfaction of the hardships of some outdoor way of life. Many American ballads have a strongly journalistic quality; they subjugate the use of suspense and verbal artistry to the building up of supportive detail. The folk in this country seem comparable to the upwardly mobile peasants in Linda Dégh's Hungarian villages: they no longer wish to hear imaginative impossibilities but prefer something like, and probably based on, a newspaper account.[12] They do not want to be "fooled" into empathizing with a fiction, still less an outright fantasy.

A partial exception to the general run of American ballads is the bold, comical, and most definitely fictional account of "Tying a Knot in the Devil's Tail."[13] This is a sort of occupational ballad run wild, in which the skills of two cowhands give them power over the devil himself. The devil in the ballad is spiteful but impotent, rather like the unfortunate devil who steals "The Farmer's Curst Wife" in the Child ballad of that name (Child no. 278). In this case the supernatural is treated as a joke. There is no question of belief, of "paying something extra," in E. M. Forster's terms; rather the effect is to forestall any subsequent efforts to create a serious story around the devil or any other traditional non-human being. Humor acts to defuse the sense of wonder that marks fantasy. If there is to be humor in a work of fantasy, it must be kept separate from the component of the marvelous, as Tolkien isolates the often bumptious hobbits from the stern and magical elves. Mixing simple cowboys and fallen angels, without any mediating characters or principles, can only produce the ludicrous incongruity effectively exploited by this ballad.

"Tying a Knot in the Devil's Tail" has more in common with the tall tale, which is a particular form of the folktale, than with other ballads. Tales, like ballads, thrive best in regions of little literacy, where they need not compete with the written word. In this country, the tale and the ballad are found most commonly in the Southern mountains, from Virginia to Missouri, where isolation and poverty have allowed an oral culture to continue relatively undisturbed. Folksong as a popular mode of entertainment, however, was not seriously challenged by mass communication until the development of electronic recording and broadcasting, whereas folk literature found itself in direct competition with popular journals and newspapers early in the nineteenth century. The long narrative forms like the fairy tale, requiring a skilled narrator and a willing audience, tended to be replaced in our oral tradition by shorter, simpler forms like the tall tale or the joke, and jokes themselves became briefer and more dependent on the punch line and the quick laugh.

In most places where long folktales are still told, wonder tales or *Märchen* form an important part of the repertoire. England is not noted for its *Märchen* as are the Celtic, Scandinavian, and Central European countries, but fine versions of such tales as "Beauty and the Beast," "Cinderella," and "The Juniper Tree" have been collected there.[14] The *Type and Motif Index of the Folktales of England and North America* lists greater numbers of *Märchen* types here than in the parent country, but its compiler, Ernest W. Baughman, suggests that the American variants reflect an earlier stage in English tradition.[15] American storytellers, more isolated than their English cousins, preserve more of the old tales, just as they preserve older songs or forms of speech. As with ballads, though, the stories have undergone Americanization.

Settings in the American folktales are adapted to the frontier scene; they are full of forested hills and cleared fields. As Richard Chase has pointed out, even the kings and giants who carry over from Europe live in log houses and spend their time breaking "newground."[16] The hero of one cycle of stories, Jack, is less a fairy tale hero than a classic American trickster, adaptable and unscrupulous, a local boy who gets by on his wits without supernatural aid. Some of the Jack tales veer from *Märchen* to tall tale, as when Jack goes hunting and takes a full bag with a single bullet (Chase, p. 151).

Most susceptible to the process of rationalization are the nonhuman figures of the European *Märchen*. A few witches survive, and some scaled-down giants, but the evil magician tends to blur into the comic devil we have already met in ballads, and the only dragon evident is altered almost beyond recognition into the "Old Fire Dragoman," a pipe-smoking old man with an ogreish temperament (Chase, p. 106).

A typical treatment is the variant of "The Three Wishes" collected in Arkansas by Vance Randolph. In it the three wishes are given to a foolish old couple and promptly wasted, as in European versions, but the emphasis in the story is shifted from the magical possibilities to pragmatic considerations. The ham produced by the first unintentional wish is not wasted but carefully wished back on the plate. Whereas the magic in the European tale serves to illustrate a fine array of ironies involving greed, this American retelling blurs the message by informing us that hocus-pocus, and not the basic motivation, was at fault:

> So pretty soon the old man went down to the road, and there was a letter in the box. It was from their married daughter, and she had sent them some money. She says there is plenty more where that came from, as her man has got a good job now. So it looks like everything turned out all right after all, even if the old folks did make a mess of them three wishes.[17]

Even these stripped-down wonder tales failed to generate much interest among American writers. While much of our nineteenth-century literature is based on styles and themes of folk narration, for the most part *Märchen* was passed over in favor of *Münchausen*. Constance Rourke has traced the adoption by American writers of the standard mask and motifs of the great local liars, who made a fine art out of straight-faced exaggeration.[18] There is a strict etiquette of response to the tall tale—to smile or laugh or fall for the story is to ruin its effect. Tall tales treat the supernatural as a species of willful falsehood; they cut through all the stages of partial and temporary belief that mark the literature of magic. "You're a fool if you believe this," is one underlying message.

One group of tall tales did, however, generate a sort of tentative fantasy, and that is the Paul Bunyan cycle. Originally a set of "brief, sidelong tall-tale capsules," unconnected and rarely circulated, the stories about Paul Bunyan were drastically reshaped by an advertising agent for the Red River Lumber Company into the more or less coherent narrative we think of today.[19] Paul Bunyan is thus a creature of popular media, not folk culture. He may be said to symbolize nineteenth-century exploitation of the American continent, but in a manner which demonstrates neither the vitality of traditional invention nor the complexity of artistic creation. Poets—Frost, Sandburg, Auden—who have taken up the Bunyan theme have met with little success, and no literary prose fantasy derives from it. The Bunyan stories are not really very promising material for the fantasist. The only violation of reality in them is a matter of size. There is no special world, no inhuman characters, no controlling plot, no pattern of magic and metaphor. Paul remains limited by his origins: the lying tale may be whittled down to the briefest anecdote but it resists fuller development.

Stories which are given credence by tellers and hearers are known to folklorists as legends. Actually, a legend may often be told by a skeptic, but always with an awareness that someone somewhere—old-timer, child, churchgoer, or "gentile"—maintains its truth. As I mentioned before, a primary source for English fantasy is the vast and colorful body of fairy legend. Katharine Briggs has cataloged the major tribes of fairy folk in British belief, from the piskies of Cornwall to the *siths* of the Highlands.[20]

Among them a fantasist can find supernatural beings great or small, beautiful or grotesque, benevolent or threatening, to weave into his story. The fairy tradition also holds that uncounted mortals have slipped from our world to Elfland, and the lucky ones back again: the path from England to the Other World is a well-worn one. But American storytellers have dropped the fairies from their repertoires, with the result that fairyland— that is, the entire realm of Faërie or enchantment—has become distant and abstract, no longer the glittering hall under the next mountain. The disappearance of supernatural beings is characteristic not only of Anglo-American culture, but of all European immigrant groups: "Irish-Americans remember the fairies. Norwegian-Americans the *nisser*, Greek-Americans the *vrykólakas,* but only in relation to events remembered in the Old Country.... Apparently the ethnic supernatural figures are too closely associated with the culture and geography of the Old Country to migrate."[21]

Some of the fairy folk set out to emigrate to this country. Katharine Briggs recounts the story of a family, plagued by a household goblin, who decided to escape to America. As they start to leave, they inform a neighbor of their plans, and a voice from the churn pipes in, "Aye George, we're flitting."[22] But neither that cheerfully malevolent sprite nor any of his kind, save perhaps Whittier's woeful Irish fairies, ever showed up in our tradition. Their lack leaves our rivers and hills curiously empty: we may explore or exploit them but never meet their spirits face to face.

America is not without legends, however. Richard Dorson classifies American legend into four phases: the colonial period, dominated by religious beliefs; the early national period, when regional heroes represented a new democratic faith; the later national period, a time of economic and occupational lore; and the contemporary period, marked by druglore and counter-culture protest.[23]

Cotton Mather's six-volume *Magnalia Christi Americana*, incorporating his father Increase Mather's *An Essay for the Recording of Illustrious Providences*, is our primary source for the legendry of early New England, and it is a body of materials dominated by the supernatural. Local legends of the seventeenth century, derived for the most part from English originals, included "[d]ivine judgments and providences, witches and witchcrafts, ghosts and poltergeists, a personalized Devil and his train of invisible demons ... " (Dorson, p. 12). Puritan theology dictated the character of our early lore. First of all, it required a firm belief in the immanence of the supernatural: the early divines could not conceive of a true religion which denied God's (or the Devil's) active role in the workings of the world. Second, it affirmed that the supernatural concerned society as much as it did the individuals involved: the Puritans were God's chosen tribe, sent to do his business, and each member of the community must either enter into a covenant with Him and be sainted or refrain and be damned. Third, the universe was strictly divided into good and evil, God and his elect and Satan and his infernal minions, among whom the Indians held a prominent place. Even the American landscape was split along moral lines into the clearing—the holy City on a Hill—and the forest, Satan's dominion of delusion and sin. Fourth, both God and the Adversary dealt directly with mankind, God speaking through miracles and His revealed word, and Satan meeting with his slaves in the forest. Just as Protestant churches abolished mediaries and made each man his own priest, Puritan legend largely eliminated spiritual middlemen: angels, heavenly saints, and, of course, fairies. Stories originally attached to such beings were attributed to God or else became the work of the devil. Satan was allowed to keep his assistants because it suited his role as a masquerader and confuser of men to have an army of lieutenants or avatars.

On the one hand, Puritanism strongly encouraged belief in the supernatural as an essential tenet of faith, while, on the other hand, it severely limited the range and character of supernatural lore. With all innocent play of magic reserved for God, any other preternatural phenomena must be considered acts of ill will or revenge. Cotton Mather records poltergeists plaguing the homes of the unrighteous, ghosts and bleeding corpses revealing their murderers, threatening apparitions, and the dark deeds of witches. Whereas in Europe witches were believed to be able to cure as well as kill, and to perform magic sometimes simply for their own amusement, changing themselves, for example, into cats or crows, all witchcraft was viewed by the Puritan divines as the devil's work: "They did not swallow wholesale the old wives' tales and notions freely circulating among the folk, with which they were fully acquainted, but rather endeavored earnestly to screen out 'superstitions' and 'fabulous' elements from genuine evidences of sorcery and diabolism" (Dorson, p. 32).

Though there are many fascinating motifs associated with New England witch lore, like the invisible horse ridden by a bewitched girl in the presence of Cotton Mather himself (Dorson, p. 40), most of it is dark and repellent. After such gloom and the excesses of the Puritan witch trials, eighteenth-century skepticism seemed truly an enlightenment. Early national writers concentrated on the rational and practical problems of nation building and for the most part ignored such superstitions—beliefs, that is, that transcended direct experience and common sense—as remained in oral circulation, and evidence indicates that tradition, too, began to slight the supernatural.

Legends from Dorson's second period correspond with broadside ballads in their emphasis on local incident and character and with the tall tale in their wry humor. Witches and ghosts were no longer in the foreground. In their place were "bear and coon hunts, scrapes with Indians, travel by stagecoach and steamboat, the bench and the bar in the backwoods, politicking, quarter-racing, gambling, rough-and-tumble fights, shooting contests, Yankee pedlars, doctoring in the swamps, rustics agape in the city, courtships and weddings in the back country, horse trades, camp meetings, tricks on merchants, frolics and country dances, itinerant actors, small-town newspaper editors, 'darkies' on the plantation..." (Dorson, p. 58). Such motifs were to generate first a popular literature and eventually the beginnings of a unique American literary art.

When, a hundred and fifty years after the Salem witch trials, John Greenleaf Whittier attempted to gather together the remaining *Supernaturalism of New England* under the influence of European romantic antiquarianism, he could not throw off his notions of pragmatic truth: "not even for the sake of poetry and romance would I confirm in any mind a pernicious credulity, or seek to absolve myself from that stern duty which the true man owes to his generation, to expose error, whenever and wherever he finds it."[24] Thus he works at undermining belief in portents, hauntings, "domestic conjurations," the dwindled remnants of a once awesome body of lore, even as he seeks them out as evidence of "the deep, silent workings of the inner life—the unsounded depths of that mysterious ocean, upon whose solemn shores the loud footfalls of Time find no echo" (p. 30).

Whittier's ambivalence toward his subject is typical of his time. Nineteenth-century Americans felt the pull of the mysterious and occult, but they generally preferred the supernatural safely contained within some institution or other, church or pseudoscientific society. Whittier shows some degree of acuity in labeling his subject "supernaturalism," rather than merely the supernatural: the *ism* illustrates an American fondness for systematizing the ineffable. Instead of recounting old and eerie tales, we tend to organize our apprehensions and aspirations under such headings as millennialism, transcendentalism, mesmerism, or spiritualism. Whittier cites several such movements, with apparent approval, as heirs to Puritan belief: "Look at Magnetism, with its fearfully suggestive phenomena, enacting daily in our midst marvels which throw far into shadow the simple witchcraft of our ancestors" (p. 32).

James Russell Lowell shared Whittier's skepticism toward the delusions of the past, though he looks with longing at some of the more delicate conceits of British lore and literature:

> Credulity, as a mental and moral phenomenon, manifests itself in widely different ways, according as it chances to be the daughter of fancy or terror.

> The one lies warm about the heart as Folk-lore, fills moonlit dells with dancing fairies, sets out a meal for the Brownies, hears the tinkle of airy bridle-bells as Tamlane rides away with the Queen of Dreams, changes Pluto and Persephone into Oberon and Titania, and makes friends with unseen powers as Good Folk; the other is a bird of night, whose shadow sends a chill among the roots of the hair, is choked by the night-hag, pines away under the witch's charm, and commits uncleanness with the embodied Prince of Evil, giving up the fair realm of innocent belief to a murky throng from the slums and stews of the debauched brain. Both have vanished from among educated men. . . . [25]

Too sophisticated for fairies and too good-hearted to call up the "murky throng" that obsessed their ancestors, many American writers avoided any use of supernatural legend in their work. Some made it a point of honor, a part of their poetic code, not to betray their perceptions of the real world. Walt Whitman, in the 1855 Preface to *Leaves of Grass*, found:

> any miracle of affairs or persons inadmissable in the vast clear scheme where every motion and every spear of grass and the frames and spirits of men and women and all that concerns them are unspeakably perfect miracles all referring to all and each distinct and in its place. It is also not consistent with the reality of the soul to admit that there is any thing in the known universe more divine than men and women.[26]

Puritanism, rationalism, transcendentalism—each in its turn acted to circumscribe or suppress the stock of supernatural legend motifs that America inherited from Europe. Contemporary legendry is dominated by one-line statements about persons or places—that a famous child star was killed in Vietnam or a certain town was named from the initials of its first settlers—and by those pithy distillations of the grotesquery of modern life known as "belief tales." The latter often appear in newspapers as straight news items: tarantulas hitch a ride in a bunch of bananas, a grandmother's corpse is stolen by mistake, alligators colonize the sewers of a major city, an escaped psychopath terrorizes couples in lover's lane. This kind of legend translates well into fiction. Thomas Pynchon's *V.* makes use of the subterranean alligators, and Faulkner's *As I Lay Dying* transforms the missing grandmother theme into classic art. But eerie, acute, or effective as belief tales can be, they are tied to everyday life and offer no clues to the maker of a fantasy world.

Linda Dégh, taking her clue from Jung, points to anecdotes of Unidentified Flying Objects, many of them told and retold, or printed and reprinted, as true narratives, as an important form of modern legend, and one which indicates a great deal about twentieth-century beliefs.[27] The world view implied by UFO stories is not religious or mythological, but scientific. We have replaced our divinities with extraterrestrials, who may appear in lore as destroyers or saviors. Our Other World is the rest of the universe, and its magic is an advanced form of science. Similarly, in recent American literature, technology takes over the functions of magic, and fantasy transforms into science fiction, a genre with entirely different conventions and aims. Science fiction is predominantly speculative, looking forward and outward. Fantasy is more introspective and traditional; it attempts to revivify old metaphors and reembody old mythologies.

American folklore of all genres has proven to be a rich mine for the writer, so long as he is content to follow its concerns. Many writers, however, chafed at its limitations, and some made the attempt to create a pseudofolklore of their own by adopting foreign materials, focusing on typical items, or outright inventing. Charles M. Skinner's *Myths and Legends of Our Own Land* (1896), for example, seems to be a combination of all three. Skinner shared Whittier's interest in the supernatural and his indifference to documentation, but he did not inherit the older writer's scruples about truth. He wrote at a time when collectors were ransacking Europe for paintings and sculptures in an attempt to make America more "picturesque": his collection of tales is the literary equivalent of this endeavor. Richard Dorson sums up the *Myths and Legends* as a set of "pretty tales cloaking the American hills, coasts, rivers, and prairies with romantic associations culled from a past skimpy by European standards but approaching a respectable three centuries in his day."[28]

Skinner includes considerable lore that is authentic, such as comic anecdotes or Indian captivity narratives, and in those his descriptions display a feeling for landscape that Dorson calls "Hawthornesque" (p. 69), but when he writes of castles in Maine and wizards on the Hudson he reveals European influences imperfectly assimilated. No American storyteller ever gave one of his characters such a speech at this Faustian utterance from the misplaced fire elemental in the tale of "The Ramapo Salamander":

> I tread the darkness of the universe alone, and I peril my redemption by yielding to this love of earth. Thou art redeemed already, but I must make my way back to God through obedience tested in trial. Know that I am one of those that left heaven for love of man![29]

Neither the diction nor the subject suggest the hand of tradition.

Most of Skinner's supernatural tales revolve around sentimentalized Indians: pure maidens and stalwart warriors who would be more at home in a medieval romance than in the American forest. Like Longfellow's "Hiawatha," Skinner's Indian legends are an awkward mixture of New World materials and creaky Old World conventions. Other tales are frankly borrowed from literary creations: Hawthorne's "The Great Carbuncle," Joseph Rodman Drake's "The Culprit Fay," and Irving's "Rip Van Winkle," among others, make their way into his collection. Only Irving gets an acknowledgement.

Reprinting themes and motifs in a piece of popular literature like the *Myths and Legends* can constitute a kind of tradition in a primarily literate country like this. Stories which, like the UFO lore mentioned above, strike a chord in the reader may be said to have a currency equivalent to that of oral tradition, even if the stories never circulate by word of mouth. Most of Skinner's choices, however, are unlikely candidates for further distribution. Hawthorne's story, for instance, which is a slight but engaging allegory on avarice, becomes in Skinner's reduction a pointless yarn, a tall tale stripped of humor. Samuel Adams Drake, another nineteenth-century collector of American legends, but one considerably more careful in crediting his sources, believed that "The Great Carbuncle" was actually an Indian legend known among white settlers, and that Hawthorne was indeed incorporating a bit of folk belief into his story.[30] It is significant, if so, that Skinner chooses Hawthorne's moralized version over the raw original.

"The Culprit Fay" is the best known of several early attempts to transplant fairies to the American landscape through poetry. Joseph Rodman Drake's saccharine rendering of the trials and triumph of a diminutive fairy first appeared in 1835, was reprinted the following year, and was reissued periodically until well into this century. As a mark of its popularity among certain circles, it was even set to music as a cantata for women's voices. It has some of the earmarks of a true fantasy: the Hudson River at night becomes a fairyland (rather like an economical stage director changing scenes by switching lighting); there are several classes of nonhuman characters: fays, water sprites, sylphs; there is a plot which parallels the "impossible task" portion of Propp's fairy tale morphology. But there is no human protagonist to put things in scale—that would upset the drawing room coziness of the miniaturization—nor is there any particular system of significance. The story is affected and trivial, and occasionally, because of the failure to establish a consistent perspective, grotesque. We are asked first to believe that the fairy renegade of the title has fallen in love with a mortal maid, and then that he is small enough to have "lain upon her lip of dew,/ And sunned him in her eye of blue...."[31] Such inconsistencies of imagining would soon be filtered out of a real legend; in an attempted fantasy they point out the need for the control imposed by adopting traditional forms.

If "The Culprit Fay" could pass through tradition, it might emerge in a tighter, tougher form, not a fantasy, but a legend to fuel other fantasies. As it is, despite the promise in its opening descriptive passage, it lacks the geographical concreteness, the location in space that is a mark of the traditional fairy legend. Its primary sources are the seventeenth- and eighteenth-century set pieces by Drayton or Herrick that launched a fad for tiny, powerless, faintly comical fairies. Drake, like his predecessors, sacrifices wonder for whimsy. His imagination gets bogged down in cobweb hammocks, acorn helmets with thistle plumes, and boats made of "muscle" shells. This "tricksy pomp of fairy pride" (p. 12) is a dramatic contrast to the spare, clean action of authentic lore.

Such sentimental fairy verse appeared in many of the popular literary periodicals of the early nineteenth century, often under pseudonyms, as if the authors felt they were condescending. John Milton Harney (calling himself merely "An American") published his *Crystalina; a Fairy Tale* as early as 1816.[32] William Gibson's *A Vision of Faery Land* did not appear until 1853.[33] Throughout this period, and even later, there appears the same overly precious treatment of the subject. In some poems, the fairies become mere decoration; in others, a clever conceit. S. G. Goodrich, for example, uses certain connotations of the word *fairy*—tininess, bright colors, speed—to create a mock parable of the "Birthnight of the Humming Birds," in which a tribe of Irish fairies come to America to hunt jewels, get caught by the sunrise, and are permanently transformed.[34] This is neither legend nor fantasy, but rather an extended form of the same kind of whimsy that makes Emily Dickinson describe the hummingbird's wings as a "fairy gig," a whimsy that she abandons in her later and stronger poem on the same subject.[35]

These mannered fairy poems represent an attempt to fill a gap in American tradition, a gap first felt, seemingly, not by the folk but by professional writers. Drake and the rest tried, by means of a set of borrowed poetic devices two steps removed from living folk tradition, to interpret the American landscape, which seemed to them, in contrast with Europe, empty and spiritless. They created neither a lasting art nor a viable legendry. A writer with more skill, more awareness of real traditional materials, and a little luck could, however, transfer European motifs to an American setting and produce something quite as memorable as legend. William Austin's "Peter Rugg, the Missing Man," for example, is a Massachusetts Flying Dutchman, a man condemned by an ill-advised oath to race around New England in the teeth of a great storm in a vain attempt to get to Boston by nightfall.[36] The hard-edged realism of the story, as opposed to the moonlit fuzziness of the fairy poems, renders it eerily effective: the supernatural is all the more powerful for being played against a backdrop of solid New England practicality.

Another American character who becomes unstuck in time (is that a particular national fear?) is at the center of our best-known literary legend, "Rip Van Winkle." Washington Irving's story has been retold, versified, dramatized, and painted enough times to suggest that Rip has fixed himself securely in the American consciousness, even though Irving took his theme, not from American, but from German traditional sources.[37] Irving himself comments on the similarity of Van Winkle's adventures to stories attached to Frederick Barbarossa, one of many sleeping heroes scattered around Europe.[38] Once again scenery and characterization work to naturalize the import. And Irving's sharp eye and deftness of style allow him to orchestrate a legend of much greater complexity than "Peter Rugg." Indeed, Irving brought the fairies to America, in the guise of Hendrick Hudson and the crew of the Half-moon. Hudson, with his confused nationality and his mysterious disappearance, carries just the right air of antiquity and strangeness to act the role of demigod in that part of the world he claimed for the Dutch. By selecting the old explorer, rather than some conventional, diminutive fairy king, Irving recaptures the danger and grotesquery of the best European narratives. We are never sure whether the silent carousers are ghosts or nature spirits bowling thunder in the mountains. They might be good or evil or mockingly indifferent. Whatever the case, they are formidable and alien, and Rip is lucky to have escaped at the loss of only twenty years of his life—especially after violating the traditional tabu against eating and drinking in the Other World.[39]

The mountain hollow where Rip's adventure takes place is indeed a fairyland in miniature, and "Rip Van Winkle" is as much fantasy as literary legend. Its plot line is easily translated into the terms of Propp's morphology: interdiction (Dame Van Winkle orders Rip out of Nicholas Vedder's tavern), lack (Rip's lack of a happy home), departure (the hunting trip), acquisition of a magical agent (appearance of Hudson and his men), transference to a designated place (entry into the amphitheater), contest (the drinking bout), branding or marking the hero (Rip's sudden aging), liquidation of misfortune or lack (Dame Van Winkle's death), return of the hero, unrecognized arrival, and, finally, recognition of the hero. There is no final wedding and accession to the throne, because Rip's tale is one of abdication rather than assumption of responsiblity.

The hidden amphitheater in the mountains is the actual enchanted world in the story, but the Catskills themselves are at least on the threshold of fairyland. Irving paints the scene in such a way as to prepare for the intrusion of the supernatural: "On the other side he looked down into a deep mountain glen, wild, lonely, and shagged, the bottom filled with fragments from the impending cliffs, and scarcely lighted by the reflected rays of the setting sun" (pp. 58-59). The mountains, weird and isolated, of "magical hues and shapes," are contrasted with the rich, serene, mundane Hudson Valley, "where the blue tints of the upland melt away into the fresh green of the nearer landscape" (p. 52). An earthly green sets off the unearthly blue of the mountains that Irving said he always considered "the fairy region of the Hudson."[40]

Irving was a writer of atmosphere, and his fairyland is mostly a matter of color and cloud. It is his hero, Rip, who gives the story its tangible quality. Rip is earthy and ordinary, like most fairy tale heroes; his motivations are none too high, but his heart is good. He stumbles into the world of magic, and we perceive it through his senses—a cleft in the mountains, a leering goblin face, a flagon full of liquor, a stiffness in the joints on awakening: the extraordinary mixed with the familiar.

I have already noted Irving's successful creation of a race of supernatural beings. Some of the magical aura that hangs over Hudson and his band is due to well-placed narrative devices: the solitary crow that introduces them, their silence, their association with tricks of light and with thunder, their distorted countenances: "one had a large beard, broad face, and small piggish eyes; the face of another seemed to consist entirely of nose, and was surmounted by a white sugar-loaf hat set off with a little red cock's tail" (p. 61). More importantly, they evoke memories of older stories of sleeping warriors, hauntings, and wild hunts, told and believed in Europe, if not in America. Something once believed is more likely to be believable—that is, self-consistent, concretely portrayed, and exciting to the imagination—than a purely literary convention like the cobwebs-and-cowslips brand of fairy.

Hendrick Hudson is an appropriate figure to preside over Rip's encounter with the preternatural world. An explorer from the first days of American settlement, he represents the transition from Old World to New, from the known to the unknown. He is a heroic figure, a wandering Odysseus who contrasts with Rip Van Winkle's inverted Odyssey. For the primary meaning of the story is Rip's refusal of the challenge, his relinquishment of the fairy tale goals, marriage and maturity. The enchanted sleep is an initiation, not into manhood, but into an irresponsible old age. Hudson the historical figure escorts Rip out of the course of history. Hudson the explorer puts an end to Rip's explorations and sends him back to the fireside. In Irving's hands magic is an effective ironic tool, injecting high contrasts and sharp transitions into the story that could not otherwise be there.

Irving demonstrates that the writer can transcend his store of traditional materials. If he is sensitive to the dynamics of his native lore, he can revise it, rearrange it, and insert motifs from other cultures, where they will not strain the basic fabric. But it is not an easy operation: Irving himself managed it with such success only once, and "Rip Van Winkle" is only a sketch. It takes place in a tiny corner of the country, among a people not yet assimilated to American life; yet even among those isolated Dutchmen there is skepticism toward Rip's story, especially among the younger and more prosperous members of the community. Were the tale to trespass beyond its geographical and temporal limits, entering into modern mercantile America, the delicate blend of magic and humor would be undone. What passes in the haunted Catskills would never survive New York City. Irving shows how American fantasy can be created, but not how it can be made full scale, nor how the sense of wonder may spread to the broader American scene.

Our folk songs, stories, and beliefs, especially our beliefs, portray a population increasingly pragmatic and impatient, interested mostly in the here and now, susceptible to sentimentality, but only if convinced that its tears are being jerked by real events. If the dark vision of the Puritans still haunts us in our midnight dreams, that is all the more reason for scoffing in the daylight. Most of our popular literature falls into the same pattern: indeed, the line is thin between the broadside ballad and the newspaper eulogy, or the oral and written tall tale. Both kinds of narrative, folk and popular, have shaped American habits of expectation and belief and have created a serious problem for the artist, Irving or even Drake, who wishes to reach beyond practical concerns and the limits of daily existence.

THREE

Belief, Legend, and Romance

OF THE VARIETIES of folklore that feed into literary fantasy, the most important in determining its character is legend. Tales provide a rationale and an outline, ballads suggest an appropriate diction and tone, but legends, because they are told as true, offer whole magical worlds saturated with belief. Legend settings are vivid, self-consistent realms already adapted to the presence of the marvelous. It may seem inappropriate to speak of belief or truth in regard to a genre whose distinctive trait is that it is not believable, not true, but several varieties of both truth and belief exist in literature, and where one kind is absent the others are all the more important.

Nearly every writer of fantasy has felt compelled to offer some kind of defense of his work, to demonstrate that the marvelous is not arbitrary or irrelevant to human life. Samuel Taylor Coleridge's phrase "willing suspension of disbelief" is a misleading one if it is taken to mean that Coleridge saw belief as a solid bar across the imagination, to be hauled up out of the way for short periods of time, then dropped back into place when the amusement is over. When Coleridge wrote one of his supernatural ballads he wanted to call all the reader's faculties into active play, with belief neither excluded nor suspended. He knew there can be truth in a fiction, and that there is a middle ground between absolute disbelief and full credence. He said of his portions of the *Lyrical Ballads:*

> the incidents and agents were to be, in part at least, supernatural; and the
> excellence aimed at was to consist in the interesting of the affections by the
> dramatic truth of such emotions as would naturally accompany such situa-
> tions, supposing them to be real.[1]

33

Coleridge points out that the supernatural, properly treated, can partake of an emotional truth, a fidelity to human experience, that overrides the apparent unreality of the subject matter. In the "Rime of the Ancient Mariner," for instance, we can not only perceive, but also believe, the horror, despair, and awe generated by the experience. We know them for truth, truth of the human heart, as Hawthorne would say, even though very few of us have been becalmed, and none in such a sea. Thus there is at least one kind of belief which is not bound by our rational knowledge of the possible and the impossible.

Coleridge's poem suggests another kind of truth that may reside within a work of fantasy. There is something about the Ancient Mariner's tale that lies deeper than emotion. It is not just that Coleridge has accurately gauged the probable response to his improbable situation. Rather, we sense in the situation itself an experience, masked but recognizable, that we seem to have lived through. Freudians might say that it represents a stage in our emotional development, disguised as fiction. Jungians would say instead that the experience hinted at is a racial memory retained in the unconscious mind of each of us. Either way, Coleridge's poem contains, or expresses, archetypes: patterns of subjective truth, not observed, but felt deep inside. Maud Bodkin pointed some of them out in her 1934 *Archetypal Patterns in Poetry*: the white bird of omen, the oily, monstrous sea, the inspiring wind.[2] These archetypes stand out clearly in part because of the unreality of their setting. Coleridge's fantastic world is a little like the worlds of myth in that regard: simple and stark and fundamental.

What is true of a supernatural poem also holds for a prose fantasy. It, too, must be emotionally valid, and it should, to be effective, embody some kind of archetype. Eleanor Cameron, a writer and critic of fantasies, says that "though fantasy takes place in a world apparently divorced from reality, it is limited if it does not contain, aside from its own imaginative truth, the truth of the human condition."[3] For someone accustomed to the mode of fantasy, whether traditional or literary, it is not only possible, but often advantageous, to move one's creation away from the observable world into the realm of the impossible, where archetypal, human truths tend to lie a little closer to the surface, as in dreams.

Coleridge, in the same essay quoted above, divided the imagination into two parts, a primary imagination that perceives and a secondary one that invents (p. 167). J. R. R. Tolkien postulates a similar division in the power of belief. Using Coleridgean terminology, Tolkien describes a "primary belief," which can be applied to a tree, to the laws of entropy, or to a myth, and a "secondary belief," which is applied at will to the creations of the (secondary) imagination:

What really happens is that the storymaker proves a successful "sub-creator." He makes a secondary world which your mind can enter. Inside it, what he relates is "true": it accords with the laws of that world. You therefore believe it, while you are, as it were, inside.[4]

This means that the reader can by no means merely suspend disbelief. He must, to some extent, commit himself to the material he is reading. If he accepts the emotional scheme of the work, and if there is archetypal force to draw him in, then he is able to devote a measure of secondary belief where no primary belief is possible or expected. This is perhaps what E. M. Forster means by the extra payment required by fantasy: a pledge of faith in the author's imaginative insight and a willingness to believe that truth can be reached by indirect and fantastic paths.

The author can do more, however, than convince us that his extra toll is worth paying for its ultimate rewards. He can lighten the burden by depicting the setting and incidents of a story so vividly that we can support inner conviction with the evidence of the senses. All the great fantasies do so: as we have seen, Washington Irving, in "Rip Van Winkle," made excellent use of descriptive accuracy to draw the reader in. C. S. Lewis calls this narrative device "realism of presentation," and he gives as an example the dragon in *Beowulf* "sniffing along the stone."[5] Such unexpected but appropriate detail brings the story into sudden focus. It lets us bring our experience to bear on the imaginary world of the tale by making connections and analogies—the sniffing dragon is like a wolf or bear on the hunt and can be comprehended and feared in the same way. The more of our knowledge we can apply to the fantasy, the easier it is to achieve secondary belief. We cannot picture the unknown unless we hear it described in terms of the known. As Lewis comments, "Try to imagine a new primary color, a third sex, a fourth dimension, or even a monster which does not consist of bits of existing animals stuck together. Nothing happens."[6]

This is why the bowls of porridge obey the laws of physics in their cooling in "Goldilocks and the Three Bears," why the Princess in *The Princess and the Goblin* goes on hands and knees up an especially steep flight of stairs, why Ransom gets sunburned on his flight to Lewis' *Perelandra*, and why Rip Van Winkle's gun rusts during his long sleep. Each of these bits of realism helps nail its story to reality. By putting the imagined in a coherent framework of the known, we allow ourselves to exist briefly on a plane with it: we enter the Other World only when there is air to breathe, food to eat, and ground to walk on. For the same reason, fantasies are usually told in a conservative manner, without the shifts in time and point of view, the verbal tricks, and the violations of illusion that characterize much modern literature. Those things are devices to break up the solidity of complacency or despair that writers find in contemporary life. Fantasy makes its one great rift with the perceived world and neither requires nor tolerates others.

The delight of fantasy is not in disordering, but in reordering reality. It reinforces our awareness of what is by showing us what might be, and uses the imaginary laws of the created world to postulate hidden principles on which our own might be organized. To do so, however, it must be belief worthy on every level except the one that marks "realistic" fiction. Its impossibilities must be reacted to in a recognizably human manner, and they should embody archetypal actions and values. This is no easy task for any work of literature, but the fantasist can call tradition to his aid. He can reanimate old tales of wonder. He can observe and imitate the characteristic devices of ballad or epic. And, most importantly, if he is living in a time when a body of legend is being reevaluated, he can catch bits of that body on their way down from full credence to discredit. When a writer (and his readers) knows that there are no fairies in the forest, yet knows or remembers people that still hold the old fairy faith, then he is free to toy with the idea of fairies, modify it and invent around it, and still make use of the lingering half-belief it evokes.

Legends about the fairies, or any other supernatural force, express the way peasant peoples felt about their lives and the powerful, mysterious, world around them. A perceptive writer of fantasy can take hold of remembered legends and extract the truth that remains in them. That is the final kind of truth in a fantasy, the cultural belief expressed in traditional motifs. The writer can call it forth and direct it as he wills, but he cannot create it where it does not exist. For this reason American fantasy has been circumscribed by the legendry it draws on, and sometimes converted into a different mode of writing altogether.

Irving was one of several early American writers interested in stories of the marvelous. Hawthorne, Poe, and Melville also wrote brief works of fantasy, and, indeed, one of the primary characteristics of American writing is its departure from the social realism of most English novels. Yet the major works of these writers are not fantasy, any more than they are Trollopian novels of manners. They are usually called "romances," like those medieval poems that move without effort from the worldly life of the court to the spiritual wonders of fairyland. American romance, too, exists in two worlds. It is bordered on one side by the mimetic novel, and the contrasts and relationships between the two have often been pointed out, but the other border, which is the line between romance and fantasy, has never been adequately surveyed. The great works of romance make use of the techniques of the marvelous and yet fall outside the realm of fantasy.

We have already seen how Irving uses details of presentation, borrowed or reworked traditions, and a carefully limited field of action to ease the supernatural into his story. But he does one other thing, at the tale's end, to ally the reader with him: he anticipates the reader's own skepticism. He drops a hint in his final paragraph that he himself remains unconvinced: "[Rip] was observed, at first, to vary on some points every time he told it, which was, doubtless, owing to his having so recently awakened."[7] If we follow the hint, we are obliged to discount the heart of the story and interpret the whole as the account of an ingenious lie. Irving is evidently unwilling to commit himself entirely to the world he has created, so he gives us a wink as he draws the curtain.

Coleridge makes no such disavowal in his supernatural poems; European fairy tales do not end with a disclaimer; and Tolkien roundly condemns "any frame or machinery suggesting that the whole story...is a figment or illusion."[8] In "Rip Van Winkle," the truths of presentation and emotion outweigh the final momentary failure of commitment, and the story remains a satisfactory fantasy. In other stories, though, like "The Legend of Sleepy Hollow," or the "Adventure of the German Student," Irving effectively punctures secondary belief with his ironic asides. The latter story ends with a complete debunking: "I had it from the best authority. The student told it me himself. I saw him in a mad-house in Paris."[9] This is not fantasy, or even romance, but literary satire of a very deft sort.

Only in "Rip Van Winkle" and perhaps "The Devil and Tom Walker," which draws on the forest devil of the Puritans, did Irving find enough legendary authority to support an original American fantasy. In the rest of his work we find legends aplenty—Dutch, German, English, Spanish—but nowhere else does he transform traditional materials into personal statement the way he does in Rip's tale. None of the other legends, of English ghosts or Moorish djinns, seemed to touch so directly on Irving's life and the culture around him. Much of the time, though he wrote before the study of folklore had been systematized, he comes across more as collector than as creator, roaming the world in search of marvels he could not find at home.

Edgar Allen Poe's stories, like Irving's, are nearly all brief, and their range of subjects is narrow and repetitive: enclosure, possession, necrophilia, disintegration. Like Irving he often undercuts a story by questioning the veracity of the narrator or protagonist; his work is full of dreams, hallucinations, and hoaxes that frame apparently fantastic sequences of events. The virtuosity of his atmospheric technique suggests a smoke screen to cover his shortage of and lack of faith in the supernatural materials he worked with. Not the protofolklorist that Irving was, he borrowed his motifs from literary treatments, in Gothic novels and magazines, of European legend. When he made use of the *Märchen* form, as in his brief fable "Eleanora," he copies the highly symbolic, static, decorative style of German Romantics like Novalis.

Perhaps the nearest thing to fully realized fantasy among Poe's works is "The Fall of the House of Usher." Read as a fantasy, this is a tale about a haunted world, where a house and its owner are magically linked, where poetry and music have power over physical being, and where an ancestor's pride can feed on his descendants. The setting of the story is marked off from this world not so much by particular impossibilities as by an overall impression of malevolence so intense as to leave the narrator gasping in dashes: "I looked upon the scene before me—upon the mere house, and the simple landscape features of the domain—upon the bleak walls—upon the vacant eye-like windows—upon a few rank sedges—and upon a few white trunks of decayed trees—with an utter depression of the soul which I can compare to no earthly sensation more properly than to the after-dream of the reveller upon opium—the bitter lapse into everyday life—the hideous dropping off of the veil."[10] That the overwhelming force of the place is no illusion is confirmed by that traditional Gothic truth teller, the mirror: in this case, the "black and lurid tarn" into which the narrator gazes "with a shudder even more thrilling than before—upon the remodelled and inverted images of the grey sedge, and the ghastly tree-stems, and the vacant and eye-like windows" (p. 398).

At the center of this lurid landscape stands the House of Usher, magically preserved despite its age: "No portion of the masonry had fallen; and there appeared to be a wild inconsistency between its still perfect adaptation of parts and the crumbling condition of the individual stones" (p. 400). Fungi drape the house, like the visible stigmata of age. House and landscape clearly belong to another dimension, set apart from earthly things (especially American things) by antiquity and inherited evil. Poe, even more than Irving, uses atmosphere to lay the groundwork for unbelievable events. Colors, emblematic objects, and a strong dose of the "pathetic fallacy" announce to the reader that he is in a world where ordinary laws of matter and behavior have been wrenched into some new pattern.

All that remains to establish a fantasy world is to proclaim it, that is, to reveal through place names, snatches of imaginary history, or unambiguously magical events that the story is indeed unfolding in fairyland. Of place names there is only one, Usher, which designates place, edifice, character, and, in Poe's onomatopoetic fashion, the hushed anticipation pervading the story. The name is not invented but Biblical, a clue that the tale may be not so much fantasy as parable. It is certainly the name of no real place that we know of, but conversely there is no clue to tell us that there could not be a baronial house named Usher somewhere in the world. Other names in Poe are more other-worldly, like "the dark tarn of Auber,/ In the ghoul-haunted woodland of Weir,"[11] or the "wild weird clime that lieth, sublime,/ Out of Space—out of Time," called "Dream-Land."[12]

The House of Usher stands in the middle of that same nightmare landscape that Poe spent most of his time as a poet trying to convey without clearly describing. In the poems he openly terms it a "Fairy-Land": "Dim vales—and shadowy floods—/ And cloudy-looking woods,/ Whose forms we can't discover...."[13] In prose, however, he is reluctant to label it as such.

As for imaginary histories and impossible events, again it is difficult to say they are present in the story. We are told no history; rather the narrator pieces together a symbolic account of past events from paintings, music, a ballad, and a quasi-medieval romance. All of these are unearthly, but they are given no value of truth or falsehood within the story, as are, for instance, the elven ballads or comic hobbit songs in *The Lord of the Rings*. When Roderick Usher sings of "The Haunted Palace," where

> ... travellers now within that valley,
>   Through the red-litten windows see
> Vast forms that move fantastically
>   To a discordant melody;
> While, like a rapid ghastly river,
>   Through the pale door,
> A hideous throng rush out forever,
>   And laugh—but smile no more ("Usher," p. 407)

he anticipates Tolkien's description of the ruined tower Minas Morgul. But whereas Tolkien is writing of a place on a par with his narrative action, Poe is creating imaginary worlds within imaginary worlds, so the world of the song and the world of the singer generate different expectations. There is a correspondence between the Haunted Palace and the falling house, but the "vast forms" and "hideous throng" of the former have only a symbolic existence in the latter. The dragon of the imaginary "Mad Trist" is analogous to Roderick's afflicted sister, but they are obviously not the same.

Analyzing the events of the story, we can see that the House of Usher is somewhere between our world and fairyland. Unlike Irving, who only momentarily steps out of the frame of his story, Poe flaunts his doubts. Every seemingly magical event in the story is loaded with ambiguities:

Roderick Usher's belief that he was bewitched by his house is "conveyed in terms too shadowy here to be re-stated" (p. 403); the glowing vapors that surround the house "are merely electrical phenomena not uncommon" (p. 413); and the heavy doors that open spontaneously, "as if in the superhuman energy of his utterance there had been found the potency of a spell," are really moved by "the work of a rushing gust" (p. 416). We are in a world where every happening has two explanations: one unbelievable but appropriate, the other rational but absurdly inadequate.

Other markers of fantasy appear with the same ambiguity. There are no alien or supernatural beings; yet Usher and his sister are by no means natural. Madeline is both invalid and undying monster; Roderick is a man grappling with insanity and also a magician whose countenance is unconnected with "any idea of simple humanity" (p. 402), who is served by silent and, for the most part, invisible retainers. The narrator of the story, though he does nothing even faintly heroic, is like a fairy tale hero in that he is an ordinary man cast among wonders, through whose eyes we see the Other World. He is even more like the hero of legend, Tam Lin or Thomas the Rhymer, who enters fairyland unwillingly, is powerless while there, and escapes amid great danger. His adventure has none of the bright wonder of *Märchen*, nor any visible trace of its structure, but much of the supernatural terror of legend.

The magical world of fantasy is a world of meaning, where everything interacts with everything else in coherent patterns, whereas Poe's is a world of antimeaning. The movement in most fantasies is toward understanding or revelation of the ruling principles in the fantasy world, the alignment of positive and negative values that are its motive powers. In Poe's story there are no particular values, and the two main characters arrive at such disparate conceptions of the world that they consider one another madmen. Usher, whose world view represents a fantasy reading of the story, sees a malevolent universe, in which man's imagination stands alone against the forces of disintegration and death. In him, Poe has reproduced the Puritan belief in black magic without its meliorating belief in divine providence. The narrator, who generally represents a nonfantastic, rational reading of the story, sees an impersonal universe, likewise tending toward destruction but without malice. In his view, man's reason holds the barriers against the darkness: he is the heir to the Enlightenment trying to shed its light on chaos.

"The Fall of the House of Usher" operates by superimposing two frames: the fantastic and the rational. As fantasy it is limited by Poe's unbelief, the same unbelief that so often made him turn Gothic conventions toward parody. When Poe attempted to write unambiguous fantasy, as in some of the poems, he found it possible to do so only by making his fantasy world so vaporous as to evade questions of belief. The fantasy side of "Usher" is narrow, narrower in its scope than even "Rip Van Winkle": without the richness of scene, variety of character, or intricacy of plot that mark the English fantasies.

As naturalistic narrative the story is equally limited, little more than a portrait of an isolated madman. What is more, the plot is full of melodrama and coincidence, as if Poe wished, not to hide his conventions and devices, but to highlight them: to defy secondary belief. Only when the two frames are put together does the story take on power and significance. The two flat readings, interacting like slides on a stereopticon, generate a new perspective. Poe wished to write about perception, order, belief; he could not do so by accepting any one stance even for the duration of the story.

Poe's fiction is full of experiments with frame and structure. Starting usually with the same core of materials—the murders, ghosts, and madmen of popular Gothic fiction, colored with his own obsessive concerns—he can rationalize them as detective story, psychological study, hoax, or science fiction, depending on whether he establishes common sense, tricks of perception, untrustworthy narration, or technology as the dominant frame of reference. The point in all of these genres is that we can explain away the mysteries of life and death. But in Poe's most striking words, like "The Fall of the House of Usher," rationality is evenly matched with fantasy: the two structures coexist and reverberate against one another.

This productive ambiguity characterizes modern romance. As I said before, ancient and medieval romances freely mix the mundane and the supernatural. Modern romance, too, tries to juxtapose the real and the magical—unlike fantasy, which keeps them walled off from one another—but it can do so only through this kind of duplicity of structure. Like the modern mind of which it is a product, it carries within it two hostile world views, an acquired scientific one and an inherited magical one, both of which must be appealed to for a fully satisfactory and believable statement about the universe.

If we look in Poe for the various kinds of belief-worthiness described at the outset of this chapter, we find little or no attempt at realism of presentation; some degree of traditional verification, though more through literary than folk conventions; an acute, if bizarre, kind of emotional truth, with roots in both the fantastic and the rational sides of the story; and a highly successful evocation of archetypes. These add up to a sort of dream realism: everything has an insubstantial, watery, moonlit quality far from the sturdy solidity of fairy tales and their immediate literary descendants. Poe did not run into problems romanticizing America because he did not use it: his landscape refers neither to New World nor to Old, but only to the geography of his own mind.

Nathaniel Hawthorne, on the other hand, wrote full-length and unmistakably American fiction, but he did not have an easy time of it. Before each of his romances he lodges a complaint about the unsuitability of the American scene for imaginative literature. His complaint is twofold. A sentence in the preface to *The Marble Faun* conveys something of the nature of both halves:

> No author, without a trial, can conceive of the difficulty of writing a Romance about a country where there is no shadow, no antiquity, no mystery, no picturesque and gloomy wrong, nor anything but a commonplace prosperity, in broad and simple daylight, as is happily the case with my dear native land.[14]

On the one hand, he is saying, we lack the complexities of society that come from antiquity and inherited wrongs, which are the stock in trade of the social novelist. Writers from Cooper to James voiced the same complaint. R. W. B. Lewis points out that Hawthorne expresses the novelist's dilemma most clearly through the hero, Redclyffe, of *Dr. Grimshawe's Secret:* "Redclyffe's nostalgia is for the kind of 'density' he finds in the atmosphere of an English country estate; a thickening of life and character caused by the hidden vitality of the past. In such a place, Redclyffe supposes, 'the life of each successive dweller was eked out with the lives of all who had hitherto lived there . . . so that there was a rare and successful contrivance for giving length, fullness, body, and substance to this frail matter of human life.' "[15]

On the other hand, Hawthorne also longs for "shadow" and "mystery," requisites not of the novel but of fantasy. He envies European writers, who could wander at will into the marvelous:

> In the old countries, with which Fiction has long been conversant, a certain conventional privilege seems to be awarded to the romancer; his work is not put exactly side by side with nature; and he is allowed a license with regard to every-day Probability, in view of the much improved effects which he is bound to produce thereby. Among ourselves, on the contrary, there is as yet no such Faery Land, so like the real world, that, in a suitable remoteness, one cannot tell the difference, but with an atmosphere of strange enchantment, beheld through which the inhabitants have a propriety of their own.[16]

Hawthorne is here using "Faery Land" metaphorically, as a name for the sphere in which all fiction operates, but his description of it fits fantasy best of all: like the real world, but remote, improbable, enchanted. Only in this imaginary realm does Hawthorne find it possible to express his insights into the human heart.

The valuable thing about romance, for Hawthorne, is that it can depart from observable reality; it "has fairly a right to present... truth under circumstances, to a great extent, of the writer's own choosing or creation. If he think fit, also, he may so manage his atmospheric medium as to bring out or mellow the lights and deepen and enrich the shadows of the picture." Especially, the author can "mingle the Marvellous" in order to make associations not otherwise apparent. The marvelous should be used with restraint, he says, but an author "can hardly be said, however, to commit a literary crime, even if he disregard this caution."[17] Hawthorne's theory fits both romance and fantasy, both tentative and whole-hearted violations of everyday reality.

Hawthorne shared with Irving a fascination with the legends he found in Europe. Itally, for example, was so full of magical and mysterious associations that he saw it as "a sort of poetic or fairy precinct, where actualities would not be so terribly insisted upon, as they are, and needs must be, in America."[18] In his later years, frustrated by an increasing inability to capture American life in his kind of writing, he turned for more congenial sites first to Italy, in *The Marble Faun*, and then to England, in *Dr. Grimshawe's Secret* and *The Dolliver Romance*, neither of which he was able to finish. There was romance and mystery in Europe, but it did not lend itself to his chosen themes. The one accessible fairyland for Hawthorne was located in his own region, but in the past.

Most of Hawthorne's shorter stories verge on fantasy. "Fancy's Show Box" is a sermon on guilt, made more tangible by personifications of Fancy, Memory, and Conscience. "The Celestial Railroad" is a satire on modern philosophies, reviving with some wit the setting of Bunyan's *Pilgrim's Progress*, and, like it, continually trying to break out of the limits of allegory into independent fantasy. "The Hall of Fantasy" and "A Virtuoso's Collection" also unfold along allegorical lines, but of Hawthorne's own devising. These four stories show a kind of evolution from outright moralizing to the submerged message typical of fantasy.

One of the finest stories, "Young Goodman Brown," is more fully realized yet, but in it Hawthorne, like Poe, has planted so many seeds of doubt that it should rather be called romance. It is tied to legend, and so is "The Great Carbuncle," which I have already mentioned as an example of legend radically altered by the literary artist but nevertheless attaining a degree of popular currency in its revised form. "The Great Carbuncle" is not so ambiguous as romance, but neither is it quite true fantasy. It tends to break apart into a plot, based on the premise of a supernatural jewel hidden high in the mountains, and a message about avarice that tends to overwhelm the story line. It is both legend and allegory, and the two halves work at cross purposes. If those two components could be coordinated we would have something very much like fantasy as the English fantasists understood it: a tale or legend imbued with moral significance. And that is precisely what we have with the story of "Feathertop," subtitled "A Moralized Legend."

From its magical beginning to its ironic end, "Feathertop" sustains a fantasy world. It opens with a cheerful bit of witchcraft:

> "Dickon," cried Mother Rigby, "a coal for my pipe!"
> The pipe was in the old dame's mouth, when she said these words. She had thrust it there after filling it with tobacco, but without stooping to light it at the hearth; where, indeed, there was no appearance of a fire having been kindled, that morning. Forthwith, however, as soon as the order was given, there was an intense red glow out of the bowl of the pipe, and a whiff of smoke from Mother Rigby's lips.[19]

Another world? Yes, whether we say that Mother Rigby's witchcraft establishes hers as the Other World or that the invisible Dickon is its emissary into our own.

Dickon's world, though Hawthorne does not stress the fact, is Hell. He is an imp, Mother Rigby's familiar, and the coals he uses to light her pipe are embers of hellfire.[20] Any seventeenth-century New Englander could tell you as much, but Hawthorne pretends ignorance: "Mother Rigby always liked to flavor her pipe with a coal of fire from the particular chimney-corner, whence this had been brought. But where that chimney-corner might be, or who brought the coal from it—further than that the invisible messenger seemed to respond to the name of Dickon—I cannot tell" (pp. 226–27). Hell, as it existed in the minds of Hawthorne's ancestors, was no place for fantasy. The richest fantasy worlds contain both poles, good and evil, else there would be no room for conflict; nor would it do to have one's characters eternally damned just for dealing with magic. They must have a choice within the fantasy framework, not between it and salvation.

Therefore Hawthorne modifies Puritan belief to suit his aims. He avoids mention of Hell, or identification of Dickon as an evil spirit. The Devil he refers to by his common nickname, the Black Man, but not in the traditional context of meetings in the forest or infernal bargains. The only reference to him in the story is in connection with a garment said to be his: "an ancient plum-colored coat of London make, and with relics of embroidery on its seams, cuffs, pocket-flaps, and button-holes, but lamentably worn and faded, patched at the elbows, tattered at the skirts, and threadbare all over" (p. 225). This devil is a gentlemen, even a bit of a fop, but in reduced circumstances. He is not the raw and elemental force of Puritan accounts.

The witch, too, has undergone a meliorating change. Puritan witches were supposed to be wholly evil, single-mindedly going about their master's business, which was to torment and tempt the people of God. Hawthorne has gone back to a less theological conception of the witch as a potent wonder worker with a mind of her own. Like witches in older European lore, Mother Rigby works spells merely for her own comfort—like the pipe coal conjuration—or amusement. It is to amuse herself that she brings to life the title character, Feathertop.

Feathertop is a scarecrow, with a broomstick for a backbone, various sticks and implements for limbs, straw for innards, and a pumpkin for a head. He is dressed in the Black Man's own jacket. Mother Rigby originally intends him to stand guard in her garden, as a scarecrow should. Hawthorne brings in a nice piece of realism of presentation in this connection, corroborative evidence, as it were: "It was now the latter week of May, and the crows and blackbirds had already discovered the little, green, rolled-up leaf of the Indian corn, just peeping out of the soil. She was determined, therefore, to contrive as lifelike a scarecrow as ever was seen, and to finish it immediately, from top to toe, so that it should begin its sentinel's duty that very morning" (pp. 223-24). Feathertop proves such as accurate and comical caricature of mankind, though, that Mother Rigby decides to make better use of him than she had planned. "He's capable of better things," she says. "What if I should let him take his chance among the other men of straw and empty fellows, who go bustling about the world?" (p. 227).

The finest scene in the story is surely the account of Feathertop's animation. Hawthorne uses every means to make his description believable. Again there is the smooth joining of imagined and observed detail that constitutes realistic presentation, as the pumpkin head breathes in life from Mother Rigby's pipe, first in the faintest puffs and then in "a volley of smoke extending all the way from the obscure corner into the bar of sunshine. There it eddied and melted away among the motes of dust" (pp. 383-84).

There is realism, too, in Mother Rigby's reaction to her creation. She begins in a spirit of fun, both enjoying and mocking her scarecrow: "'Puff, darling, puff!' said she. 'Puff away, my fine fellow! Your life depends on it!'" (p. 227). As the spell begins to work she claps her hands in a mixture of Faustian glee and pure craftsmanlike pleasure at her success. When the scarecrow makes a feeble attempt to stand, her impatience is roused: "... the strong-willed old beldam scowled, and beckoned, and flung the energy of her purpose so forcibly at this poor combination of rotten wood, and musty straw, and ragged garments, that it was compelled to show itself a man, in spite of the reality of things" (p. 229). Lastly, and most tellingly, she shows a curious motherly tenderness toward disillusioned Feathertop when he returns from his adventures:

> My poor, dear, pretty Feathertop! There are thousands upon thousands of coxcombs and charlatans in the world, made up of just such a jumble of worn-out, forgotten, and good-for-nothing trash, as he was! Yet they live in fair repute, and never see themselves for what they are! And why should my poor puppet be the only one to know himself, and perish for it? (p. 245)

If we may trust Hawthorne, his story is derived from legend, and has the weight of tradition to add to its truthfulness of detail and of emotion. "Upon my word," says Hawthorne midway through Feathertop's transformation, "if the legend were not one which I heard on my grandmother's knee, and which had established its place among things credible before my childish judgment could analyze its probability, I question whether I should have the face to tell it now!" (p. 229). Hawthorne is certainly using the appearance of traditionality as an aid to his storytelling, whether or not he derived his principal motifs from oral sources, in much the same way that he uses his custom-house experience to lend solidity to *The Scarlet Letter*.

Baughman's *Type and Motif Index of the Folktales of England and North America* does not list any instances in recorded American lore of animated scarecrows or magical pipes.[21] But in the broader category of living, full-size dolls, a European scholar, Max Lüthi, offers two examples, one a local legend from Switzerland and the other a modern fairy tale from Greece.[22] The latter is similar to "Feathertop" in that a woman of power creates and animates an artificial man to take his place in the world, in this case as her husband. But, as Lüthi points out, this is only the beginning of a more complex tale along typical *Märchen* lines (p. 88). Fairy tales do not end with single events, but must fulfill the upward cycle described by Propp.

The local legend stays closer to Hawthorne's tale. In it, a group of cowherds assemble a manlike form from odds and ends and then perversely and wickedly baptize it, thereby bringing it to life through what is essentially an act of witchcraft. The creature then kills one of them and escapes to wreak evil in the valley, as Feathertop might have worked evil in the city if he had not been hindered by a conscience. The story of Feathertop is one which could be incorporated in a longer and sunnier fairy tale or fantasy, had Hawthorne been so inclined, or it could be told to generate a thrill of horror in the reader, as the Swiss legend does, and as Poe might have chosen to do with the same materials. Hawthorne, though, does neither. He leans toward the fantasy side, clearly suppressing the darker implications of the New England witchcraft he takes for his magical machinery, but he avoids the integrative happy ending that marks a typical literary fairy tale. Instead, he writes a wry, comical, faintly tragic tale of eccentrics and society. Feathertop and Mother Rigby are misfits, one too sensitive and the other too independent and creative to fill their assigned social roles.

The elements of fantasy in "Feathertop" are used, as Hawthorne says, to highlight the important parts of the story. Through them Hawthorne is announcing that his story is not an imitation of the world, but a distillation of his feelings about life. On the other hand, even in this most fantastic of his tales, he is not content merely to follow traditional patterns of storytelling, as some fantasists have done. "Feathertop" is a satisfying and unusual reworking of legend into a meaningful and original literary composition, more distinctive and concrete than, say, Ruskin's *The King of the Golden River*, but not so rich or well sustained as one of William Morris' better fantasy pieces. It is equivalent, perhaps, to one of the short stories of another moralizer of legend, George MacDonald, though with a different flavor: sharper, thinner, more American. If Hawthorne was satisfied with "Feathertop" (and he had reason to be), then it would seem likely that he might go on and write longer works in the same vein, the American counterparts of MacDonald's *The Princess and the Goblin* or *Lilith*. But he did not. Instead he wrote *The Scarlet Letter*, a much different and, indeed, greater work.

Constance Rourke observed that Hawthorne stands somewhere between the realistic mode of most British fiction and the nonrealistic mode of poets like Coleridge or Keats, which is also the mode of fantasy. She sees Hawthorne's position as a dilemma:

> Though he drew upon a traditional material, Hawthorne could not rest at ease as the great English poets have rested within the poetic tradition that came to them through the ballads and romances, or as the great English novelists have drawn upon rich local accumulations of character and lore. The materials at his hand were not rich or dense or voluminous: time had not enriched but had scattered them. The effort to create imaginative writing out of such a groundwork must inevitably have been disruptive for an artist like Hawthorne; it was making bricks of straw.[23]

Hawthorne did have difficulty with sustained creation, as indicated by the complaints in his many prefaces. In the end, he found himself unable to finish any of several unsatisfactory romances. But great obstacles often generate great solutions. Out of the thin fabric of American society and the thinner fabric of American legend, Hawthorne was able, at his artistic peak, to stitch together a new and vital kind of fiction, like Poe's dream romance in its doubleness of vision, but longer, fuller, more vivid, and more central to the American experience.

To understand *The Scarlet Letter*, or any of Hawthorne's major fictions, it is necessary to understand both elements of the synthesis, the social novel and the fantasy. The novel side predominates in all of the full-length romances, and consequently that is the side which has been given the most attention by critics already predisposed in that direction by theories of mimesis or the Great Tradition of realistic fiction. But the strongest of Hawthorne's romances is the one in which the realistic and magical components are most nearly balanced, while his weakest are marked by the inadequacy of their legendary materials.

Everyone is familiar with the daylight events that make up one half of *The Scarlet Letter*: an offstage act of adultery, the birth of an illegitimate child, a trial, a meeting of the guilty lovers, a cuckold's intricate revenge, a public confession—all operating under a primary theme of guilt, contrition, and forgiveness. The same theme dominates the fantastic side of the story, but the events in it are, in comparison, wild and exotic.

The magical story embedded within *The Scarlet Letter* begins at the end of the accompanying essay on "The Custom-House," when Hawthorne, ostensibly in his own voice, describes the finding of the embroidered letter:

> It seemed to me,—the reader may smile, but must not doubt my word,—it seemed to me, then, that I experienced a sensation not altogether physical, yet almost so, as of burning heat; and as if the letter were not of red cloth, but red-hot iron.[24]

Thus, before the story is even under way, we have a clue to the presence of the extraordinary. We have been warned that the letter is not merely what it seems, but has somehow absorbed the passion and suffering of its wearer. This is magic, the modification of the physical world directly through will or emotion, and, though Hawthorne allows us to smile, that is, to retain our primary disbelief in such enchantment, he will not allow us to doubt within the story, on a secondary level, that the scarlet letter is more than a material object.

When the story opens, and Hester Prynne appears at the door of the jail with the letter on her breast, Hawthorne enlarges on the supernatural function of the letter: "It had the effect of a spell, taking her out of the ordinary relations with humanity, and inclosing her in a sphere by herself" (p. 54). That is an ambiguous sentence, and it has a place in both the natural and supernatural systems of event and meaning in the romance. Hawthorne means, first, that the letter had an effect similar to that of a spell, and, second, that its isolating effect was truly magical. The structure of the sentence parallels and enforces the double nature of the story.

Usually Hawthorne's effect is simpler: he offers rival explanations of an event as perceived by bystanders or participants and refuses to select among them. A part of the spell of the scarlet letter is to give Hester an awareness of evil within her fellow townspeople. That is the fantasy reading, and it occurs to Hester herself:

> Walking to and fro, with those lonely footsteps, in the little world with which she was outwardly connected, it now and then appeared to Hester,—if altogether fancy, it was nevertheless too potent to be resisted,—she felt or fancied, then, that the scarlet letter had endowed her with a new sense. (p. 86)

But she cannot be sure: is it a new sense or is it just an overactive imagination? An even more fantastic explanation of her revelations occurs to her:

> Could they be other than the insidious whispers of the bad angel, who would fain have persuaded the struggling woman, as yet only half his victim, that the outward guise of purity was but a lie, and that, if truth were everywhere to be shown, a scarlet letter would blaze forth on many a bosom besides Hester Prynne's? (p. 86)

Insight or illusion, fantastic or explainable: Hawthorne will not choose, nor can his reader, if he wishes to comprehend the tale in its fullness. Hawthorne intends us to guess that some of Hester's new insight is due to her new awareness of small signs of guilt, unnoticed before, in the faces around her, but he is not willing to state unequivocally that such skill is a purely natural thing. It is more magical than we have realized, he says.

The same technique is most evident in the final chapter of the book. A twin of the scarlet letter has been revealed on the bare chest of Arthur Dimmesdale. "Most of the spectators," comments Hawthorne, "testified to having seen, on the breast of the unhappy minister, a SCARLET LETTER—the very semblance of that worn by Hester Prynne—imprinted in the flesh" (p. 258). A few "highly respectable witnesses" (p. 259) claim to have seen nothing, but Hawthorne more or less discounts their testimony. However, we are not told how the letter came to be branded there; instead, we get three accounts, one skeptical and two fantastic, from the witnessing crowd:

> Some affirmed that the Reverend Mr. Dimmesdale, on the very day when Hester Prynne first wore her ignominious badge, had begun a course of penance,—which he afterwards, in so many futile methods, followed out,— by inflicting a hideous torture on himself. Others contended that the stigma had not been produced until a long time subsequent, when old Roger Chillingworth, being a potent necromancer, had caused it to appear, through the agency of magic and poisonous drugs. Others, again,—and those best

able to appreciate the minister's peculiar sensibility, and the wonderful operation of his spirit upon the body,—whispered their belief, that the awful symbol was the effect of the ever active tooth of remorse, gnawing from the inmost heart outwardly, and at last manifesting heaven's dreadful judgment by the visible presence of the letter. (pp. 258-59)

The first of these three explanations is too anticlimactic, at least to Hawthorne's taste and mine, to stand alone; the second too much like a fairy tale to match the complexity of Hawthorne's characterizations; and the third too obviously allegorical. But taken all three together, they are more than adequate to convey the depth of Hawthorne's psychological and moral insight. There is a truth in ambiguity, which he exploits, adding it to details of presentation, emotion, and archetype to make his work belief worthy.

The tale of fantasy that operates within *The Scarlet Letter* goes something like this: a woman, having committed adultery in Puritan Boston, discovers that her act has made her vulnerable to the devil's magic. By naming no earthly lover, she implicitly accepts an unearthly one. She is now a witch, whether she wishes or no; the letter on her bosom is the devil's mark and the child in her arms is a soulless changeling. The Black Man himself, or one of his servants, takes the form of or possesses her husband, who then proceeds to work toward her complete damnation and that of her lover Dimmesdale, through magic learned from the Indians, Satan's forest minions. Another emissary of the devil is Mistress Hibbens, the Governor's sister, who calls Hester to join her nightly revels. Hester, like Faust, gains from her bargain a new and wide-ranging knowledge of the universe. Her daughter Pearl is a source of both torment and hope for her. She is an alien creature, ranging from imp to elf as the mood strikes her. Pearl is amoral, but, though the devil's child, not evil. Because of her, Hester refrains from exercising her witch powers.

Hester, Pearl, and Dimmesdale have three significant meetings. Once they stand together on a scaffold at midnight, and a glowing letter "A" appears in the sky. A second time they meet in the forest, where Hester calls on the vegetative powers of nature to free them from the devil's spell. She herself might have been freed, but Dimmesdale is too weak, and Pearl calls her back to the world of moral responsibility. Finally, they meet, again on the scaffold, in broad daylight, in front of the gathered townspeople. Dimmesdale's confession, at the cost of his life, breaks the spell on them all: he reveals the stigma on his breast and expires, Hester rejoins the community of mankind, Pearl, like the little mermaid, sheds tears and gains a soul, and the Black Man turns away in defeat. The scarlet letter, no longer the devil's mark, has been turned by suffering into an amulet of good, which Hester wields for the benefit of all.

Not a bad fantasy, well supported by legend, and with a clear fairy tale movement of isolation, trial, and return. But as fantasy it is slight. The fantasy world is empty of non-human beings, except for Pearl and the offstage devil. There is little action, and fantasy, which is usually dominated by the element of story, demands action. *The Scarlet Letter* should not be judged solely by the criteria of fantasy any more than by those of the English domestic novel.

By juggling two patterns of narrative, Hawthorne can, at will, focus on interior or exterior phenomena: on the play of values commanded by the metaphor of magic or on subtleties of behavior that evade simpler methods of moral analysis. He can set two simultaneous currents of action going in opposite directions: in the forest scene, for instance, Hester and Arthur's moment of greatest material happiness is also their time of gravest moral danger. Or he can move his two plots in parallel, as in the conclusion, when Pearl becomes both an heiress and a fully human being.

In none of Hawthorne's other romances do the magical and mundane stories blend and balance so well. Outside of the fairyland of the past, Hawthorne's plays of fantasy tend to seem artificial and intrusive. Maule's curse, in *The House of the Seven Gables*, is a good bit of legend from an earlier time, but it seems largely irrelevant to the daily doings of nineteenth-century Salem. The hypnotism of *The Blithedale Romance* is mere stage craft. Italy was, as Hawthorne says, a more congenial spot for romance. Whether or not Donatello's ears, in *The Marble Faun,* were pointed, his transformation from alien to human is acted out quite satisfyingly—more so than that of the irritating Pearl. *The Marble Faun,* though it is severely flawed in other ways, is a good example of fairy tale and novel moving in opposite directions to good effect. As a fantasy, the story tells of a young man's journey to maturity. Donatello leaves home, meets the princess, slays the evil magician, flees, and ultimately, one hopes, gains both kingdom and bride. In the real world, however, Donatello's act is a crime, and his story is not fairy tale but tempered tragedy.

An ordinary novel is more likely to be ironic or pathetic than tragic. As Northrop Frye points out, tragedy requires characters larger than life, partaking of the nature of gods as well as men.[25] The fall of a tragic hero is a ritual act, as well as a fictional event. Modern writers can no longer invoke the gods and fates to elevate their protagonists to tragic stature. But they can, as Hawthorne does in both *The Scarlet Letter* and *The Marble Faun,* superimpose the archetypal patterns of fairy tale and legend over mundane action and get something of the same effect. This is the real secret of the success of modern romance: the range of significance that it, unlike the naturalistic novel, has available to it.

The master of this kind of fictional overlay was Herman Melville. Melville began by writing adventure stories, not fantastic, but exotic, vivid, and immensely popular. *Typee* and *Omoo* are daydream books, and, as C. S. Lewis pointed out, people want their daydreams to have the appearance of possibility, no matter how far above the reality of their lives those dreams might be.[26] The burning critical question in early reviews of *Typee* was whether its events had indeed transpired as Melville said they did. After two such books, Melville grew tired of the limitations of the autobiographical-adventure format. He had begun reading history, philosophy, and literature, and his mind was bursting with speculations that simply could not be fit into another *Typee*. Like Hawthorne, he turned to romance.

Melville seems to have understood, if his readers did not, that the South Sea setting of his earlier books was largely his own creation. Though *Typee* fans subsequently saw Polynesia through Melville's eyes, the missionaries whose work he denounced had a far different vision of his pagan paradise. At any rate, Melville proposed, in *Mardi*, to make a fairyland of his private Polynesia, as Hawthorne did of his Puritan New England. In a letter to his publisher he said:

> I have long thought that Polynesia furnished a great deal of rich poetical material that has never been empl[o]yed hitherto in works of fancy.... Well: proceeding in my narrative of *facts* I began to feel an incurable distaste for the same; & a longing to plume my powers for a flight, & felt irked, cramped & fettered by plodding along with dull common places.... [27]

Mardi is a strange book: overgrown, diffuse, and brash in its judgments. It begins as straight adventure: two sailors jump ship in mid-ocean and find a beautiful Nordic maiden about to be sacrificed by an island priest. They rescue the girl, Yillah; kill the priest; and from then on the action begins to grow fantastic. Yillah disappears, and the hero takes on the name of a local demigod, Taji. He also switches traveling companions, joining up with a minor king, a poet, a historian, and a philosopher, all burlesques of their kinds and extremely talkative. Two rival groups take an interest in Taji: the three sons of the murdered priest, who threaten him with spears, and three veiled handmaidens of the goddess/queen Hautia, who lure him with flowers. Taji and his friends, debating all the way, pursued by love and death, search the entire world, as represented by the Mardian archipelago, for the vanished Yillah. Here the story again changes direction, turning into a sort of travelog satire of religion, politics, war, and commerce. At the end of the story, nothing is resolved. Taji rejects Hautia's pleasures, the ascetic paradise of a Christian utopia, and even his friends to continue his search for Yillah, who may well be dead by this time. We last see him, still pursued and pursuing, heading toward more adventures and the next chain of islands.

Mardi is three different stories at once, a high seas adventure, a broad-ranging satire, and a fantasy. Melville could write adventure; he had already proved that, But he did not yet have the subtlety of wit to carry off successful satire, nor did he find in his South Pacific milieu the materials for a full or believable fantasy. The fantasy plot consists primarily of repeated manifestations of the three hunters and three maidens (who communicate in a Polynesian form of the popular Victorian pastime of flower-language), and increasingly obscure visions of the pale Yillah, who has undergone a sinister sea change:

> Swift I fled along the valley-side; passed Hautia's cave of pearls; and gained a twilight arch; within, a lake transparent shone. Conflicting currents met, and wrestled; and one dark arch led to channels, seaward tending.
> Round and round, a gleaming form slow circled in the deepest eddies:— white, and vaguely Yillah.[28]

Because Melville was not quite ready for fantasy or satire, and because his goals of amusement, mystification, and speculation tend in this book to work at cross-purposes, the amalgam breaks down. Taji's quest is too open ended, its motivation too unclear, to glue the book together. Melville seems purposely and perversely to avoid the triumphant resolution of a fairy tale, although the original meeting with, rescue of, and loss of Yillah is clearly in the *Märchen* mode. Too little, also, is made of promising elements like the priest's prophecy, Hautia's witchcraft, and Taji's apotheosis. *Mardi* simply confused contemporary readers, although in retrospect we can see it as a prospectus for greater works to come.

With the relative failure of *Mardi* on the market, Melville decided to return temporarily to unembellished and down-to-earth narrative. He planned his next novel, *Redburn*, as "a plain, straight-forward, amusing narrative of personal experience—the son of a gentleman on his first voyage to sea as a sailor—no metaphysics, no conic-sections, nothing but cakes and ale."[29] He privately considered it a potboiler. After the color and freedom (however much he had abused that freedom) of romance, he was unwilling to chain himself once more to the real world, but "when a poor devil writes with duns all round him, & looking over the back of his chair—& perching on his pen & diving in his inkstand—like the devils about St. Anthony—what can you expect of that poor devil?—What but a beggarly 'Redburn.' "[30]

Melville followed *Redburn* with *White-Jacket*—not beggarly, but not what he truly wanted to write. Then, with the pot once more boiling securely, he wandered off again into his watery fairyland.

Melville had more luck chasing after a white whale than a white maiden. *Moby-Dick*, though fantastic to a lesser degree than *Mardi*, is a better example of how fantasy can be put to work by an American author. It is more strongly rooted in reality and in tradition than the earlier work, and thus rings truer both in detail and in overall movement. *Moby-Dick* has been analyzed too often and too well for me to go into much detail here. Daniel Hoffman, in particular, has noted its use of European romance and myth, and the earthy, comic themes of American folklore.[31] Melville fused classical archetype with subliterary stereotype—Zeus the white bull and the white steed of the prairies, Prometheus and Sam Slick, Perseus and Daniel Boone—to create a story both universal and uniquely, richly, saltily American.

. *Moby-Dick* is not just a double story, like *The Scarlet Letter*, but one inlaid and overlaid many times. The thread of fantasy in it is thin in relation to its bulk, though striking. The ocean, as in *Mardi*, is the Other World. Melville makes excellent use of the fluidity, the indeterminacy of the sea; from chapter to chapter it shifts from romantic landscape to object of scientific study to mirror and analog of the solid land to enchanted realm. Within this world of possibilities, there are two primary acts of magic: prophecy and damnation. Prophecies abound in the book. Ishmael's childhood dream of a phantom hand is prophetic, Ahab's name is said to be prophetic, mad Elijah prophesies to the sailors going on board, Starbuck sees omens all around him, prosaic Stubb dreams of the white whale, the eerie spirit spout presages Moby-Dick's appearance, the Shaker prophet of the *Jeroboam* foretells gloom for his own ship and doom for the *Pequod*, birds and seals give signs of approaching death, and Fedallah predicts with oracular duplicity both his own and Ahab's demise. These prophecies and omens mark a world of occult relationships between man and object and from past to future. They have an important bearing on Ishmael's speculations on destiny and free will, and they form a darker counterpoint to his pantheistic reveries.

Ahab must go through an incredible number of decisions (in the religious, or antireligious, sense) and ceremonials to get himself damned, unlike the Puritans, who considered it sufficient to have been born. He has been baptized into Fedallah's demonic fire worship in a ceremony that left him scarred from head to foot, he has tempered his harpoon in human blood in a travesty of Christian ritual, he has cried out in pagan worship to the lightning, he has vowed to place his quest before all human considerations, and still there is danger of repentence. Nevertheless, he goes to his destruction still defiant, and takes the ship and its crew with him, all but Ishmael, who is saved from damnation by the greater mysteries of love.

Ahab and the whale are the two poles of the book and each has some degree of magical association, but their conflict is more spiritual and universal than fantastic, as we usually think of fantasy. They stand outside the limits of the fantastic story that runs through *Moby-Dick*. Fedallah, the Parsee, is more clearly fantastic. Not a rounded human character, he is a fairy tale menace, an Arabian-nights wizard, and an embodiment of the force and fascination of fire. In this last role he is joined by the other three harpooneers in a tetrangle of elemental influences. Dark, solid Dagoo is the earth; wild, aquiline Tashtego is air; and island-born Queequeg is the water in which Ishmael is reborn. Melville uses Renaissance cosmology here in place of legend to fuel his fantasy. It has the same aura of former belief, the same sense of magical, meaningful pattern which, because it is no longer tied to any orthodoxy, can be modified at will to fit the needs of the story. The harpooneers belong to the Other World; not fairies but more primitive demigods.

Among Melville's later works, a sketch, "The Lightning-Rod Man," and a full-length work, *The Confidence-Man*, are good examples of fiction incorporating the fantastic. They are the same story, really: a man who is more than a man seeks to test mankind's faith by offering security in this world or the next. The lightning-rod salesman claims to be able, through his devices, to direct lightning where he wills, like Jupiter Tonans, Jupiter the Thunderer, which is the name the skeptical narrator gives him. He is not really Jove, the director of the elements, but another Peter Rugg, vainly trying to outrun fate. Hawthorne referred to the Peter Rugg story in his sketch "A Virtuoso's Collection," and Melville must also have been aware of the tale. Whether or not he intended the reference, he relies on the storm-crow motif, the ill-omened Rugg-like weather-bringer, to lend a touch of eeriness to his portrait of the lightning-rod man, who is otherwise a standard Yankee huckster like the one in a superficially similar sketch by Mark Twain.[32] That touch of eeriness becomes a broad stroke of demonism by the story's end: "The scowl grew blacker on his face; the indigo-circles enlarged round his eyes as the storm-rings round the midnight moon. He sprang upon me, his tri-forked thing at my heart."[33]

Melville is making a statement in this tale, something to the effect that if a man seeks to hide himself from fate he becomes a flesh-and-blood ghost, a wandering lost soul like Peter Rugg, and if he tries to undermine another man's dignity with his false security he becomes a devil to be cast out: "I seized it; I snapped it; I dashed it; I trod it; and dragging the dark lightning-king out of my door, flung his elbowed, copper scepter after him" (p. 180). It is not a meaning that can easily be presented without a touch of fantasy: even my restatement of it relies on the terms "ghost" and "devil." Contemporary readers of "The Lightning-Rod Man" resisted both meaning and fantasy, just as they had with *Mardi* and *Moby-Dick*. A reviewer in

The Criterion called it "a very indifferent paper,"[34] and Fitz-James O'Brien, in an essay in *Putnam's Monthly*, complained of "the grotesque absurdity and incomprehensible verbiage of the 'Lightning-Rod Man.' "[35]

It must certainly have been in response to such hostile and insensitive reaction to his romances that Melville inserted into *The Confidence-Man* a brief statement—one of his very few—on his literary goals and techniques. "Strange," he says, "that in a work of amusement, this severe fidelity to real life should be exacted by anyone, who, by taking up such a work, sufficiently shows that he is not unwilling to drop real life, and turn, for a time, to something different."[36] He shows here awareness of the basic precondition of fantasy—the reader's willingness to accept the writer's imaginative manipulations of reality, his overturning, even, of fundamental facts, in order to point out some emotional or moral truth. He goes on to say that it "is with fiction as with religion: it should present another world, and yet one to which we feel the tie" (p. 244). But Melville found that his audience was not about to pay the extra bit of secondary belief necessary for him to develop fantasy, either on its own or submerged in romance.

The Confidence-Man was written, in part, as a criticism of the narrow and naive realism of American society. It takes place on board the riverboat *Fidèle*, on April Fool's Day. Again, Melville seems to have found a floating stage more conducive to his fluid view of reality. The fantasy in the work is all related to the title character, who is, like the lightning-rod man, both human sharper and supernatural visitant. All of his insights, actions, and guises are explainable in rational terms: the insights as shrewd guesswork, the actions as the machinations of one who plays the confidence game for the sheer challenge and sport of it, and the disguises as stage make-up and costuming; but from first to last Melville indicates that the natural explanation is inadequate without a corresponding supernatural one.

The confidence man's initial appearance—advent is a better word—is described in magical, mythic terms: "At sunrise on a first of April, there appeared, suddenly as Manco Capac at the lake Titicaca, a man in cream-colours, at the water-side in the city of St. Louis" (p. 1). This purely American character, the sharper and shifter described by Daniel Hoffman,[37] is given more-than-human stature and significance through analogy to gods of other times and places: here Manco Capac, and later Christ and Lucifer.

His physical appearance, though that is by no means to be trusted in this romance, seems to mark him as other-worldly:

> His cheek was fair, his chin downy, his hair flaxen, his hat a white fur one, with a long fleecy nap. He had neither trunk, valise, carpet-bag, nor parcel. No porter followed him. He was unaccompanied by friends. From the

shrugged shoulders, titters, whispers, wonderings of the crowd, it was plain that he was, in the extremest sense of the word, a stranger. (p. 1)

No baggage—where, then, do his subsequent disguises come from?

Disguise is not an adequate name for them: they are transformations, incarnations, avatars of the god of Confidence. The repeated encounters that make up the book, the endless variations on a theme of greed conquered by fraud, do follow a sort of progression in the aspects of this god, from light to dark, from the innocent and impotent lamb-like man to the ominous and all-powerful Cosmopolitan:

The next moment, the waning light expired, and with it the waning flames of the horned altar, and the waning halo round the robed man's brow; while in the darkness which ensued, the cosmopolitan kindly led the old man away."
(p. 336)

The fantasy that moves through *The Confidence-Man* is the story of a godlike being who visits the earth for a day, through a series of magical transformations learns its ways and the motivations of its inhabitants, and in the end puts out its sun and leads the inhabitants away, like foolish and naughty children, to an unknown destination. Woven around this tale is a comic satire on American manners and morals, a dark parable on religion, and a panorama of life in the booming West. In spite of the multiple aims, *The Confidence-Man*, unlike *Mardi*, hangs together; indeed it is more coherent than *Moby-Dick*, though not so grand or satisfying. It is held together by an overriding conception, embodied in the confidence-man, that operates simultaneously in every sphere of the story. Grounded in Melville's experience, broadened by his readings, animated by elements from popular lore, and granted power by the world's mythologies, the confidence-man boldly challenges America's confidence in its own commonplace reality.

These early writers of romance faced, and to some degree solved, the problems involved in creating American fantasy. First of all, they worked out a theory of literature which placed imaginative insight above straightforward reporting and set the embodiment of ideas, rather than the delineation of character, at the center of the fictional universe, which they liked to call fairyland. By their lights, they could write works that fell anywhere along a continuum of reality and fantasy, according to the dictates of subject and theme. This does not seem like such a questionable theory now, but it went counter to the taste and traditions of most of the reading audience of the early nineteenth century.

Most often they chose to work at a midpoint on the spectrum, neither wholly mundane nor commitedly fantastic. But fantasy cannot be dropped into a narrative in separate little nuggets, like chocolate chips in a cookie. A fairy tale can be recounted within a longer tale, but it becomes no more than an utterance by one of the characters, an extended figure of speech. The fantasy in a romance must operate from beginning to end, parallel to and challenging other narrative streams. It must be a fully outlined story, however slight its development. The second thing these writers had to do was alter the basic fairy tale form to fit their purposes, to express truths more complex, more ambiguous than the fairy tale's affirmation of marriage, maturity, and society. In works from "Rip Van Winkle" to *The Confidence-Man*, we can see that *Märchen* structure truncated, counterpointed with tragedy, made cyclic, or inverted. American heroes go on quests for immaturity, quests with no ending, quests of self-destruction; rarely do they fight the dragon and win the girl, though that is always the pattern of expectation the writer works from.

Thirdly, writers of romance, like fantasists, need characters outside the ordinary human mold, and the romancers ransacked American history and legend and drew as well on Americans' growing familiarity with the myths and legends of the rest of the world, in order to populate their fairylands with potent and believable, as well as fantastic, figures. Among their greatest successes are an explorer's ghost, a live scarecrow, a changeling child, a white whale, and a satanic salesman—an interesting crew, new and unusual, the hard-won beginnings of an American fairy nation. Hard-won they certainly were. The story of their creation is one of extensive search, painful introspection, frequent failure, and popular neglect. Each work of early fantasy or romance was sent out hopeful into the world like poor Feathertop, only to be met with gasps of horror and incomprehension. Only gradually did tastes shift, in part because of the efforts of Poe, Irving, Hawthorne, and Melville, and romance become an acceptable mode of communication.

Romance, with its doubts and doubleness, its shifting levels of primary and secondary belief, differs in its aims from pure fantasy. Nevertheless, in solving their own literary problems, the romance writers helped clear the way for more fully developed fantasies, stories concerned not so much with shadows and ambiguity as with sheer wonder, told with a full measure of belief. They showed how American songs, tales, and legends, no matter how intractible, might ultimately be coerced into tales of the marvelous. They demonstrated, too, that truths about this world—and even this country—can find their way into fairyland, and, sometimes, shine more clearly there than here.

FOUR

Fantasy for American Children

AMERICAN ROMANCE offered a compromise between realism and fantasy. It enabled artists who were not content with setting their creations in the flat, sunny, everyday world to superimpose on it a shadowy, timeless, inner world of magic and myth. But by the end of the nineteenth century the romance tradition had dwindled to a set of formulas in the hands of milk-and-water writers like Hawthorne's son Julian or his would-be successor Edward Bellamy. Hawthorne's Puritan Other World slipped farther into the past, beyond the powers of lesser writers to invoke it, and Melville's slippery ocean universe was dispelled by the invasion of steampowered merchant ships. The elements once fused into romance broke apart and formed new genres: realism, psychological suspense, and science fiction. Other genres grew out of the dawning discovery that America had, after all, a past and a society: local color, naturalism, and the genteel social novel. Some writers ceased to comb American folklore for its remaining fragments of supernaturalism and began to build a new literature out of its more solid elements—humor, verbal play, lively characterization, and generous sentiment.

Where, then, did the element of wonder go? There is awe in the contemplation of a vast and powerful nature and there is fascination in the complex workings of the mind; but open and avowed wonder, the sense that the world holds timeless mysteries, that an object may be a key to something greater than itself—did that burn itself out of our literature after *Moby-Dick*? It did not; rather it was consigned to an audience who, it was assumed, did not need to worry itself about the problems of a growing, altering society. The Victorian era discovered children as a unique and enthusiastic audience, for whose benefit the author could overcome his own doubt and sophistication and plunge whole-heartedly into the world of wonder. What might be suspect for adults was condoned for children, regardless of the fact that adults wrote, bought, and often read the new crop of wonder stories with as much delight as did their children.

In England this was the era of Lewis Carroll, John Ruskin, and George MacDonald. Their books soon began to make an impact on this side of the Atlantic, but the history of American literary fairy tales more properly begins with two books by Nathaniel Hawthorne.

A Wonder Book and *Tanglewood Tales* are retellings of Greek myth for children. Hawthorne took great liberties with his materials, redirecting and adding events, modifying characters, and altering the tone from "classical" grandeur to "Gothic" enchantment, all in order to produce stories suited to a child audience.[1] He even read each day's work to his own children, "by way of a test."[2] To tamper with the classics and to write, not doggerel or moral lessons, but carefully worked stories specifically for children—these were bold actions in America in the 1850s. American children of that day had little of their very own to read, and that little was, for the most part, grim. There was James Janeway's *A Token for Children*, full of hellfire and brimstone; there was John Cotton's *Spiritual Milk for Boston Babes*, later incorporated into the *New England Primer*; there was Mother Goose in various forms, and Isaac Watts's *Divine and Moral Songs*; there was, inescapably, the Bible, and Bunyan's *Pilgrim's Progress*, not a bad adventure if one could keep the allegory suppressed.[3] More recently, there was an almost endless series of travelogs and ill-disguised lessons from the pen of Samuel Griswold Goodrich, who called himself Peter Parley. At one time Hawthorne himself contributed a bit of hackwork to be published under the Parley pseudonym.[4]

Goodrich seems to represent a majority point of view on the subject of children and their reading. He was immensely satisfied with his own work and despised fairy tales, some of which had appeared in American chapbook editions as early as the eighteenth century.[5] Goodrich's dislike of fairy tales sprang from squeamishness, rationalized into a moral stance:

> Somewhat later one of my companions lent me a volume containing the stories of Little Red Riding Hood, Puss in Boots, Blue Beard, Jack the Giant Killer, and some of the other tales of horror, commonly put into the hands of youth, as if for the express purpose of reconciling them to vice and crime. Some children, no doubt, have a ready appetite for these monstrosities, but to others they are revolting, until by repetition and familiarity, the taste is sufficiently degraded to relish them.[6]

Not content to avoid such stories of horror—or wonder—he attempted to drive them out entirely. He wrote, or commissioned others to write,

"Parley's tales of travels, of history, of nature, and art, together with works designed to cultivate a love of truth, charity, piety, and virtue," hoping with these to "displace the bad books, to which I have already alluded—the old monstrosities, Puss in Boots, Jack the Giant Killer, and others of that class."[7] It was in answer to this set of mind, perhaps partly in answer to Goodrich himself, that Hawthorne took up the task of adding to the child's store of wonders by turning mythology into fairy tale.

A Wonder Book is constructed as a framed narrative, each tale being told by a college student to a group of children at Tanglewood, in rural Massachusetts. Hawthorne takes great care to establish the Berkshire scenery through which the teller and his audience ramble in all seasons of the year, perhaps in hopes that the localized imagery will carry over into the myths themselves, and thus bring them closer to the contemporary child reader.

For instance, in introducing the story of Perseus, he dwells on the autumn landscape around Tanglewood, where Eustace Bright entertains his juvenile listeners. The emphasis is on height and distance and the dreamy grandeur lent by passing clouds:

> Four or five miles off, to the southward, rose the summit of Monument Mountain, and seemed to be floating on a cloud. Some fifteen miles farther away, in the same direction, appeared the loftier Dome of Taconic, looking blue and indistinct, and hardly so substantial as the vapory sea that almost rolled over it. The nearer hills, which bordered the valley, were half submerged, and were specked with little cloud-wreaths all the way to the tops. On the whole, there was so much cloud, and so little solid earth, that it had the effect of a vision.[8]

This is the familiar technique, used so well by Washington Irving, of entering the world of fantasy through landscape reverie.

But here, unlike "Rip Van Winkle," the fantasy emerges on a different narrative level from the nature description. Not until Eustace Bright begins his story is the magical promise fulfilled. Blue, Olympian Monument Mountain and Taconic, wreathed like gods, lead us directly to the gods and mountains of ancient Greece. The lofty viewpoint from Tanglewood porch prepares us for a yet loftier one when Perseus dons the winged sandals of Hermes, or Quicksilver, as Hawthorne calls him:

> Perseus looked upward, and saw the round, bright, silvery moon, and thought that he should desire nothing better than to soar up thither, and spend his life there. Then he looked downward again, and saw the earth, with its seas, and lakes, and the silver courses of its rivers, and its snowy mountain-peaks, and the breadth of its fields, and the dark cluster of its woods, and its

cities of white marble; and with the moonshine sleeping over the whole scene,
it was as beautiful as the moon or any star could be.[9]

One can imagine Eustace Bright gesturing as he catalogs the beauties of the
earth, pointing out ponds for lakes and seas, brooks for rivers, the rocky
Berkshires for snowy peaks, and white-painted New England churches for
marble cities. The whole story is shaped, as a good embedded tale should
be, by its framework, and classical Greece borrows its life from contemporary America.

At its best this technique is promising. It creates a fairyland which is
neither Greece nor America, but linked to both: a meeting place of the
modern and the magical. Sometimes America intrudes too much, injecting
false notes of prudery or sentimentality, or references too concrete and
localized to blend, like King Midas's breakfast of "hot cakes, some nice
little brook-trout, roasted potatoes, fresh boiled eggs, and coffee."[10] But in
other scenes, like Perseus's flight, or homely Baucis and Philemon's visit
from the gods, Hawthorne weaves together alien magic and familiar landscape with more confidence than he demonstrates in any of his writings for
adults.

Whereas in the romances he is concerned with subtleties of character
and motivation and with the uncertainty of perception, in his children's
stories Hawthorne lays those concerns aside and works instead to make
magic into something solid and tangible. He leaves out most of those
seems's and *if*'s and *as if*'s, which, though they are useful in introducing a
taste of wonder, also prevent it from ever taking a firm hold. Writing for
children, Hawthorne gives himself over to fantasy. Once an element of
magic appears, like Midas's golden touch, Hawthorne spends his time, not
in blurring its effects, but in following them up step by step to their final and
necessary conclusion. The golden transformations are simply assumed,
and we watch as the gift slowly turns from blessing to curse. If there is
seeming and misapprehension, it is that things seem less wonderful than
they really are. Old Philemon, for example, cannot be sure that his visitors
are gods; they are, but his failing mortal sight is not acute enough to tell:

> Philemon perceived, too, that he had on a singular pair of shoes; but as it was
> now growing dusk, and as the old man's eyesight was none of the sharpest, he
> could not precisely tell in what the strangeness consisted. ("The Miraculous
> Pitcher," *A Wonder Book*, p. 123)

The shoes are winged, the visitor's staff is wound with living snakes, the
humble pitcher is turned into a vessel of plenty, and once their eyes are
opened Baucis and Philemon perceive and believe it all. And so, for the
course of the story, does Hawthorne: the open-mindedness of the child

audience, combined with the calm authority of his sources, allows for a measure of secondary belief not given to the fantastic elements in any other of Hawthorne's writings.

Hawthorne gains something in pitching his story for children—sureness and deftness in the handling of the supernatural—but he loses as well. The atmosphere of the Puritan tales, dark and alive, is missing, as is the insight that lets morals grow naturally and inevitably out of the allegorical ground. Nor does Hawthorne seem to know how to let the original grandeur and mystery of the myths carry them along. His notion of children seems to be that they are ready for whimsy but not for mystery; whereas most modern critics of children's literature would say that the very opposite is true. Hawthorne falls into several traps, the defects of the one great virtue of having imaginatively returned to childhood. He consistently errs toward the diminutive and the prosaic, making Pandora and Epimetheus into child playmates and taking Danaë's golden shower right out of the Perseus story. The most successful of the stories are those which are most like fairy tales to begin with, like those of Perseus, Midas, or Baucis and Philemon, with their mysterious benefactors and marvelous gifts. The best are not high fantasy, not grand or heroic or deeply moving, but low and comfortable fantasy, childhood and household tales like the Grimms' *Kinder- und Haus-Märchen.*

Hawthorne led the way for a great many American children's writers in the nineteenth century. Largely from his innovations, a tradition grew up of fairy tales that were not absolutely original or genuinely American, but not entirely derivative either.

Two collections of tales in fact predate *A Wonder Book*, though neither was of the same quality or had anything near the impact of Hawthorne's work. Both books are in a sense authorless: one because it consists of retellings of traditional European tales and the other because its author chose not to have her name attached. C. B. Burkhardt refers to himself not as author, but as translator and reteller of his *Fairy Tales and Legends of Many Nations,* [11] and the name that appears on *Rainbows for Children* is that of its editor and discoverer, Lydia M. Child. [12]

Burkhardt's book is of the sort that plagues folklorists—no sources given, no indication of the extent of editorial changes, only the stories themselves, obviously polished, listed as "A Legend of Brittany," or "A Legend of Italy." The stories are competently told, though not so interestingly as the best of traditional narrators can recount them. One tale, "The Picture of the Lord," stands out as fundamentally different from the others. It is assigned no nationality, but is subtitled "A Legend of Art." The art referred to is that of the protagonist, a painter, but the subtitle might as well refer to the fact that the story is obviously a composed one, unlike the traditional tales in style and setting. The painter is a young village boy named Benjamin, who finds success abroad in Italy, becomes corrupted there, and returns home to die repentant. His nationality is not given, but it could well be American—in fact, the name and the early stages of his career suggest Benjamin West, the early American expatriate painter. The story is strongly moralized: the supernatural element is a devil in disguise who raises Benjamin's fortunes in order to gain his soul. Burkhardt's collection is symptomatic of its time in that the one story that may be American is not a fairy tale at all, but a minor gothic romance.

Rainbows for Children is a series of fairy tales, not traditional in style, but rather of the dainty, allegorical, confectionary manner we have already seen in the fairy poems that appeared in the early nineteenth century. Only occasionally does the prose of the Rainbows carry more commitment than the verse of "The Culprit Fay." For a few brief moments the stories begin to suggest the richer conceptions of Ruskin or MacDonald, though never with the same overtones of myth.

The first of the Rainbows, called "Fiamma, or the Vase of Golden Water," begins well. Fiamma, though neither her name nor the description of her home suggest America, has a very American problem. She has heard and read about fairies, but she cannot find any. "Fiamma was always running away to the woods, peeping into caves, and under the roots of trees, hoping to find an entrance into fairy-land" (p. 11). That is just how an author might feel, peeping into oral tradition and into the pages of books in search of a usable fairyland. What Fiamma eventually finds in a hole in the ground is a colony of those gauzy, tiny fairies that are so reminiscent of swarms of gnats. She is sent by the fairies on a quest for magic water, gets a quick tour of the world, and comes back to cure her blind sister and spread love and joy everywhere. That is part of the trouble with all of the Rainbows for Children: they are filled with an American do-gooder spirit that tends to circumvent the self-doubt and introspection necessary for the production of a meaningful fable. In her introduction, Mrs. Child points to the major flaw in the work, damning it with dated praise: "Thus does the spirit of hopeful progress diffuse itself through all departments of literature, and even the fairy-wand points to a happier state of society."[13]

Fairy tale collections multiplied throughout the second half of the nineteenth century. An anonymous set of Stories: Fairy Land appeared in 1855.[14] It seems to have been close to folk sources, or quasi-folk ones like the chapbooks. The stories are brief—some more nearly riddles than true tales—and Germanic, and relatively free from imposed morals. No advance in style or technique, they are nonetheless a useful corrective to the preciousness of the Rainbows for Children or even A Wonder Book.

Children exposed to their rude vigor and pith might be less content with self-consciously literary, didactic treatments of magical themes.

A woman named Jane Austin published a set of very readable tales in 1859 under the title *Fairy Dreams; or, Wanderings in Elf-Land.*[15] This collection is notable for its variety, ranging from the earthy peasant style of the Grimms to the courtly French style of Perrault and the *Cabinet des Fées*. It shows an increasing sophistication on the part of American authors; they had begun to know what a fairy tale could do and how it was built. If they had not yet begun to extend the form, they had at least caught up with their European counterparts in their ability to imitate.

I think that by 1870, when a book called *The Fairy Egg* was published by "Three Friends." all but the least discriminating of young readers would have recognized it as an inferior article.[16] Such rambling stories and coy Little-Bo-Peepery were a step backward; surely no one wanted to read about the sort of flower fairy who could say: "Come, little Pansy, it is high time you woke up. The Crocus, the Daisy, the Violet, and even the Lily have been awake some time, and you are still sleeping" (p. 57). Nevertheless, the "three friends" went on to publish several equally offensive sequels, which followed *The Fairy Egg* into obscurity.

If anything contributed most to the familiarization of American readers and writers with the potential riches of fairy tale, and thus freed our literature from sugar-candy imitations, it was the birth of the children's magazine. Children who could get hold of *The Riverside Magazine* or *St. Nicholas* read original works by Hans Christian Andersen, Lewis Carroll, Rudyard Kipling, and Christina Rossetti, as well as almost every major American writer of the day. Fairy tales of all degrees of merit played such an important part in the composition of *St. Nicholas* that T. F. Crane, introducing a selection of "Italian Fairy Tales," said:

> I fear some of the readers of *St. Nicholas* will exclaim, on reading the title of this article, "What, more fairy tales?" and will instantly suspect the writer of designing to pass off on them some moral lesson under the thin disguise of a story, or to puzzle their heads with some of the genuine marvels of science in masks of hobgoblins, kobolds and magicians.[17]

Crane's stories avoid both the perils he cites: they are neither morally nor scientifically didactic, but plain translations of actual Italian tales. A longer story, published in *St. Nicholas* the same year, falls into a bit of moral instruction, but is, nevertheless, more interesting than Crane's. It is "Rumpty-Dudget's Tower," by Julian Hawthorne.[18]

"Rumpty-Dudget's Tower" was written in England, during a relatively happy period in Hawthorne's life, and it seems to have benefited both from

his mental state and his surroundings. It is more original, more spontaneous than most of his writings for adults and remains one of his best known
stories.[19] He seems, like his father, to have felt some sort of release in
writing for the young.

European influence is obvious in the story. The title character is
derived from the evil little dwarf known in England as Tom Tit Tot and in
Germany as Rumpelstiltzkin. He is an imp, a minor devil in dwarf guise,
but Julian Hawthorne plays down the theological dimensions as Nathaniel
did before him in "Feathertop." The name "Rumpty-Dudget" is probably
inspired by "Rumpelstiltzkin," but with added comic overtones of
"Humpty-Dumpty," "high dudgeon," and "fuss-budget." Hawthorne describes him with a fine touch, a grotesquery both humorous and sinister:

> He was an ugly little dwarf, about as high as your knee, and all gray from
> head to foot. He wore a broad-brimmed hat, and a gray beard, and a gray
> cloak, that was so much too long for him that it dragged on the ground as he
> walked; and on his back was a small gray hump, that made him look even
> shorter than he was. (p. 227)

Rumpty-Dudget lives in a high tower across a hedge from the castle
where Princess Hilda, Prince Henry, and Prince Frank live with their two
guardians, a fearsome cat who protects them by day and a fairy aunt who
visits them in their sleep. Rumpty-Dudget has stolen away a thousand
children and stuck them in a thousand corners of his tower; now his goal is
to steal one of his three neighbors to fill the thousand-and-first and final
corner.

On the most dangerous day of the year—his birthday, when the cat
must be away from sunrise to sunset—he creeps through a hole in the hedge
and nearly tempts the children to accompany him. Foiled by the cat, he
throws a spot of black mud on each child before vanishing. The next year
on his birthday, those black spots give him enough power over the children
to lead them into naughtiness, and he succeeds in carrying Henry away to
his tower.

The children's garden and castle then disappear, leaving a desert of
gray stone and thorns. Frank and Hilda, now repentant, are sheltered by
the cat and assigned tasks in order to save their brother. Frank stands a
long and painful vigil, while Hilda goes on a humiliating quest to the Queen
of the Air Spirits and the King of the Gnomes. Having succeeded, they
rescue Henry and the thousand other captives and find that Rumpty-
Dudget's black spots have vanished from their faces. Cat, Aunt, Air Queen,
and Gnome King all turn out to be disguises of their mother, kept before
from assuming her true form by Rumpty-Dudget's enchantments. She
takes them away, and all, of course, live happily ever after.

The folk and literary echoes in this tale are many. Rumpty-Dudget we have already mentioned; his tower and the forbidden garden remind one of "Rapunzel"; the captured children suggest those in "Hansel and Gretel"; the fairy aunt is a variation of the French fairy godmother; Tom the cat is Puss-in-Boots; Prince Henry is tricked and trapped in the tower like Burd Helen; he is rescued by his siblings as she was by Childe Rowland; and the shape-shifting, protective, all-pervasive mother figure is a favorite device in all of George MacDonald's works. Despite this eclecticism, the story hangs together fairly well. It is not just the sum of its motifs; the way they are linked shows some real understanding of fairy tale structure and meaning. In this one short story, Julian Hawthorne approached the kind of invention-within-tradition that MacDonald raised to a high art.

Other fairy tales continued to appear in *St. Nicholas* as various writers tried their hands at imitating the work of European and, now, a few American fantasists. Being imitations, few of these stories attain the quality of the originals, but each helped increase the store of fantastic materials available. Some are quite readable, if derivative, like Charles Carryll's *Davy and the Goblin*, unabashedly subtitled "What Followed Reading 'Alices's Adventures in Wonderland.' "[20]

Davy is primarily nonsense rather than fairy tale. Davy, like Alice, dreams his way into a curious, shifting Wonderland full of talking animals and grotesques. He is guided by a little grinning goblin who seems in the waking world to have been one of the andirons in the fireplace. Carryll is no Carroll—not one of his creations has as much life as even a minor character of the original Wonderland—but he does have a flair for the perpetual surprise that is an important nonsense ingredient. One of the best parts in the book is when Davy, running from a crowd of toffee people, empties his pockets:

> First he pulled out what seemed to be an iron ball; but it proved to be a hard-boiled egg, without the shell, stuck full of small tacks. Then came two slices of toast, firmly tied together with a green cord. Then came a curious little glass jar, filled with large flies. As Davy took this out of his pocket, the cork came out with a loud "pop!" and the flies flew away in all directions. Then came, one after another, a tart filled with gravel, two chicken-bones, a bird's nest with some pieces of brown soap in it, some mustard in a pill-box, and a cake of beeswax stuck full of caraway seeds. (pp. 38-39)

The calm listing of absurd detail suggests some pattern not quite evident, and certainly there is a nonsense logic to the above list. We might expect to find just these mistreated edibles and not-quite-useful objects in a boy's pocket (or his dream of a pocket), though Davy denies having put them there. They suit him, and they seem equally appropriate when discovered later as the principal exhibits in a museum. *Davy and the Goblin* is generally stronger on detail than on overall conception, since it is easier to borrow an author's techniques than his point of view.

Another nonsensical book, but of a different sort, is Virginia Baker's *Prince Carrotte: and Other Chronicles.*[21] Prince Carrotte's story is a vegetable romance, full of courtly honor and derring-do. The "other chronicles" take up events in the neighboring realms of the fruits and nuts. The book is an interesting experiment, but not a real success. The distance between the battlefield and the larder is never really bridged.

Prince Carrotte did not appear in *St. Nicholas*. By the 1880s readers of that magazine had been introduced to the work of two writers who carried the European style fairy tale far beyond mere imitation or experiment. Frank Stockton and Howard Pyle wrote tales more readable today than those of any of their predecessors. Their stories are still not especially American in setting or language, but Pyle and Stockton seem to be at home in the woods and villages of fairy tale Europe. They have made it theirs: no longer provincials but cosmopolitans, they adopted foreign materials with confidence and vigor.

Stockton wrote his first fairy tales for *The Riverside Magazine*: these were later collected and published as *Ting-a-Ling Tales.*[22] Of his early work he later said:

> I was very young when I determined to write some fairy tales because my mind was full of them. I set to work, and in course of time, produced several which were printed. These were constructed according to my own ideas. I caused the fanciful creatures who inhabited the world of fairy-land to act, as far as possible for them to do so, as if they were inhabitants of the real world. I did not dispense with monsters and enchanters, or talking beasts and birds, but I obliged these creatures to infuse into their extraordinary actions a certain leaven of common sense.[23]

Stockton here neatly outlines his own primary strengths. First, his mind was full, he says, of fairy tales. Growing up in the tolerant climate of Philadelphia, in the more permissive middle years of the nineteenth century, he seems, Peter Parley notwithstanding, to have been well exposed to fairy tales. He knew them: knew how the prince sets out from home, how the magical helper appears, how the dragon acts—all the elements that give a fairy tale form and flesh it out. He learned these things not through study but through early and repeated immersion, not too unlike the process by which a peasant child becomes a storyteller. He did become a storyteller, making things up for his own amusement on his way to and from school.[24] And among the first stories he told himself were magical ones.

The best of Stockton's fairy tales have that quality of rightness that marks a good traditional tale: things have to happen just so, no matter how unusual or unexpected. The quality in his writing that most reinforces this of-courseness is the second point above: that creatures of fancy must behave as if fairyland were the real world. It is the real world, for them, as any fictional landscape must be real if the fate of its inhabitants is to matter. What Stockton proposed to do in his fantasies is to grant them secondary belief. Because most of his stories concentrate on character, his theory concentrates on character, but it is the same theory we have seen before in Coleridge, in Lewis, in Tolkien. It links Stockton more closely to the old *Märchen* tradition than any of the American writers we have talked about up to now, not necessarily in degree of actual contact but in sympathy and understanding. It also helps to give his stories a distinct, unmistakable Stockton touch. That is no paradox, because Stockton saw the "real world" with most unusual eyes, and because his characters, Griffins, Minor Canons, Bee-Men, Junior Sorcerers, and all, are transformations of Frank Stockton.

That first collection of stories, the *Ting-a-Ling Tales*, is not so successful as some of the later ones. It has a fairly standard Arabian Nights setting, a set of old though still workable plot lines, and, alas, diminutive fairies. Only Ting-a-Ling, among the latter, shows much originality, partly because Stockton begins to explore the ramifications of his size. He is, at first, like his many tiny predecessors: mostly for decoration, sporting flower caps and riding butterflies. But soon Stockton, following his own advice, begins to speculate on what it would be like to be so small and to consort with normal-sized humans and even with a giant. There is all the difference in the world between tininess as a literary device and carefully considered miniaturization. The latter has produced several fine works of fantasy: Gulliver's visit to the Liliputians, T. H. White's sequel to Swift, *Mistress Masham's Repose*, and Mary Norton's *The Borrowers*. None of those works is in any way cute or precious, and neither, when Stockton becomes involved in his story, is *Ting-a-Ling*.

One of the happiest touches in the *Ting-a-Ling Tales* occurs when Ting-a-ling, needing transportation, decides to bridle a wild grasshopper. At this point the grasshopper has given Ting-a-ling one good kick and is again grazing warily:

> There he was, with his eyes still rolled back, and his leg ready for another kick, should Ting-a-ling approach him again. But the little fellow had had enough of those strong legs, and so he slipped along the fence, and, getting through it, stole around in front of the grasshopper; and, while he was still

looking backward with all his eyes, Ting-a-ling stepped quietly up before him, and slipped the bridle over his head! It was of no use for the grasshopper to struggle and pull back, for Ting-a-ling was astraddle of him in a moment, kicking him with his heels, and shouting "Hi! Hi!" (pp. 48–49)

There are several factors working for Stockton in this brief passage. First, there is humor, which often accompanies miniaturization once the coyness is stripped away. Second, there is recognizable experience: Ting-a-ling is any sorer-but-wiser rider approaching a canny horse. Third, there is deft use of natural fact to underline the strangeness of the whole experience. The one phrase that most effectively fixes the whole scene in mind is that which has the grasshopper "looking backward with *all* his eyes." Fourth, there is an underlying mythic reference that lends a measure of stature (divorcing stature from considerations of size) to Ting-a-ling. Ting-a-ling is Bellerophon. When Nathaniel Hawthorne retold the Pegasus story in *A Wonder Book* he ran the risk that his own additions might interfere with a tale already well told and fixed in the minds of his readers. In Stockton's case there is no such danger, only the lightest seasoning of myth adding wonder to his fancy.

The best of Stockton's fantasy tales, both published in *St. Nicholas* in the 1880s and reprinted many times, are "The Bee-Man of Orn" and "The Griffin and the Minor Canon."[25] In these two tales Stockton left behind the strictly traditional fairy tale frame. One has the impression that both tales took place somewhere just off the main line of once-upon-a-time, off in a backwater rarely visited by heroes or princesses. Both are gentle, ironic, and haunting, and completely free from the occasional lapses of secondary belief that mar the *Ting-a-Ling Tales*.

The Bee-man of Orn is an eccentric: old, unattractive, and alone except for the bees that swarm around him. He is also perfectly content until there happens by his hut a Junior Sorcerer, who, practicing his art, decides that the Bee-man must at some time have been transformed. The Bee-man, troubled, sets out to discover his original form. He is a conscientious man, and feels that "It is not right for any one to retain a form which does not properly belong to him" (p. 55). On the theory that his original state will draw him, just as he is drawn to bee trees, he examines a wealthy Lord, a Languid Youth, a Very Imp, a Ghastly Griffin, and various other curiosities, but nothing attracts him at all except a baby which he has rescued from a dragon. That, he decides, was his original form, and the Junior Sorcerer obligingly turns him into a baby. Years later, no longer Junior, the Sorcerer revisits Orn and finds an old man, swarming with bees, happily eating honey. "Upon my word," he exclaims, "he has grown into the same thing again" (p. 65).

The Minor Canon is as unassuming as the Bee-man, though not so eccentric:

> He was a young man of a kind disposition, and very anxious to do good to the people of the town. Apart from his duties in the church, where he conducted services every week-day, he visited the sick and the poor; counselled and assisted persons who were in trouble, and taught a school composed entirely of the bad children in the town, with whom nobody else would have anything to do. Whenever the people wanted something difficult done for them, they always went to the Minor Canon. (p. 5)

It is to this meek and obliging priest that the townspeople turn when a terrible Griffin from the wild comes to see his stone effigy over the door of the church.

It happens that the Griffin, whose judgment is superior to that of the townspeople, takes a liking to the Minor Canon, and for that reason settles down in the town, to everyone's discomfort but the Minor Canon's, who finds the Griffin a fascinating companion. The townspeople demand that the Minor Canon depart for the wilds, in hopes that the Griffin will follow. The Griffin, however, stays, and takes over the duties of his friend, but in a manner not quite so meek. School performance improves wonderfully under his command, and the numbers of sick and poor shrink to nearly nothing after he begins to visit.

But it is the Griffin's habit to eat twice a year, at the equinoxes, and summer is fast approaching an end. The people fear for their children, and they offer to prepare anything else the Griffin might wish. His answer to them is that the only thing in the town that ever appealed to him was the departed Minor Canon: "He was brave, and good, and honest, and I think I should have relished him" (p. 17). At this the people explain how they sent the Minor Canon away, being careful to indicate just where they thought he had gone. Taking with him the stone griffin from the church, the Griffin flies off to the wild, not to eat the Minor Canon, but to rescue him, for by this time he is weak from hunger and exposure.

The Minor Canon returns to town, and the townspeople, still afraid of the Griffin, do him all honor and reverence. He dies a bishop, loved at the last for his own sake as well as for the Griffin's. The Griffin, having refused to eat the Minor Canon just to suit the townspeople, does not care to eat anything at all: "So, lying down with his eyes fixed upon the great stone griffin, he gradually declined, and died. It was a good thing for some of the people of the town that they did not know this" (p. 22).

These two stories interweave tradition and invention. The Griffin and the Junior Sorcerer are more or less traditional; the Griffin was modeled after the carvings on the cathedral at Chester, which Stockton visited in

1884.[26] The Minor Canon is a bit of English town life, transferred with ease into fairyland. The Bee-man is Stockton's own creation, but he may have roots in the bee hunters of the American frontier, like Paul Hover in Cooper's *The Prairie*. Stockton is able to juxtapose figures and motifs from America, from England, and from European legend because he has found a proper stage for them all: the quiet, rural, Old World setting of fairy tale, colored by his own imagination.

Stockton never tried to set his tales in an American fairyland, nor did he ever write a full-length fantasy. His fairy tales are delicate, and not suitable for expansion. When he wrote longer stories, they were in better-established modes like science fiction or domestic comedy.

Howard Pyle's fantasies seem to be of stronger cloth than Stockton's, and he did eventually write a book-length fantasy, though it is not one of his better-known works. Pyle began as an illustrator, learning his craft on the job as did a much more important artist, Winslow Homer. Like Homer, Pyle evolved a bold and interesting style out of the sentimental conventions of nineteenth-century magazine illustration. Pyle's particular strength was in recapturing bygone eras, especially the Middle Ages. His drawings are reminiscent of Dürer's in their strong line and rich detail, and of illuminated manuscripts in their sense of texture and design. His art became quite popular, and in later years he started a school of illustration, teaching, among others, N. C. Wyeth, Jessie Willcox Smith, and Maxfield Parrish.[27] He and his students had much in common in style and aims with the Pre-Raphaelite Brotherhood, especially with William Morris, though they lacked the pretensions of their English counterparts.

Pyle turned to writing more or less by accident. He needed material to illustrate that would give full play to his particular techniques and taste, and he hit upon fairy tales. According to Elizabeth Nesbitt, he read or had read to him as a child the Arabian Nights, *Robinson Crusoe, Gulliver's Travels,* both *A Wonder Book* and *Tanglewood Tales,* and Ritson's and Percy's collections of English ballads.[28] His imagination, even more than Stockton's, was molded around giants, gods, heroes, and bandits. His first fairy tales are all traditional, retold from folklorists' collections like Thorp's *Northern Mythology.* Appearing first in *St. Nicholas* and then in book form in *Pepper & Salt* are simple and supple reworkings of "The Skillful Huntsman," "Claus and his Wonderful Staff," "How Dame Margery Twist Saw More Than Was Good for Her," and "Farmer Grigg's Boggart."[29] The last two of these are still popular legends: the former concerns a mortal midwife to the fairies and the latter is the familiar "Aye, George, we're flitting." A second book of stories, *The Wonder Clock,* matches the first in quality.

Pyle wrote as he illustrated, clearly, in detail, and with just enough archaism to set the stories off from ordinary experience. He did careful research for both pictures and text, and brought medieval Europe to life for an American audience. The end of the nineteenth century was a great time for all things foreign: America was trying to shed its parochialism by collecting European art, making the grand tour, and reading Henry James. Much of this passion for the foreign was simply dilettantism, or undiscriminating eclecticism, but there were also those who, through careful study and imaginative insight, truly embraced the past or the alien. Howard Pyle was one of those.

Pyle's best works are his consolidation of the Robin Hood legends, still the best prose rendering; his version of Arthurian material (he was not the first American to try his hand with the Matter of Britain: Sidney Lanier's *The Boy's King Arthur* is still a children's standard); and his sober reconstructions of medieval life: *Otto of the Silver Hand* and *Men of Iron*. None of these is fantasy, though there are fantastic elements in *The Story of King Arthur and his Knights*, but the effort Pyle made to imaginatively reenter the vanished world of the Middle Ages also prepared him to make a longer journey to fairyland than he had made in the early tales.

I read *The Garden behind the Moon* as a child, and it made such a vivid impression on me that I cannot read it objectively now. It is episodic, certain parts overbalance others, and some may find it overly sentimental, but my mind insists on classing it with George MacDonald's best, or at least his second best. The opening idea is certainly memorable:

> When you look out across the water at night, after the sun has set and the moon has risen high enough to become bright, then you see a long, glimmering moon-path reaching away into the distance. There it lies, stretching away from the moon to the earth, and from the earth to the moon, as bright as silver and gold, and as straight and smooth as a turnpike road.[30]

Most of us have noticed the moon-path, if we have seen the moon rise over still water, but no one except David, the hero of *The Garden behind the Moon*, has ever taken it to its end.

The three main characters of *The Garden* are all set apart from those around them. The Princess Aurelia, as beautiful a child as was ever born to a fairy tale King and Queen, is completely unresponsive. Her wits, it turns out, are behind the moon, and it takes a hero to get them back (an echo of Ariosto). Hans Krout, an old village cobbler, is touched, moon struck. He is considered insane by the villagers who cannot see what he sees. It is Hans who first shows the moon-path to David. David is a "moon-calf," slow and gentle, a divine fool. Only Hans and the babies of the town appreciate David's specialness.

David takes the moon-path one night, after having tried it once, lost faith, and fallen into the sea. This time he succeeds, and he finds the moon to be an enormous house, with a caretaker who is the Moon Angel. For a while David stays in the moon house, polishing stars with lamb's wool and looking out through the windows at scenes on earth. Sometimes he is allowed to go out the back stairs into the Garden behind the Moon, a Paradise filled with children. He meets, and falls in love with, the girl who is Princess Aurelia's true self. But during David's stay in the moon he has grown up, and adults cannot enter the Garden. He must go on a quest to find two great treasures, the Wonder-Box and the Know-All Book, which were stolen at the beginning of time by the gigantic Iron Man, who now also holds the Princess prisoner.

The quest is accomplished with the aid of an old woman who washes the souls of men (a motif from Celtic legend), a beautiful black-winged horse (another echo of Pegasus), a second old woman who lives in the giant's Iron Castle (a motif found in "Jack and the Beanstalk" and elsewhere), and his own bravery. When the box is recovered, everything vanishes. The Princess is back in her castle, her wits now intact, and in possession of the locked Wonder-Box. David is back in the village, where no one knows he has been gone and all think him an idiot. But he has the key to the Wonder-Box, and all works out. David and the Princess are married, and the Know-All Book, which is the key to all happiness, is found to hold their words to one another in the moon garden: "When we grow up we shall be married" (p. 188); and that is of course the goal of all traditional fairy tales.

The mood in *The Garden behind the Moon* is bittersweet. The Moon Angel, like MacDonald's North Wind, is also a name for death, and the first and hardest of David's tasks is to pass through him to the other side. Pyle wrote *The Garden* after the death of his son, and was working out some kind of consolation for himself.[31] The book begins with aloneness, eccentricity, and bereavement, and only through great trial reaches fulfillment. It is a very personal work, and for that reason may not appeal to a great many readers. But it is also the first sustained work by an American to make use of the fairy tale's potential for meaning and enchantment. It represents the highest development of the European style children's tale: all of the rest of the works discussed in this chapter make some attempt to touch on American themes, settings, or characters.

Stockton and Pyle proved they could find fairies—or Griffins—in Europe, and write about them as well as any European. Writers who tried to transport fairy materials to this continent were not so successful. They represent an alternative tradition of children's fantasy, but one which developed more slowly and painfully than the eclectic school. As early as

1838, James Kirke Paulding, friend and sometime collaborator of Washington Irving, made a bold attempt to transplant a fairy troupe to the American wild. He was writing not for children but for the same educated, playful, sentimental audience to whom Irving directed his sketches and Joseph Rodman Drake his "Culprit Fay." He falls somewhere between the two, neither as masterful as Irving nor as mawkish as Drake.

There is a great deal of apology in Paulding's presentation of *A Christmas Gift from Fairyland.* He hides behind, not one, but two comic pen names. He is "Sampson Fairlamb" editing a manuscript submitted by "Simeon Starkweather"—and even then claims to be translating from a birch bark original discovered in Kentucky. All of this would lead one to expect unusual, backwoods fairy tales, perhaps a little like the "Jack tales" actually told in the Southern mountains. But Paulding sticks instead to familiar patterns: fairy godmother, captured princesses, shepherds, and crones.

The first and fullest of the tales is "Florella, or The Fairy of the Rainbow," which is mostly set in a conventional fairy court of the French style, all wit and ornamentation:

> When Florella retired to her splendid chamber, which was hung with blue and silver curtains, with tassels of gold thread, and furnished with a bed and chairs, covered all over with plates of burnished gold, she cast herself on the bed, and wept to think that her father had affianced her to a man, who looked as if he was made of green cheese, whom not even wine could inspire with wit or gallantry, and who thought more of a lady's foot than her head or heart.[32]

This is workmanlike, if old-fashioned, fairy tale writing, and if the story went on the same way Paulding would seem to belong with the internationalists already discussed in this chapter. But midway into the tale, when Florella and her lover require the services of her fairy godmother to get them out of difficulty, they are magically transported to America, and once there both the magic and the writing get bogged down. A convenient bird announces to the Princess that:

> Thou art now in the NEW WORLD, far distant from kings and court etiquette, where to be useful is to be dignified; and where, when thy duties are performed to thyself and others, thou mayest without fear or reproach, enjoy all innocent sports and recreations, relieved from the chains that have fettered thy youthful spirit, and made thee a slave to all those artificial restraints, from which the rest of thy fellow creatures are free.

Any wonder that was developing in the tale is quashed by this Election Day rhetoric. In the end the young couple are freed at the loss of enchantment, rather like the pair in Hawthorne's "The Maypole of Merrymount."

Paulding must be remembered more for the will than for the deed. He was one of the first to express a partiality for fairy tales, for supernaturalism in its older, richer forms: "For my part, if we must be the tools of superstition and credulity, as seems to be our destiny, I confess I prefer the ancient, to the modern mode of playing on those instruments" (Preface).

Paulding had more success in dealing with comic Dutchmen and New Englanders in *The Book of Saint Nicholas*, again pseudonymous.[33] Here he sticks to ground already surveyed by Irving and by Clement Moore, whose "A Visit from St. Nicholas" established the Dutch saint as an American elf, entitled to a yearly suspension of disbelief. The stories in *The Book of Saint Nicholas* are done with a surer hand than those in *A Christmas Gift*, possibly because they are farther from fantasy.

One way to connect the American landscape to the supernatural is to reach back to Indian legend, as Hawthorne did in "The Great Carbuncle." In the 1850s, Henry Schoolcraft's collection of Indian oral materials was edited into *The Indian Fairy Book*.[34] The landscape is supernaturalized, but the stories are couched in a sweetened, conventionalized form that reveals a lack of engagement on the part of the reteller. Despite their settings they remain exotic, nearly as foreign to the American imagination as stories from the South Pacific.

Conversely, two stories from the same decade have a strongly American quality even though they are set somewhere in the East Indies. These are *The Last of the Huggermuggers* and its sequel *Kobboltozo,* by poet, painter, essayist, and former Brook Farm utopian Christopher P. Cranch.[35] The hero of both volumes is a lively Yankee sailor boy named Jacky Cable who is shipwrecked on an unknown island. On the island is a race of giants, now dwindled to two individuals, Mr. and Mrs. Huggermugger. The Huggermuggers prove to be gentle and courteous, unlike the island's other residents, a group of spiteful dwarfs (still slightly larger than human sized). The dwarfs, especially the shoemaker Kobboltozo, wish to be giants and rule the island. Jacky and the few shipmates who were cast away with him are picked up by a passing ship, and Jacky meets Zebedee Nabbum, an agent for P. T. Barnum. Together they return to the island to try to persuade the Huggermuggers to come to the United States and make everybody's fortune. The evil Kobboltozo, however, has discovered the secret of the giants' size—it come of eating a certain kind of shellfish—and thus, according to prophecy, has doomed them. Mrs. Huggermugger sickens and dies. Disconsolate, Mr. Huggermugger agrees to go with Jacky and Zebedee, but dies on board ship.

In the sequel, the two entrepreneurs revisit the giant's island to find that all the dwarfs have vanished except Stitchkin, the tailor. After Huggermugger's departure they had broken into his house to hold a victory feast. Kobboltozo and his friend Hammawhaxo discovered a secret tunnel under the house and went off to look for the magic shellfish that would make them giants. The other dwarfs, too, went off in search of the secret; they neglected their duties and eventually either got lost or killed one another off, all but Stitchkin. Jacky and Zebby find a repentant Hammawhaxo, who tells of his and Kobboltozo's adventures. Leaving the giant's hall, they passed through a kingdom of gnomes, earth spirits whose love is in their precious metals and jewelry. Then they reached a sea cave, and met the mer-king, who warned them that "He who is a dwarf in spirit/ Never shall the isle inherit" (p. 67). Despite the warning, Kobboltozo thought he had found the right shellfish. We last see him, shrinking away to nothing, seated on a pile of shells and proclaiming himself lord of all he sees.

Cranch's stories have several strong points: in particular the characters of Jacky Cable and Zebby Nabbum. Jacky is the bold young sailor, a younger version of characters in the sea novels of Cooper and Melville. Zebedee is the all-American huckster, shifty but sympathetic. He deals in freaks and frauds, and so is prepared to meet authentic wonders when he comes across them. Both characters quickly accept the extraordinary and are even quicker to assess its potential money value. By telling his story from their perspective, Cranch loses some potential awe but gains an easy familiarity with the unknown. Then, in the second book, when he wishes to expand the dimensions of his story to include witches, elemental spirits, and a moral, he shifts the narration to Stitchkin and Hammawhaxo, who are more nearly in the fairy tale mold, more immediately involved in events, and more susceptible to wonder than the pragmatic sailor and showman.

Cranch eases the fantasy into his story gradually. He begins with a familiar character, almost a stock character but with touches of individuality. The opening events are more adventurous than magical. The unusual is introduced in a way more typical of science fiction than fantasy: in a faraway place natural objects, like sea shells, are discovered to be of extraordinary size. The technique is more Jules Verne than George MacDonald. Giants appear, but they are naturalized giants, appropriate to their surroundings, domestic, and nonthreatening. Next we meet their counterparts on the other end of the size scale, and here a new element enters. The dwarfs have fairy tale names.[36] Indeed they are fairy tale dwarfs: comical, evil-tempered craftsmen. If it were not for the framework around them they would be little more than copies of European originals, like Julian Hawthorne's Rumpty-Dudget. Cranch utilizes the contrast between these storybook dwarfs, with their magical adventures, and the calm, rational Americans. We get the story from outside and inside both, as objective travel narrative and as fairy tale. Cranch's books are agreeable light fantasy (the lightness is somewhat disturbed by the sad fate of the giants) with strong American ties, though still set off in an exotic setting where things could happen that were not quite conceivable closer to American soil. Nor could they happen to Americans—Cable and Nabbum are never more than spectators, essentially unaffected by what they see.

In May Wentworth's book of *Fairy Tales from Gold Lands*, magical events happen, again, to foreigners and outsiders.[37] These fairy tales take place, however, in California, a place that was both exotic and American. Wentworth sneaks her magic in, not through adventure, but through local color, concentrating on the mountains, missions, and mines that set the Southwest apart from the rest of the country. In her introduction she announces that she will draw on the unusual history and natural phenomena of California, pushing them over the line into the field of magic: "The scenes of most of these Tales, will be laid in California, a land full of romance and beauty. It is not strange to hear from the miners of 'the early days,' tales as marvelous as those of the 'Arabian Nights' " (p. v).

Miners' tales are often amazing; however, they tend to be concerned with freak luck and natural disaster rather than supernatural beings. It is likely that Wentworth derived her tales from written sources, though she may have used elements from oral tradition to lend atmosphere. Her first tale is along the lines of Irving's tales of the Alhambra, neatly transposed to the California coast. The characters are all Spanish, with a Moorish duenna for a villain and one of Boabdil's treasures for a goal. Because of the Old World quality of mission life, no special tricks are needed to make the fairy tale credible.

Other stories make similar use of Chinese miners and Indians. Only one story has a hero who is what would at the time have been considered "really" American, "Emperor Norton." Norton is a miner who saves a king of the local little people, who are much like the gnomes in *Kobboltozo*. In reward he is made Emperor of Mines, but only so long as he keeps his crown dry. He fails, of course; the crown vanishes, and his adventure is considered by everyone else to be a delusion, and so it might have been. That seems to be the difference between Norton and all the other characters in the book: because he is a member of skeptical American society, his story must have the loophole of delusion or dream.

Another better-known local colorist, Edward Eggleston, wrote fanciful stories set in the rural Midwest, with an imaginative use of everyday objects. Among the "Queer Stories" are a parliament of chairs, a wonderful monolog by a tea kettle, several moralized nursery rhymes in prose, and the adventures of a walking stick that takes on the character of its minister owner.[38] Unfortunately, all are framed as dreams, so none has the author's full engagement. They remain curious and amusing fragments. A similar work by Virginia W. Johnson, *The Catskill Fairies*, has various tribes of fairies telling their stories to a snowbound little boy.[39] After an adequate opening describing the boy's home, the book breaks apart into unconnected episodes, all ultimately just a midwinter's night's dream. It is a rather disappointing sequel to Irving's treatment of the same Catskill scenery.

There may be many more nineteenth-century attempts at fairy tales with American settings, but it is unlikely that any are nearly as successful as Cranch's, or as those of the best of the European style fantasists, like Stockton or Pyle. Two that might be representative are Laura E. Richards' *Toto's Merry Winter* and Lily F. Wesselhoeft's *The Fairy-Folk of Blue Hill*.[40] The former is another set of disconnected stories told around the fire by Toto, a little boy; his blind grandmother; and various animals that make up their household. The book lacks the spark of Richards' light verse and is an improvement over *The Catskill Fairies* only in that there is no suggestion of dream. The Wesselhoeft book is an oddity: giants and gnomes in prehistoric New England, trooping around and creating assorted local landmarks. Interestingly enough, this book too has a character called Toto: Toto the Slim, an elf. Perhaps one or the other of these books could have provided the name for a later and better-known Toto in *The Wizard of Oz*.

As a general rule one might say that the more strongly rooted in American life and scenery a story is, the less amenable it is to fantasy, and conversely, the more an author's mind leans toward the fantastic, the farther he must reach for materials and setting. There are the polished, cosmopolitan tales of the *St. Nicholas* crowd and the rough and apologetic stories of Paulding and his successors. In between there is Cranch, who puts an American character in a fairy tale setting. He succeeds, but it is an uneasy compromise, and the results are devastating to the local residents, the Huggermuggers and dwarfs (this may be an unconscious reflection of guilt at American treatment of our own native population). Cranch's technique was taken up again on a grander scale in Mark Twain's *A Connecticut Yankee in King Arthur's Court*, a book which all by itself demonstrates the strong hostility between American thought and pure fantasy.[41]

A Connecticut Yankee is in many ways a book that falls into disjointed parts: half light-hearted romance, half philippic; half condemnation of medieval society, half nostalgic idealization; half tract on the benefits of modernization, half industrial dystopia. Twain is divided, as well, on the ideas of fantasy and imagination, and this ambivalence in particular affects the structure of the story itself.

The Connecticut Yankee, a grown-up version of the phlegmatic and resourceful sailor Jacky Cable, is, like Jacky, thrust into an alien world where other rules might seem to apply, rules that include magic. Once there, his thoughts, again like Jacky's, turn to ways of utilizing the situation for his own advantage. But where Jacky accepts the island of the Hugger-muggers on its own terms and is the inactive catalyst, only, of the destruction of its residents, the Connecticut Yankee sets out to transform Arthur's England into a copy of nineteenth-century America and in the process willfully kills upwards of 25,000 Englishmen.

It is interesting that Jacky Cable, who arrives on the island by perfectly natural means, is immediately willing to believe in its magic properties, while the Yankee, who is miraculously moved thirteen hundred years into the past and twice as many miles to the east, steadily refuses to credit the possibility of any violation of what he considers natural law. From the time he introduces himself to the end of the book, he reveals himself to be just the sort of observer who is constitutionally unfitted to narrate a fairy tale, and yet what else, ultimately, is his story? He is "a Yankee of the Yankees— and practical; yes, and nearly barren of sentiment, I suppose—or poetry, in other words" (p. 5). Our reaction to this statement is that the Yankee is a flawed character who, in the course of the book, ought to be restored to full sensibility. We might suppose that Twain is misleading us, and that the Yankee's sensitivity will prove, like Huck Finn's moral sense, to be superior to the standards by which it is being judged. But no. The Yankee is, as he says, devoid of poetry. He is the Philistine side of American culture personified, and, when it comes to magic, he will not believe.

At the beginning of the book there is a contrast to the Yankee in the person of "M. T.," a persona of the author who meets the Yankee in contemporary England and is the audience for his narrative. "M. T." is, unlike the Yankee, receptive to poetry and the romance of the past. He is the fictional equivalent of Howard Pyle, immersing himself in the wonders of another culture:

> From time to time I dipped into old Sir Thomas Malory's enchanting book, and fed at its rich feast of prodigies and adventures, breathed in the fragrance of its obsolete names, and dreamed again. (pp. 2-3)

But whereas Pyle made the imaginative journey to the Middle Ages and returned with a treasure of pictures and stories, "M. T." can only look from afar. It is the skeptical Yankee who makes the trip.

That may be good artistic strategy. "M. T." is already willing to accept whatever he might find in Malory's romance world, and for that reason has nothing to learn from or contribute to that world. The Yankee, on the other hand, is so foreign to any kind of fairyland as to provide it with a strong contrast and a potentially fruitful compromise. He can offer it initiative, courage, and democratic principles. Fairyland offers him, and the America he represents, color, miracles, and the kind of nobility that even the Yankee can see in King Arthur. The contrast is developed as fully as one might wish, but where is the compromise? Nowhere. The Yankee continues to reject the ground rules of the world he is in. Having been told he is in Camelot, he says, "*Something* in me seemed to believe him—my consciousness, as you might say; but my reason didn't" (p. 15). And reason continues to govern him. Merlin, to him, is a doddering fraud. An enchanted castle is a pigsty. A magic fountain is a leaky well. He pierces Sir Sagramor's veil of invisibility with an ordinary and deadly bullet. "Somehow," he says, "every time the magic of fol-de-rol tried conclusions with the magic of science, the magic of fol-de-rol got left" (p. 396). Got steamrollered, is more like it.

Because he rejects the rules of the land, he leads it to chaos, until finally the land rejects him. Merlin the supposed powerless old fool, puts an end to his supremacy with a few "curious passes in the air" (p. 446) that send the Yankee to sleep for thirteen centuries. He wakes up in his own time—in the world he was trying to create—and dies broken hearted.

A Connecticut Yankee was ostensibly written for children, but it imposes on them the kind of hard Yankee unbelief that other writers of children's books were able to evade. It relies on a fantasy framework, and yet denies any outcropping of magic within that frame. There is more of wonder in the naturalistically framed *Huckleberry Finn*, in the superstitions, never quite disavowed, of Huck and Jim, than in all of *A Connecticut Yankee*. It seems that to Twain, who was perhaps closer to mainstream American culture than any writer before him, it was not possible to accept the fantasies of other times and other traditions, whether in the role of the unsympathetic Yankee or the yearning "M. T." If fantasies were not rooted in native things, they could not penetrate to the heart of American problems and must eventually turn sour.

By the end of the nineteenth century it still remained for any author to produce a full-length work of satisfying and unmistakably American fantasy. But by that time the seeds of such a work had been planted. There was the possibility, at least, of American magic in Hawthorne's and Melville's romances. There were American scenes and characters in the dream stories of Eggleston and other local colorists, and in the powerful, if unsatisfactory, *Connecticut Yankee*, whose author grew out of the local color beginnings. And there was a growing understanding of and affection for the fairy tale among readers and writers of children's books and magazines. What was needed was someone who could put these things together. To do that would take a special kind of genius, not superb plotting or exquisite insight into character or verbal flair, but sheer storytelling, magic-making power. And not until the end of the century did someone come along with just the right combination of background and ability. Coming out of nineteenth-century fairy tales, but an evolutionary step above them, the first unquestionably American fantasy appeared in 1900, L. Frank Baum's *The Wizard of Oz.*

FIVE

Oz

In 1900, when L. Frank Baum, with two successful children's books already in print, approached his publisher with a new project, the publisher turned him down. "He advised the author it was the consensus of the book trade that children were satisfied with the fairy tales already on the market, and that their parents would not buy anything as unconventional as an American fairy tale."[1] According to his biographers, Baum and his illustrator, W. W. Denslow, finally had to put up their own money for printing and binding.[2] We have seen in the last chapter how many fairy tales were on the market, and how few of the good ones were significantly American. But where the publisher might have looked at the facts and said to himself that American fairy tales do not work, and that there were enough of the other kind, Baum made the opposite conclusion. If there were a great many fairy tales already, that meant they were well liked, and if there were no new, native fairy tales, then it was high time one was written.

Baum was right. Even though it was considered, as Mrs. Baum later recollected, "too different, too radical—out of the general line,"[3] his American fairy tale became one of the best-known and best-loved children's books of all time and marked a turning point in the development of American fantasy. For the first time, as Edward Wagenknecht points out, an American writer "can honestly be said to have created a world...."[4]

It is the nature of that created world that enables us to say, with emphasis, that *The Wizard of Oz* is an American fairy tale. It does not take place in Kansas, any more than *A Connecticut Yankee in King Arthur's Court* takes place in Connecticut. It only starts there. But there is something about Oz itself that makes it more American than Mark Twain's

Camelot or Christopher Cranch's Huggermugger Island. Somehow L. Frank Baum put together a fairyland, like none before it, that we recognize as our own, a fairyland so stamped with the national culture that the English, those connoisseurs of fairylands, often find it more bewildering than wonderful.[5] But Oz struck such a chord in American readers that they went on to demand a dozen sequels by the author, a number of musical comedy adaptations, three filmed versions (one of which is now a national icon), and countless continuations by lesser writers.

In a sense, all of the works mentioned in the previous chapter led up to the creation of Oz. Before 1900 there was no coherent American fantasy world; afterward there was.

It remains to be shown how Baum, unlike his predecessors, created a fairyland with such solid outlines that it remains recognizable in reproduction after reproduction, like a drawing still clear after a thousand tracings. Where did it come from? To begin with, it is defined through contrast with a place we know well, at least after Baum's opening description. Oz is, as Dorothy says to Toto in the film version, certainly not Kansas. Kansas is:

> nothing but the great gray prairie on every side. Not a tree nor a house broke the broad sweep of flat country that reached the edge of the sky in all directions. The sun had baked the plowed land into a gray mass, with little cracks running through it. Even the grass was not green, for the sun had burned the tops of the long blades until they were the same gray color to be seen everywhere.[6]

This is just the opposite of the atmospheric magic that introduces "Rip Van Winkle." It is a way of describing landscape, in terms borrowed from Baum's naturalistic contemporaries, that cries out for relief. Baum is doing what a painter does when he paints a large, flat, colorless area on a canvas: he is creating negative space which acts to make any positive design all the more vivid. Kansas is gray, so we begin to think about color. It is flat, so we long for contour. It is vast, so we wish for something on a human scale. It is featureless, so we imagine the absent trees and houses. It is harsh, so we think of fertility. Before the paragraph is done, we have been given, by contraries, a picture of Oz.

When Dorothy arrives in Oz, all of our expectations are met. Baum's description emphasizes the exact contrast:

> The cyclone had set the house down, very gently—for a cyclone—in the midst of a country of marvelous beauty. There were lovely patches of green sward all around, with stately trees bearing rich and luscious fruits. Banks of gorgeous flowers were on every hand, and birds with rare and brilliant plumage sang and fluttered in the trees and bushes. A little way off was a

small brook, rushing and sparkling along between green banks, and murmuring in a voice very grateful to a little girl who had lived so long on the dry, gray prairies. (p. 100)

As the story goes on, the opposition of Kansas and Oz continues in subtler ways. Kansas is a dead land, where even the grass is scorched and gray. Oz is a place of such fertility that a scarecrow can come alive spontaneously. Kansas is a place of isolation, where people do not talk to one another. In Oz, Dorothy is able to talk not only with people, but with all of the animals as well. In a later book, *The Road to Oz*, the first clue that Dorothy and her companions have left Kansas and entered fairyland is a city of speaking foxes:

"What a queer notion!" cried the Fox-King, beginning to laugh. "Whatever made you think this is Kansas?"

"I left Uncle Henry's farm only about two hours ago; that's the reason," she said, rather perplexed.

"But, tell me, my dear, did you ever see so wonderful a city as Foxville in Kansas?" he questioned.[7]

In addition to all this life and color and wonder, Oz is fabulously wealthy. Its farms are prosperous, its capital city littered with precious stones. No one must dress in rags, go hungry, or work harder than is good for him. Later, Baum began to develop a systematic utopian scheme for administering Oz, but the riches are there from the beginning. In *The Emerald City of Oz*, when Dorothy finally leaves Kansas for good, it is because the gap has grown too great between her poverty there and her rank in Oz, where she is now a princess. Oz is not plagued with droughts and crop failures, nor with bankers and mortgages, as Kansas most assuredly was. In Oz, a man who worked as hard as Uncle Henry could not help but succeed.

But Oz is not defined only by its unlikeness to Kansas. There are also certain striking similarities between the two. Both are landlocked, bordered, not by perilous seas, but by impassable desert. Oz expresses simultaneously the two symbolic landscapes that Henry Nash Smith says form Americans' image of the Western frontier: it is the Garden of the World set in the midst of the Great American Desert.[8]

Oz is filled, too, with homely, familiar, Kansas-type things. The flora and fauna in the first book include corn fields, peach trees, crows, beetles, wildcats, storks, and field mice. Sprinkled among the familiar creatures are a few exotics, like the Cowardly Lion, and inventions, like the fierce, heraldic Kalidahs. But Baum rarely interrupts the story to introduce some strange, unheard-of plant or animal when he can slip a common one in without fuss. What wonders there are stand out because the matrix is so down-to-earth. He seems to have been guided not at all by conventional notions of which creatures belong in a fairy tale: there is not a single nightingale, for instance, in any of the Oz stories, but an important part is played by a farmyard hen named Bill (Dorothy changes this to Billina).

Inanimate objects, too, are familiar, Michael Patrick Hearn, in his annotations to *The Wizard of Oz*, points to the magic slate used by the Good Witch of the North as an unexpectedly homely touch, along with the clothes basket that the Wizard attaches to his balloon, the Tin Woodman's funnel hat and oil can, and the Scarecrow himself.[9] All of these things except the basket are connected with magic. Chalk marks appear miraculously on the slate, the funnel and oil can are signs of the Woodman's strange transformation from flesh to tin, and the Scarecrow is an example of spontaneous animation. Other household items take on magical associations in this and later books. The Wicked Witch of the West carries, not the traditional broomstick, but an umbrella, appropriate, as Hearn points out, to her fear of water (p. 231). In later volumes a sawhorse, a patchwork quilt, and a phonograph come to life. Elements of daily life not only appear, but are intimately connected with the heart of the magic itself. The only American antecedents to this technique—or, more than technique, this philosophy of fantastic composition—are the talking chairs of Eggleston's *Queer Stories* and the contents of Davy's pockets in *Davy and the Goblin*, both undercut by the disjointed, affectless quality of dream narration, and Hawthorne's remarkable "Feathertop," which will be discussed later in connection with Baum's invention of characters.

Oz is also Kansas in that it is the agrarian promised land. It is essentially rural and democratic, though it has a capital city and a queen. Its many farmers and woodsmen act and speak with the assurance of yeomen, rather than with the cautious humility of peasants; servants are few and independent; the army has been reduced to a comical and impotent handful of officers; and titles, like Dorothy's, seem to be awarded by popular acclaim. It is too much to say, as Henry Littlefield does, that *The Wizard* is a "Parable on Populism," but it does share many of the Populist concerns and biases.[10] Taken loosely, with a grain of salt, Littlefields's readings help indicate much about the relationship between Kansas and Oz: the silver shoes are a little like William Jennings Bryan's silver ticket to prosperity, the Scarecrow is, in a sense, the troubled farmer, the Tin Woodman can stand for the industrial laborer, the Cowardly Lion is a witty analog of Bryan himself, the Wizard could be any ineffectual President from Grant to McKinley, and the band of petitioners are another Coxey's Army descending on Washington (Littlefield, throughout). I might even propose one more analogy. Dorothy, bold, resourceful, leading the men around her toward success, is a juvenile Mary Lease, the Kansas firebrand who told her neighbors to raise less corn and more hell, or an Annie Diggs, the Populist temperance reformer. Baum and the Populists promoted an active role for women in the rural utopia. Incidentally, the real surname of the Wizard of Oz is Diggs.

Baum created Oz, then, with the aid of a paradox. It is Kansas—or rather, let us say, since most of the elements we are dealing with are applicable to a broader area than Dorothy's Kansas, it is the United States—and it is also everything that conditions in the United States make us wish for. Oz is America made more fertile, more equitable, more companionable, and, because it is magic, more wonderful. What Dorothy finds beyond the Deadly Desert is another America with its potential fulfilled: its beasts speaking, its deserts blooming, and its people living in harmony.

If Oz in America, then Dorothy is its Christopher Columbus. *The Wizard of Oz* is primarily a story of exploration, and one of its principal strengths is the feeling of "wild surmise" that Keats ascribed to Cortez and his men. Dorothy is the discoverer who opens up the newest new world; later she and other children—the Cabots, Drakes, and Hudsons of this fairyland—chart the unknown regions remaining in Oz and the lands around it. All of the stories are based on movement. They whisk one away from known lands with a dizzying swoop, proceed over land, water, and air toward a brief action, then take off again for home. In *The Road to Oz*, indeed, there can be said to be no plot at all except the journey of Dorothy, Button Bright, Polychrome, and the Shaggy Man to Oz. The journey motif owes something to traditional fairy tale structure, as we will see, but it owes as much or more to an American tradition of restlessness and curiosity. Happily, the discovery of Oz undoes some of the evils that accompanied the discovery of America. The natives accept the invaders, who, in turn, leave them in possession of their lands. Profit and progress are firmly excluded, and Oz remains the sleepy paradise it began.

Selma Lanes points out in her essay on "America as Fairy Tale" that the discovery of Oz coincided with a change in America's image of itself. Not until we realized that we were not living in a fairyland of peace and plenty could we begin to draw upon the power of that archetype in our fictions. "Having long had a thin tradition of American fairy tales precisely because of a deeply held faith in the fairy-tale aspects of the American dream, we have in our time lost that faith and are creating new and more convincing American fairy tales and fantasies."[11]

Oz is at the turning point. It could only have been invented by someone who, like Baum, personally felt the gap between American ideals and American life. In this regard it is interesting to compare the Oz books, as Fred Erisman does, with another of Baum's series, the "Aunt Jane's Nieces" stories. The same values are upheld in both: generosity, simplicity, individuality, and industry; but, whereas in Oz the virtues define society, in the fictional "real world" they struggle for minor victories within a system responsive only to power and prestige. Aunt Jane's nieces rely on wealthy benefactors and on a shady detective named Quintus Fogerty to help them clean up patches of corruption, but Dorothy, in Oz, can destroy a witch with a bucket of water.[12]

The successful creation and immediate acceptance of Oz indicates that Americans by 1900 had finally begun to feel the need of an ideal world apart from America itself, as it was believed to be or as it was expected to become. Many critics associate Oz with the host of utopian writings that appeared in the final years of the nineteenth century, and indeed it is a product of the same hunger for a more equitable world that produced Edward Bellamy's *Looking Backward.* However, Bellamy's book, published in 1888, is a prospectus, set in a Boston-that-is-to-come, for America's future development. It extrapolates; it proposes; it relies on a science fiction rationale to lend plausibility to its ideas. After it appeared, Bellamyite societies sprang up all over the world, dedicated to bringing the course of history into line with Bellamy's speculations. But twelve years later there were no Baumite societies. No one proposed to govern Boston after the manner of the Emerald City. Far from having scientific verisimilitude, Oz is punctuated with marvels, each of which widens the gap between the lived world and the imagined. Both Bellamy and Baum capture the energy of the Progressive impulse, but while *Looking Backward* represents it at its most optimistic, outward-reaching point, *The Wizard of Oz* reveals a shift toward introspection and the redefinition of values.

That is not to say that Americans, including Baum, immediately and totally transferred their allegiance from this world to various Others. The perfections of Oz would not be so poignant if they did not so strongly suggest qualities of American life at its rare best. In this respect, I would say that the primary source of secondary belief taken advantage of by Baum is the powerful but receding faith in the American Dream, rather than any corpus of supernatural legend. That faith has not yet left us entirely (it is kept alive partly by having been realized imaginatively in Oz) so that if Kansas, for example, is proven to be a part of the fallen world, there is still a glimpse of earthly paradise farther on, in California or Alaska or on the moon. As a matter of fact, Oz shares many of its characteristics with the popular image of California: fertility, mineral wealth, kindly climate, and a profusion of colorful eccentrics. It is no accident that Baum moved to

California when his writings earned him enough money. If Oz were open to immigration, the Emerald City would soon be as big as Los Angeles.

That, then, is Oz, a photograph of America with its blemishes filtered out, hand-tinted with the colors of the imagination. Topographically, the four quadrants of Oz seem to represent Baum's own personal geography. The East is Baum's New York childhood, a gentle land of forest and farm, with its residents scaled down just enough to make a child comfortable. One has the impression that the land of the Munchkins is a little older, more settled, than the other regions, and there are traces there of an "old-world" heritage, analogous to the costumes and customs retained by, say, Pennsylvania Germans. Baum's own family was German, and his father made at least one trip back to the old country. Could it be that the Munchkins, though the name is rich in other associations, derive ultimately from the child statue that overlooks the capital of Bavaria from its town hall? It is known as the Munich Child—*Münch Kind*. Bavaria's "official" color, like that of the Munchkins, is blue.

If the Munchkins live in the settled East, the Winkies are Western frontiersmen. The western quarter of Oz is roughly equivalent to South Dakota, the westernmost point of Baum's early wanderings. The Winkie country is wild: "As they advanced the ground became rougher and hillier, for there were no farms nor houses in this country of the West, and the ground was untilled" (p. 220). It has hoardes of marauding beasts—wolves, crows, and locustlike black bees—and a tribe of savages (in the form of winged monkeys) who attack Dorothy's band of pioneers. In heading west, the travelers leave the protective forest and enter a harsh prairie: "In the afternoon the sun shone hot in their faces, for there were no trees to offer them shade; so that before night Dorothy and Toto and the Lion were tired, and lay down upon the grass and fell asleep, with the Woodman and the Scarecrow keeping watch" (p. 221).

Baum was not a farmer, but as one-time editor of a small town newspaper in Aberdeen, South Dakota, he was intimately concerned with the farmer's plight. As agriculture suffered in the late years of the nineteenth century from drought, high expenses, and low prices, so did his paper suffer and eventually fold. Dorothy's Kansas is evidence that he was sensitive to the problems of his rural neighbors; it is a one-sided picture of the hardships of life on the prairies. The land of the Winkies is again a reflection of pioneer life, but with an element of optimism transforming gray waste into golden plenty. Though the West of Oz seems stern and forbidding, with a malevolent nature spirit—the Witch—in command, once the witch is vanquished we see it in a new light. The Winkies, out from under the thumb of cruel necessity, prove to be friendly and helpful. They are sturdy farmers and craftsmen, and they help Dorothy rescue and repair her friends in something of the spirit of a neighborhood barn raising. The chosen color of the Winkies is the yellow of ripe grain.

North and South are less clearly defined. Dorothy does not visit the northern land of the Gillikins in the first volume, and by the time Baum began to explore it, Oz had become well established in its own right and did not reflect American geography so closely. We do know that its color is purple and that it is a mountainous, timbered, largely unsettled region. It vaguely suggests northern Michigan, where Baum spent vacations, or Minnesota, or the great untracked expanse of Canada. The South is primarily a region of isolated communities of eccentrics, like the people made all of china in the first book. There is no clear connection between the land of the Quadlings and the American South, with which Baum was not familiar. Its queen, Glinda, is revered as a near-goddess, suggesting the Southern worship of genteel womanhood, but then Oz itself becomes a matriarchy when Ozma comes to power. South, for Baum, more probably meant the hills of southern Illinois, Indiana, and Missouri, where he traveled selling china (the origin of the china country?) after the failure of his newspaper. The hostile Hammerheads who attempt to block Dorothy's southward journey are not unlike conventional hillbillies, save for their unusual physical characteristics—they are armless and have heads like battering rams on elastic necks.

The sections of Oz are unquestionably influenced by American sectionalism, though their characteristics reflect Baum's own experience rather than traditional political or economic divisions. The Munchkins do not engage in New England style manufacturing nor the Quadlings in sharecropping: neither would be in keeping with an idealized fairyland. Nevertheless, the analog is clear. But what of the center, the radiant Emerald City? What, to Baum, was the capital and heart of the country? The answer must be Chicago, the scene of his first successes, the home to which he returned after his sales trips, the site of a growing artistic community of which Baum felt himself an integral part. His Chicago was not the jungle of Upton Sinclair's shocking exposés, nor the brawling hog-butcher of Carl Sandburg's apostrophes. It was the shining, hopeful White City, built on the shores of Lake Michigan for the great Columbian Exposition. The beaux arts brilliance of the White City inspired another writer to dream of utopia: to Henry Demarest Lloyd it was the seed of a new society, as described in his sketch "No Mean City."[13] The buildings of the White City soon came down, and the city of fairy tale splendor passed into fairy tale, altered in color but not in meaning.

We have seen something of how Baum utilized American material to create his Other World. Other writers, like Bellamy or Lloyd, did much the same thing: they too played on national hopes and disappointments in creating fictional landscapes. But Oz is not a utopia, though it has many utopian elements. It is something more lasting, a fairyland. The difference is that Oz, like any fantasy world, allows for—rather, demands—the existence of the impossible. How does Baum integrate the impossible into a setting derived from pragmatic American experience? The best way to point out his techniques is to look at our other earmarks of fantasy: narrative structure, hero, nonhuman characters, and a coherent system of magic and significance. The fact that Baum's work, American as it is, lends itself to analysis along these lines, which were drawn originally from the British fantasy tradition, is a sign of his unprecedented entry into the mainstream of fantasy after our hundred or so years of apprenticeship.

The land of Oz is a constant throughout the series, and so may be described as if all fourteen volumes were one evolving work. But there is no overall story structure to the set; each book must be considered individually. The most important story, and the most highly structured, is that of *The Wizard of Oz*. I asserted in the first chapter that the basic pattern for most successful fantasy is derived from the traditional fairy tale, being that pattern of journey, conflict, return, and reward outlined by Vladimir Propp in his *Morphology of the Folktale*.

Baum was probably unaware of most of the scholarly work being done in his time by folklorists, and in any case he lived before the important analyses of the folktale, like Propp's, had been made. If his story corresponds in any significant measure to the traditional structure, it indicates not a studied imitation but an intuitive grasp of the fundamental dynamics of the folktale. And *The Wizard* does, indeed, follow the traditional pattern, with the additional multiplication of elements and overlaying of action we expect of a written work, though a good oral storyteller can do the same things.

The rapid opening of *The Wizard* corresponds to Propp's first set of "functions" (see chapters 1 and 2 for a simplified account of these functions). First of all, there is an original, presumably idyllic, situation. In this case, the original state occurs some time before the book begins, when Dorothy was living with her parents somewhere other than Kansas. Next is what Propp called "absentation," when one or both parents leave the formerly happy home. Dorothy's parents die, leaving her in the care of Uncle Henry and Aunt Em. On a symbolic level, Uncle Henry and Aunt Em are Dorothy's parents, but she is unable, at this point, to accept them as such: hence the importance of her final reunion with them. Next in the fairy tale morphology we have a command or interdiction of some sort, and an act of disobedience. Aunt Em calls out to Dorothy to get into the cellar, but Dorothy runs after her dog instead. At this point in a fairy tale the element of magic enters into what usually begins as an ordinary domestic scene. The villain may come snooping around or leave a trap for the hero, or, as in this case, the hero may fall by accident under the influence of a magical agent, like the cyclone which carries Dorothy to Oz.

Now the fairy tale action proper begins. Either there is an act of villainy, or else a need or lack is discovered. The hero is informed of it and dispatched to go fill the need. The first thing he usually encounters is a figure Propp calls the "donor," who tests the hero in some way, awards him a magical agent to aid in the quest, and points the way. For Dorothy, these two segments, the dispatch and the meeting with the donor, are compressed into one. The first person she meets in Oz is the Good Witch of the North. The Witch informs her of her lack—she is no longer in Kansas and there is no way to get back—and also presents her with the magical silver shoes and a protective kiss on the forehead. Then she shows her the yellow brick road and sends her off on the next stage of her adventure.

The journey to the Emerald City figures in Propp's morphology as a single function, the delivery to the appointed place of action. But Baum expands this element into a symmetrical set of complications. First, Dorothy meets her three companions: the Scarecrow, the Tin Woodman, and the Cowardly Lion. These are the hero's customary helpers, animated forms of the magical agent. They are also, in this instance, heroes themselves of parallel subplots. Each has a lack of his own—brains, heart, and courage—and to each Dorothy acts as the dispatcher, sending them off to the Emerald City. After the three companions appear we got three obstacles: wild beasts, a river, and a field of deadly poppies, before reaching the goal.

At this point in the fairy tale morphology we should meet the villain, usually an ogre or evil wizard. Dorothy finds a wizard, but instead of taking the villain's part, the Wizard of Oz assumes the role of a second dispatcher. He informs the travelers of a new need: they must kill the Witch of the West. The subsequent trip to the land of the Winkies is an embedded adventure within the main one. The secondary adventure proceeds apace, with a struggle, a victory, and a return. The Witch is dead, the quest accomplished, and the Wizard should now revert to his original role. He is defeated, his conditions met; now he is responsible for solving the problems of the heroes. With the auxiliary heroes he can do so. They get what they lack. But Dorothy discovers that she is no closer to home than before. With her, the Wizard was falsely assuming the positions of donor and villain. He has nothing to give her, nor does it solve her lack to defeat him. So we get something not unknown in fairy tales: the hero sets out once again in search of the still elusive goal.

With a fine balancing of beginning and end, Dorothy meets at last the one who can help her, and it is Glinda, the Good Witch of the South, essentially a double of the Witch of the North who launched her on her quest. Now the resolution comes, but in a divided form. Most fairy tales end with a wedding or an accession to the throne, or both. No one is paired off at the end of *The Wizard*, but the three companions all assume thrones. The Scarecrow goes back to rule the Emerald City, the Woodman becomes Emperor of the Winkies, and the Lion becomes king of the forest. For Dorothy, the resolution is one which does not appear in Propp's morphology, unless we stretch the meaning of such a term as Function K[10], "release from captivity," but we know it from such tales as "Hansel and Gretel." It is a return to the family, now seen not as cruel step-parents but as loving parents, though still in the guise of aunt and uncle.

Baum not only intuitively understood fairy tale structure, but he was also able to adjust it at will to fit his needs. The sharp break between the opening segment and the ensuing action, for example, he made serve as a crossing of the threshold into another world. By doubling and tripling certain elements he was able to take advantage of his major strengths as a writer, the portrayal of movement and the quick and comical delineation of character. The embedded plot is neatly introduced by having one character, the Wizard, take on two functional roles. The Wizard is also placed in a central position in the book, structurally and geographically, with the result that at the heart of fairyland we find Omaha-born Oz Diggs, a reminder of the opening scene of the book and a forecast of its end. Baum's skill in handling the fairy tale story line—in making it his own—surpasses, I believe, that of any of the imitators of European style fairy tales mentioned in the last chapter, just as his grasp of American character and landscape surpasses that of all his predecessors in the native, fairies-in-America line.

Baum's first stories were actually much like those of Howard Pyle or the lesser retellers from European tradition. They were transformations into *Märchen* form of familiar Mother Goose motifs, short and clever but in no way innovative.[14] At the time he was preparing *The Wizard* for publication he was also readying *A New Wonderland*, a set of stories in the familiar comic fairy court vein of Thackeray's *The Rose and the Ring* or Andrew Lang's original tales.[15] Between Oz books he also continued to write more or less traditional fairy stories, the finest of which is *Queen Zixi of Ix*.[16] These books show that Baum was familiar with the kind of competent fairy tale writing that magazines like *St. Nicholas* made popular. Indeed, Zixi herself appeared in *St. Nicholas*, from November 1904 to October 1905. If Baum had written more for *St. Nicholas* and similar prestigious journals, and if he had limited himself to their standard fare, his achievement would have been less striking, but his reputation would probably not have suffered such an eclipse among critics of children's literature.

Baum made a clear distinction between his conventional stories and those he called modernized fairy stories, like *The Wizard*, but, as he indicates in his introduction to that book, both kinds shared the same prototypes:

> Folk lore, legends, myths and fairy tales have followed childhood through the ages, for every healthy youngster has a wholesome and instinctive love for stories fantastic, marvelous, and manifestly unreal. The winged fairies of Grimm and Andersen have brought more happiness to childish hearts than all other human creations. (p. 85)

Baum is clearly thinking of "folk lore" here as something belonging to other cultures and other times. He gives it credit for originating the fairy tale, but seeks something more in tune with present-day life: "for the time has come for a series of newer 'wonder tales' in which the stereotyped genie, dwarf and fairy are eliminated, together with all the horrible and blood-curdling incident devised by their authors to point a fearsome moral to each tale" (p. 85). If he had known more of authentic oral tradition, he would have known that most tales are free of both winged fairies and morals. By reacting against the sentimental writers that he knew (more likely the Virginia Bakers and Lily Wesselhoefts of this country than the Grimm collection or Andersen), he was reaching past them to sources he had never actually seen or heard.

As Baum continued to write "modernized" tales, he grew bolder in his treatment of the fairy tale structure. *The Land of Oz* has an unconventional ending: the boy hero is revealed at last to be, not a king in disguise, but a queen, transformed by witchcraft into male form. In *Ozma of Oz* and several of the later Oz books, Dorothy becomes a sort of heroine errant, performing quests not for her own sake but for other, lesser characters; the hero role is broken up, that is, into an active but unconcerned protagonist and one or more passive but needy companions. *The Scarecrow of Oz* contains a fairy tale in burlesque, the "hero" of which is the most ineffectual character in the story. Some of the books, like *Dorothy and the Wizard in Oz* and *The Road to Oz*, suppress all phases of the fairy tale morphology except the quest–journey, but they still follow the proper sequence for that segment of the full structure. In others, like *The Emerald City of Oz, Tik-Tok of Oz,* and *Glinda of Oz,* a rival story line of conquest and siege all but overpowers the individualistic fairy tale development, perhaps reflecting America's growing awareness of international strife up to and during World War I. But the underlying pattern remains constant and occasionally, as in *Rinkitink of Oz,* reappears in classic form.

Though Baum's familiarity with fairy tale style and structure does not mean that he was in touch with the Jack tales and other American versions of *Märchen,* still he was able to do what oral storytellers often do, adapt a borrowed pattern to local conditions, local habits of thought. There are genuine bits of oral tradition in his stories, mostly on the level of language: prose rhythms, metaphors, and jokes. A structure is a very neutral thing, so that no matter where Baum learned the pattern for a fairy tale, his fantasies came out unmistakably American because of their sound, their sense of place, and, to move into the next area of concern, their characters.

The third point noted about the English fantasies in chapter one is that their protagonists, like the heroes of fairy tale, are generally the representatives of common, unexceptional humanity in worlds of miracle. They are lenses through which the reader can view the unfamiliar without having to lose his orientation in the familiar. If they accomplish prodigious feats it is only with agonizing effort—or luck. They are high-spirited, but must frequently be helped by the grander figures around them. Their greatest strengths are an active curiosity that gets them into awkward situations, and a measure of common sense that gets them out again.

The one unforgettable protagonist of Baum's books is Dorothy. Dorothy is all of the above things: ordinary, human, lucky, plucky, surrounded by protectors, curious, and sensible. She suggests Gretel (another witch killer), Cinderella, and Jack—all the intrepid *Märchen* heroes. But Dorothy and her lesser avatars, Tip, Prince Inga, Betsy Bobbin, and Trot, are more complex than characters in traditional tales. Other sides of Dorothy's character point to sources and analogs in other modes of literature.

An important literary source for *The Wizard,* and probably the primary inspiration for Dorothy herself, is Lewis Carroll's *Alice in Wonderland.* When Baum set about to construct a modernized fairy tale, *Alice* was one of the few examples available to him, although it may be called a fairy tale only in the very broadest sense, being much less closely aligned with oral tradition in detail or overall conception than *The Wizard.* Nevertheless, Baum considered Alice's adventure, "rambling and incoherent as it is," to be "one of the best and perhaps the most famous of modern fairy tales."[17] Rambling and incoherent in comparison with folk or literary *Märchen* it is, because it is nonsense: a wild mutation away from the parent form, with its own logic and order; but for Baum, who was considering it as a source book, the important thing about *Alice* is not its discovery of the absurd but its development of the fairy tale hero into a distinctive, perceiving individual. In an essay on "Modern Fairy Tales," Baum, after decrying Carroll's "whimsical" treatment of fantastic themes, says that, nonetheless:

> ... it is but fair to state that the children loved Alice better than any prince or princess that Andersen ever created. The secret of Alice's success lay in the fact that she was a real child, and any normal child could sympathize with her all through her adventures. The story may often bewilder the little one—for it is bound to bewilder us, having neither plot nor motive in its relation—but Alice is doing something every moment, and doing something strange and marvelous, too, so the child follows her with rapturous delight.[18]

In contrast with Charles Carryll, whose *Davy and the Goblins* copies all of Carroll's techniques except that of giving life to his characters (and thence to his story), Baum threw away offhand everything but the spirit of *Alice in Wonderland*, and in doing so produced a far worthier successor. Dorothy and Alice are two of the most likeable heroines in literature, two witty and contemporary character sketches of the sort one finds in the best domestic comedies. Carroll discovered that such a character could be removed from the social world into the world of dream, and Baum took things one step further (in terms of violations of reality) into a world of waking marvels.

Though Alice and Dorothy are both portraits of believable, modern-day children, there are important differences between them. Dorothy, unlike Alice, never wonders who she is, where she is going, or why the world has suddenly turned upside down. "My name is Dorothy," she says to the Scarecrow after only one day in the land of Oz, "and I am going to the Emerald City, to ask the great Oz to send me back to Kansas" (p. 118). Even while whirling through the air in the middle of a tornado, she keeps her self-possession:

> At first she had wondered if she would be dashed to pieces when the house fell again; but as the hours passed and nothing terrible happened, she stopped worrying and resolved to wait calmly and see what the future would bring. At last she crawled over the swaying floor to her bed, and lay down upon it; and Toto followed and lay down beside her. (pp. 95-96)

Alice is English; Dorothy is aggressively, triumphantly American. As the primary link between the naturalistically portrayed Kansas of the beginning and the transmogrified America that is Oz, she must be able to make explicit the comparisons between the two, and to do so she must be accepted by the reader as a valid representative of all things American. Therefore, Dorothy is not merely a fairy tale heroine, or a believable child, she is also heir to an American conception of character, especially of its own character. And what is the essential American character? Often it is the explorer, the wanderer, who penetrates ever wilder regions of the world or the mind and comes back relatively unscathed.

Rip Van Winkle, in the first successful American romance, is such a wandering hero. He too, like Dorothy, explores for a time the perilous regions of fantasy, facing the strangest events with mild surprise. Rip ages during his adventure, but he can hardly be said to be otherwise changed by it, except perhaps to be more appreciative of his lost and regained home. Rip is childlike, in comparison to those around him; he represents a vanishing peasant simplicity, organically related to that of a fairy tale hero, that lets him accept without question whatever may happen.

Edgar Allan Poe's explorers are of a different cast. Like Rip, like Dorothy, they are plunged into a universe of marvels, but their reaction is more likely to be an exultant horror than calm curiosity. A Poe hero represents the American mind in conflict with itself. Enamored, on the one hand, of system and logic, he is drawn, on the other, to the wild unpredictability of the universe. When adventure comes to him, his two desires clash. He may become totally irrational, possessed by sensation, like Roderick Usher. Or he might take refuge in blind reason, an artificial order that has no bearing on the outside world, like Usher's friend, or like the oh-so-reasonable narrator of "The Tell-Tale Heart." In both cases, the madness buried at the beginning surfaces by the end. Twain's Connecticut Yankee portrays a similar conflict between reason and miracle.

By using a child version of the explorer, Baum is able to sidestep such an intellectual dilemma. Dorothy and Arthur Gordon Pym mark the boundaries of this American type, the explorer or stranger in a strange land. Somewhere between the two we find Melville's not very mature Taji, in the water world of *Mardi*, his Ishmael, who seems to poise exactly between the dark and light views of his world, and the mature child Huckleberry Finn, under whose seeming acceptance there is a great deal of Poesque despair. What all of these characters share is their ability to discover new worlds, to move through them and learn from them, and then to emerge from them paradoxically the same as when they started. Even Pym escapes long enough to tell the tale. Some of them are Gothic heroes, some picaros, some heroes of *Märchen*, but whatever the narrative mode, the commanding motivation remains the same. It is to see what is around the next corner or over the next range, and that is true whether the hero looks ahead with fear or with delight.

Since Dorothy is female and a Westerner, she suggests one other category of character, another peculiarly American one: the pioneer woman. There are two classes of pioneer women in the popular imagination. One is faded and bleak and particularly appealing to local color writers with a naturalistic vision. That is Aunt Em. The other is lively and attractive, drawing her strength from the earth she lives so close to. That is, of course, Dorothy, who is to some degree a forerunner of the Nebraska heroine in Willa Cather's *My Ántonia*.[19] Throughout *The Wizard*, Dorothy gives her comrades guidance and encouragement, like a little mother; and if men of tin or straw could eat, or if lions were vegetarians, she would undoubtedly nurture them as well. She does an admirable job of keeping herself and Toto provided for on an arduous journey. Nurture, comfort, and guidance: these, in mythology, are the functions of the Earth Mother. If Dorothy were allowed to mature, we might imagine her something like the grown-up Ántonia, full-figured, sun-burned to earth colors, radiating order, contentment, and fertility.

She does not grow up, however. An adult heroine would, as I say, bring back all those troublesome questions of belief and reason that drove Poe's heroes mad. So Baum imposed on Oz an end to aging, and Dorothy, rather than maturing, began to fall into a rather gushing girlishness. That is one of the primary weaknesses of the later books, so important is Dorothy's earthiness to the fantasy.

How are all these conceptions of Dorothy related? The first, the fairy tale hero, is a basic guideline, like the Proppian story outline. It merely says that the hero must be perceivably one of us, and not a partaker of the strangeness of the Other World. The qualities of a good fairy tale hero keep the story moving, because he is bold and curious, and make the outcome meaningful, because he is universal. But a writer who wishes to expand the role of hero to the status of rounded character, and the brief tale into full-length fantasy, must fill in the outlines from other sources.

If the fairy tale gave Baum an outline for his main character, one might say that Lewis Carroll taught him how to draw in features and make them appear three-dimensional. Carroll's Alice comes to life because she has a family, a history, habits, opinions, and a unique point of view. These are things that are difficult to generate unless the author is familiar with the character's milieu, or unless he knows more about his fictional society than he could ever fit into a book. It is possible to so immerse oneself in a fantasy world (I am speaking of art, not psychopathology) that a member of that world can become a fully developed personality and our representative in the world, like certain of J. R. R. Tolkien's hobbits, but it is easier to draw a character more directly from life.

With an outline and a set of features, Dorothy still needed color. It is not enough to say, "I will create a character who seems to be a living, breathing American child." One must have some notion of what it means to be such a creature. Part of what it meant to Baum is to be healthy, confident, exploratory, and full of pioneer spirit, to the point of invoking the quasi-mythic conception of frontier womanhood. This side of Dorothy's character reveals Baum's regional-minded optimism: what wonderful children we are raising in the West, he is saying; they are the hope of the country. Dorothy from Kansas, Betsy Bobbin from Oklahoma, and Trot from California all move through his stories gently wreaking order and distributing love. Baum was fond of all children, but he had no such faith in those from Eastern cities. Button Bright from Philadelphia is a charming boy, but completely helpless. In the matter of character, as in setting, Baum is all the more an American writer for being a regional one as well.

What about the characters around Dorothy? Just as she is the essential tie with the familiar, they are the wonder-working helpers and adversaries who must carry us into the marvelous. How does Baum stand up on our fourth element of fantasy, the assortment of nonhuman characters? Excellently, for the most part. From the Good Witch at the beginning of *The Wizard* to the fascinating Yookoohoo in *Glinda of Oz*, his last book, Baum produced with seeming ease a host of vivid, unquestionably magical beings: he brought a scarecrow to life, made an engaging eccentric out of an insect, revealed a common tramp to be a wonder worker, and made witches seem like his own invention.

The secondary characters in Baum's Oz fall into four overlapping groups: there are Class A figures, bold, humorous, unforgettable characters who nearly assume hero status; Class B, not so grand as Class A, but still strong; Class C, a group of spear carriers, thrown in to keep the story rolling, which they do competently enough; and, unfortunately, Class D, weak or whimsical groups that never come to life at all.

In Class A I would put the Big Three: the Scarecrow and the Tin Woodman from *The Wizard* and Jack Pumpkinhead from *The Land of Oz*. These three characters establish Baum as the Dickens of fantasy. Like Pickwick and his friends, they are a perfect blend of the grotesque and the lovable. They demonstrate Baum's remarkable ability to assume the viewpoint of even the oddest creature.

What kind of personality does a living scarecrow have? Baum, without hestitating, answers that this particular Scarecrow, at least, is a close and careful observer (through those lovely, blue, mismatched, painted eyes), a wit (though his jokes are often, appropriately enough, corny), a humble fellow (having started out in life as a sort of farm laborer), but with some understandable vanity about his wizard-made brains. From having spent his early life stuck on a pole, he is something of a philosopher, of the pragmatic school:

> "I am never hungry," he said; "and it is a lucky thing I am not. For my mouth is only painted, and if I should cut a hole in it so I could eat, the straw I am stuffed with would come out, and that would spoil the shape of my head." (p. 124)

His mood is always sunny, which may be due to the fact that his mouth is painted in a perpetual smile. It is not much 'use asking whether he is always smiling on the inside, since his insides are only straw. He is a case of clothes making the man, and doing a pretty good job of it. Unlike Dorothy, who is never described in much detail since we are more interested in her impressions than in her appearance, the Scarecrow, being all outside, as it were, is described quite exactly, and with frequent subsequent references to his peculiar looks:

> Dorothy leaned her chin upon her hand and gazed thoughtfully at the Scarecrow. Its head was a small sack stuffed with straw, with eyes, nose, and mouth painted on it to represent a face. An old, pointed blue hat, that had belonged to some Munchkin, was perched on this head, and the rest of the figure was a blue suit of clothes, worn and faded, which had also been stuffed with straw. On the feet were some old boots with blue tops, such as every man wore in this country, and the figure was raised above the stalks of corn by means of the pole stuck up its back. (p. 116)

The Scarecrow's first act is a friendly wink at Dorothy, and he continues to demonstrate his feelings with broad gestures as well as with a distinctive style of speaking. Baum has a way of portraying character through costume and through repeated bits of action, like the Scarecrow's many tumbles, that is probably a holdover from his youth, when he wrote and acted in popular plays. The Scarecrow and the Tin Man are very much like a pair of comic players, a team of vaudevillians, and it is no wonder that old vaudevillians Montgomery and Stone on Broadway and Ray Bolger and Jack Haley in the movie struck such a response in the roles.

At his most human, the Scarecrow resembles a kindly farmer. The Tin Woodman resembles, to no one's surprise, a woodsman: a hunter or trapper or logger operating just beyond the cleared land. And that is what he once was, until, through a gradual replacement of body parts, he became a man of metal, with his memory and identity intact, but no longer human.

In many ways, the Tin Woodman complements the Scarecrow. The Scarecrow is contemplative, the Woodman a man of action. The Scarecrow comes from settled land, the Woodman from the virgin forest. The

Scarecrow was once inanimate matter that became a man; the Tin Woodman a man that has grown to resemble an inanimate object. The Scarecrow aspires to human intelligence, while the Tin Woodman longs for human sympathies. On that last point hangs their entry into the plot, and throughout the story questions of intellect center on the Scarecrow and questions of sentiment on the Woodman.

Many critics have pointed to the Tin Woodman as the first entry of the machine into the field of fantasy, but the Tin Woodman is not a machine, nor is he ever connected with things mechanical. Baum does bring in a mechanical man, Tik-tok, in the third Oz book, and he is a very different character from the Woodman. The Tin Woodman's distinctive characteristic is the tender human spirit within his hard and shiny body; it makes him a rather poignant character, and, since he accepts his fate without self-pity, an admirable one, a symbol of resistance to dehumanization.

Jack Pumpkinhead is not so witty as the Scarecrow, nor as staunch as the Tin Woodman, but he is their equal in strangeness. Jack is a man made of wood, with a Jack O'Lantern for a head, dressed in some unknown gentleman's cast-off clothes. He is meant only for a joke, but his comical appearance strikes the fancy of an old witch, and so she brings him to life. If that sounds familiar, it ought to, because Jack is Hawthorne's "Feathertop," given another chance at existence. Feathertop was too good a creation to disappear after just one story. Baum proves that his comical potential was barely tapped in Hawthorne's tale.

I know of no evidence that Baum read Hawthorne. He was not generally much of a reader, but he had a taste for anything partaking of the marvelous, and, as we have seen, there were few American writers besides Hawthorne who were able to make effective use of fantasy. The resemblance between the two scenes of animation is quite striking: in place of Mother Rigby's hell-fired pipe we have the Powder of Life in Mombi's pepper box, and, Mombi did not make the mannequin himself as Mother Rigby did, but other details—the pumpkinhead's calm acceptance of life and the witch's shifts from fury to glee—are identical. Baum's account even suggests something of Hawthorne's amused style:

> Jack Pumpkinhead stepped back a pace, at this, and said in a reproachful voice:
> "Don't yell like that! Do you think I'm deaf?"
> Old Mombi danced around him, frantic with delight.
> "He lives!" she screamed: "he lives! he lives!"
> Then she threw her stick into the air and caught it as it came down; and she hugged herself with both arms, and tried to do a step of a jig; and all the time she repeated, rapturously:
> "He lives!—he lives!—he lives!"[20]

Marius Bewley suggests that Jack Pumpkinhead is not the only thing in Oz to show Hawthorne's influence.[21] Many of Baum's magical events sound like possible entries in Hawthorne's notebooks: a girl's heart is frozen so she cannot love; a man meets his own cast-off head and cannot decide which of the two is the real individual; a straw man wants a brain and finds that one made of pins and needles serves him perfectly; a mechanical man moves, speaks, and thinks—but does he live? What is the difference between these conceits and those of Hawthorne such as "The Bosom Serpent"; "Ethan Brand," whose sin has turned his heart to marble; "The Birthmark" that is all that stands between a woman and perfection—and death; or the mechanical yet seemingly living butterfly created by "The Artist of the Beautiful"? The difference is partly one of tone—Baum is in every case more light hearted, less concerned with dark implications and motivations—and partly one of framework. Hawthorne wrote allegorical romance, Baum fantasy. And the difference between those two modes is in the placing of secondary belief: the one continually points beyond itself to the moral or metaphysical truths under examination, while the other pretends to signify only itself, to be no more than a recounting of "actual" events, although those events may lead to the same philosophical questions that the allegory explicitly raises.

I will say more about meanings in Baum shortly, for that is the final point of my analytical description of fantasy, but for now I will say only that Hawthorne's techniques of speculation seem to form the basis for Baum's creation of magical characters. The most important characters, like the three discussed above, always combine more than one allegorical message. They are more on the order of Chillingworth, who is at one time wronged husband, man of the wilderness, devil, and Faustian antihero of *The Scarlet Letter*, than like the one-dimensional characters of the sketches. Jack Pumpkinhead, for instance, goes beyond Feathertop's single issue: our willingness to be fooled by a handsome facade. He also plays the child to Tip, his maker, raising questions of parental responsibility and love for the imperfect child. At times he is a wise fool, a Touchstone, revealing the inconsistencies of those around him. He is, like the Scarecrow, a symbol that a man should be judged by his acts rather than his origins. And he becomes an embodiment of the paradox of mortal body and immortal soul when his pumpkin head—surely the major part of him—spoils and is buried, leaving Jack as good as new with a replacement.

Other characters play more limited roles and have less complex meanings. The group of individuals I called Class B generally have one notable attribute apiece, but each can, if given the opportunity, break into three-dimensionality. Among this class are the witches, good and evil; various animals, especially the Cowardly Lion and Billina, the forthright yellow hen; the other Americans who make their way to Oz, all of them children or eccentrics like the humbug Wizard or the Shaggy Man; solitary magicians, neither good nor evil, like Red Reera the Yookoohoo or the Lonesome Duck; the archvillains of Oz, the Nomes; and characters like the Patchwork Girl and the Frogman who might have been Class A except that they do not appear until the later, lesser books and thus are not granted the development given to the Scarecrow or Tin Woodman. The Nomes are an interesting race, strongly reminiscent of the gnomes in Christopher Cranch's *The Last of the Huggermuggers*. They are never portrayed as entirely evil creatures; indeed, the Nome King bears a curious resemblance to Santa Claus, and he can be charming on occasion. But the Nomes are Earth spirits, guardians of underground treasures, and their wealth often leads them into greed. They value jewels too much and other living creatures too little. Baum shows a nice insight into his own symbols when he makes the Nomes fear, more than any other thing, the egg, symbol of new life.

Class C characters never go beyond their single significance. They include most of the adult Ozites, who may be subdivided into Helpful and Unhelpful Strangers. Also in this group are Uncle Henry and Aunt Em after they get to Oz, where they degenerate into low humor: country folk touring a foreign country. In Class C, too, I would put some of the tribes of grotesque beings that impede the progress of Dorothy and her friends. Among these are the Hammerheads, Wheelers, Mangaboos, Gargoyles, Scoodlers, and Growleywogs. When Baum is interested in a group like the Wheelers, they can be bright spots in the narrative, like items in a well-written travelog or bestiary. When he is not, they sink into Class D.

Class D creatures are those one would rather were left out of the story. They are boring at best, and sometimes make one acutely uncomfortable. Among them are the living utensils of Utensia and the edible people of Bunbury, both from *The Emerald City of Oz*. They are in the unmemorable kitchen-fantasy tradition of *Prince Carrotte*. There are other ill-conceived individuals, like the animated phonograph in *The Patchwork Girl of Oz* and Kiki Aru, the tiresome Munchkin boy who makes trouble in *The Magic of Oz*. There are also times when a Class B, C, or even A character can behave in a Class D manner. Both the Scarecrow and the Patchwork Girl, for instance, develop a terrible case of doggerel by the end of the series.

Some characters I find difficult to classify. Ozma, Polychrome, and the other fairies who show up in Oz from time to time seem unpleasantly dainty to me now, but when I read the Oz books as a child they were among my favorites. Certainly the chorus girls who masquerade as mist fairies, cloud fairies, and flower fairies belong in Class D. They are unfortunate holdovers from the sentimentalism of the nineteenth century, harking back to *The Fairy Egg* and Drake's "The Culprit Fay."

Setting aside Class D—no one can claim that Baum was a consistent writer, no matter how good he is at his best—the remainder of Baum's imaginary host is a noteworthy achievement. Romance writers strained to find some replacement for the countless fairies, goblins, and curious beasts of European folklore. Children's writers of the later nineteenth century either borrowed wholesale from Europe or settled for whimsy. And then there is Baum reworking old motifs with unprecedented conviction and inventing new ones seemingly out of the blue. He not only created an American fairyland where there had been none, but he also filled it with Nomes in the earth, fairies in the air, and an astounding assortment of beings in between.

On the first four points of fantasy Baum rates from good to outstanding. But how about point five: meaning? By this, remember, I mean not some moral lesson but the ethical and philosophical substructure of the fantasy, from which grow world and story and characters. What kind of world view does Baum express through his use of magic?

The answer is, a limited one. Baum does adopt Hawthorne's system of symbolization, so that in whatever points a character differs physically from the norm, he is also likely to illustrate a moral issue. Jack Pumpkinhead has something to say about the pumpkin-headedness of us all, and so on for each speaking creature in Oz. But Baum's introduction of characters was haphazard and frequently dictated by his impatience with the progress of the plot. Enduring characters like Jack begin, through simple accretion, to take on some philosophical complexity, but his one-shot, ad hoc creations—the Fuddles of Fuddlecumjig are a good example, being nothing more than a literalization of the phrase "to go all to pieces"—can hardly be said to be artistic examinations of the problems of life. Nor are they meant to be. In the often quoted phrase that became the title for the standard biography of Baum, he wrote "to please a child."[22] It is for children, not for critical adults, that he upholds such uncontroversial virtues as kindness, generosity, and self-reliance. Ambivalence and sin, with their meatier dramas, he leaves to Hawthorne.

If there is a grander scheme of philosophy in the workings of Oz, it will show up in the essential rules of magic within which Baum operates, rather than in his piecemeal inventions. The following seem to me to be the fundamental magical operations throughout the series: animation, transformation, illusion, disillusion, transportation, protection, and luck. Now these are not unusual operations; they are found throughout fairy legend and *Märchen*. But Baum has set them up in a rudimentary system, and that is an important distinction between imitation of folk forms and creative fantasy.

Animation comes in several forms in the Oz books. I have mentioned two: the Scarecrow's unexplained awakening and Jack Pumpkinhead's birth under Mombi's cackling midwifery. The Tin Woodman's case may also be considered as a sort of gradual bringing to life of his new, tin self, though it is also clearly a transformation. Several other characters are brought to life by the alchemical powder that sparks Jack Pumpkinhead: a wooden sawhorse, a flying contraption made of couches and palm leaves, a patchwork girl, a glass cat, a victrola, a bear rug, and two Munchkins who were accidentally turned to stone. It might be considered animation on the two occasions when people are picked from bushes: a prince of the vegetable Mangaboos and a lovely rose princess. The Wogglebug's magnification is really a sort of animation, taking him from insignificant insecthood (the Tin Woodman would disagree with me there) to quasi-humanity, with as much increase in awareness as in size. Glinda the Good is responsible for the life of the Kuttenklips, human-sized paper dolls, and probably for several of the other oddities in her kingdom.

Things always seem to be springing to life in Oz. As I said earlier, it is a remarkably fertile place. But what is the end result of all this magical procreation? It is almost always to the good. By this means Oz has been provided with some of its most valuable and colorful citizens. No one could wish the Scarecrow still hanging lifeless on his stake, or Jack Pumpkinhead rotting on a compost heap. Not everyone is a fan of the talking phonograph, the vain glass cat, or the unpleasantly floppy bear rug, but all three have their uses. The principle here seems to be that it is better to exist than not, no matter what your form or foibles. These animations are part of a general tendency toward increasing richness of life; they represent a universe slanted toward Becoming.

We might note that many of the animations are accidental, without visible agency like the Scarecrow's, or against the intentions of those around. The roses, for instance, did not want their princess plucked into existence. Other characters are created for questionable reasons or by downright wicked characters like Mombi. But in every case, things turn out for the best. It is never wrong, in Baum's view, to create, and, indeed, it is difficult to help it.

Transformation is another matter. There are many people in Oz and its environs capable of transforming objects. Glinda, Ozma, Polychrome, and Dorothy all turn things into other things, and so do Mombi, another witch named Blinkie, Ugu the Shoemaker, Kiki Aru, the First and Foremost of the Fanfasms, Mrs. Yoop the giantess, and the Nome King. The latter group includes the wickedest people in the series; the former group the best. It would seem that transformation is a neutral art, usable for either good or evil ends. But there are two quite different sorts of transformation in Oz. What Mombi and her fellow villains do is to impose a new shape on an unwilling victim, or on themselves for evil purposes. What Dorothy and her friends do is to restore victims to their original form. (I exclude Dorothy's turning Nomes into eggs, which is a matter of self-defense. The Nomes do not have the Western respect for the individual that Oz shares with America, anyway.) The one act is a taking away, the other a giving back of something highly valued in Oz, one's true identity. To alter another's shape is to fail to respect his integrity as a living being. Only a villain like the Nome King could prefer the Scarecrow turned into a golden ornament to his own comical, lovable shape.

In a sense, transformation is the opposite of animation. To desire to change the people and objects around one is to deny their intrinsic importance, to wish them, as it were, unmade. The archetype of all transformations is that fearful operation, threatened by Mombi and performed accidentally by the ambiguous Crooked Magician, petrifaction. Turning someone to stone is the ultimate denial, and of course in Oz it must eventually be undone by the affirmative act of reanimation.

The Crooked Magician is ambiguous, and so is an interesting character named Red Reera. She is a sort of sorceress who specializes in transformations, but she is by no means evil. Roger Sale suggests that she represents Baum himself, for her transformations are harmless, temporary ones, performed for her own amusement, more explorations into the nature of reality than acts of denial or affirmation.[23] She is a fantasist of sorts, an artist, and not subject to the categories of good and evil.

Illusion and disillusion form another couplet like transformation and animation. Once more, the operation that denies reality is evil, and that which restores it is good. The implication is that reality is more wonderful than any obscuring of it, in fairyland or in the real world, a belief which would not seem to lead naturally into fantasy except for the fact that, for Baum, it never hurts to add to the store of existence through imagination. Generally the same people practice illusion as indulge in transformations. But anyone with a little insight can undo an illusion, simply by ignoring it. Several times Baum has his characters pass a seeming obstacle by closing their eyes and walking through, or poking it with a pin, or making friends with what appeared to be an enemy.

One of the shrines of Oz is the Truth Pond, a limpid little body of water that undoes transformations, illusions, and lies. It is a dangerous resort for the enchanted, because, while it can lift transformations that nothing else will touch, it imposes on those it benefits a strict adherence to truth. For those who are too wicked to be converted by the Truth Pond, there is another potent body of water, the Forbidden Fountain, which washes away evil by stripping those who drink of it of their memories, leaving them innocent as babies. Both the Fountain and the Pond carry the message that evil itself is an illusion no more formidable than a film of dirt. How else is it that Dorothy can destroy a witch with a bucket of cleaning water?

Transportation has no particular moral value in Oz, but it does act as a sign that anything in the world is possible and within reach. Dorothy's cyclone, the enchanted road in *The Road to Oz*, Ozma's magic carpet, and so on are simply variations of the traditional seven-league boots, which carry their owner to fame and fortune. Most of the modes of transportation to and within Oz are natural objects, rather than conscious agents. They represent the unpredictability of nature, which to Baum is rarely hostile but always amazing.

Protection and luck are really two views of the same thing. Glinda's spell of invisibility over Oz, the Good Witch's protective kiss, and the Shaggy Man's love magnet are the same as Ojo the Lucky's good fortune in *The Patchwork Girl*. The only difference is that luck is a more mysterious, pervasive thing, not traceable to any knowable cause. Both operations stress, again, the benevolence of the world. It is as if there were watchful parents everywhere, some visible and some invisible.

These basic principles are elaborated in the various individual stories, each of which stresses one or two particular facets of life. They do not make up a very new or rigorous philosophy. It is a child's vision that Baum is presenting, and so he shies away from any more darkness or complexity than he felt a child would be prepared to deal with. Writing for children freed Baum's imagination as it did the imaginations of many of the writers mentioned in the last chapter, but the boon was also a limitation. We have no proof that Baum *could* have written a more mature work of fantasy than Oz, with a more demanding and rewarding reordering of the world's laws, but he certainly could not do so as long as he conceived of fairy tales as the province primarily of children. So we have the Oz books: simple, sunny, utterly delightful, but narrow in their range of emotion and significance.

Yet the barrier had been broken, effortlessly punctured like a wall of illusion. Baum proved, without doubt, that an American writer could write fantasy from American materials, even if those materials were significantly unlike the well-developed tales and legends available to European collectors and storytellers. Other writers could build on his accomplishment, as he built on the efforts of those before him, could gradually bring into their

American fairylands those questions he left out. Even with his weaknesses, he is our Grimm and our Andersen, the man who introduced Americans to their own dreams.

SIX

Fantasy and Escape

AFTER BAUM'S accomplishment with *The Wizard of Oz*, other writers began to make use of the American scene in children's fantasies. Only a year after *The Wizard* appeared, for instance, Eva Katharine Gibson came out with *Zauberlinda the Wise Witch*, a fairy tale set in South Dakota's Black Hills.[1] It was either a very quick imitation or a manuscript already written or conceived but called forth by the success of Baum's book. Much the same thing happened after Bellamy's *Looking Backward* generated interest in utopias: utopias came out of the woodwork. At any rate, American fairy tales no longer seemed so outlandish to publishers and readers of children's books, and a considerable percentage of notable American fiction for children since the turn of the century has been home-grown fantasy. Some more examples will be considered in the next chapter.

After Baum, too, certain writers began to attempt fantasy or near-fantasy for adult audiences; however, without the special dispensation given to children's literature, they could not bring together the familiar and the fantastic with his kind of ease. The three writers to be discussed are typical in their struggle to turn America into a fairyland accessible to grownups as well as children. Quite often the result was escape from, rather than imaginative transformation of, American life in the first decades of this century. I cannot agree with those who say that all fantasy amounts to an irresponsible evasion of reality, but certain types of fantasy do avoid full commitment to the fictional world and thus to its moral and philosophical implications. Typical escape routes are unmotivated action, unrestrained irony, and sensationalism. These routes are followed, respectively, by

Edgar Rice Burroughs, James Branch Cabell, and Howard Phillips Lovecraft.

Burroughs, Cabell, and Lovecraft, and the lesser writers who influenced or imitated them, may be equated with children's writers before Baum. Much that they produced is vigorous and memorable, but nothing is quite so satisfying as we wish because of a split between borrowed techniques and native subject matter. One might say that the lens, fantasy, is not yet properly set on its object, and so the scene comes through either raw and out of focus or distant and unreal. Like Paulding, Cranch, and Stockton, these three are also pioneers, from whose failures and successes both another generation of writers was to learn its craft.

That anxiety I proposed before, the distress of a nation created by the Enlightenment brought face to face with the irrational that brought Poe's heroes to madness, Twain's to violence, and Hawthorne's to crippling indecision, is still at work in the early twentieth century. But there has been a change. To Burroughs, Cabell, and Lovecraft, there is something even more disturbing than the realm of the marvelous, and that something is daily life, the deadening round of existence illustrated in overwhelming detail by their contemporaries Sinclair Lewis, Theodore Dreiser, and Upton Sinclair. To Burroughs et al. nothing could be worse than writing of the actual modern world, or even suggesting it through Hawthornesque ambiguities. For this reason, even though Burroughs' heroes operate at a preconscious level, Cabell's disengage themselves from persons and events around them, and Lovecraft's die shrieking, they remain firmly planted in the realm of the impossible. Despite flaws and escapes, these writers represent a real development in the free application of secondary belief in fantasy.

Edgar Rice Burroughs had a career remarkably like that of L. Frank Baum. Both entered the field of literature late, after Western excursions and a number of unsuccessful business ventures. Both achieved their first fame, not in the older literary capitals of the East Coast, but in young, free-wheeling Chicago. Both eventually migrated to the warmer pastures of Southern California. Though Baum was a few years older, they knew one another. Burroughs mentions in a letter having been introduced to a local club by "Frank Baum, the fairy tale man."[2] Both Baum and Burroughs wrote a great deal more than was good for their critical reputations: having had their first tastes of success through writing, the temptation was to keep on turning out the volumes and series long after inspiration had faded. Among Baum's books, only the Oz stories (and some of them by courtesy) and a few other early tales bear rereading. With Burroughs the division is not so clear between his best and his worst, but his first books, like *A*

Princess of Mars and *Tarzan of the Apes*, generally outshine anything that came after. In those two stories he outlined the principles of his fictional world; all the others only fill in the chinks.[3]

What is the nature of Burrough's fictional world; that is, how does he stand on the first and fundamental element of fantasy? Burroughs seems to have several fantasy worlds. One is called Mars, or, by its natives, Barsoom (Burroughs' names are rarely lyrical but often memorable). Another is called Africa, and is supposedly a part of the real world. A third is the imagined hollow center of our own earth. A fourth is Venus. A fifth is displaced in time rather than space: it is Burroughs' own version of prehistoric Europe. Others appear briefly: the moon, Jupiter, a world in another galaxy. But, aside from names and certain surface phenomena, like the number of legs of the native animals or the size of the enemy warriors, all of these different places are regions of one uniform, Burroughsian universe.

Burroughs' universe is never more vividly portrayed than in its first expression, in *A Princess of Mars*. This story begins in a part of the country with a strong flavor of the exotic, the mountains of Arizona, among hostile Indians, mineral treasures, and mysterious caves and ruins. Burroughs, who was briefly in the cavalry in Arizona, takes a chapter to set the scene in proper local color/adventure style, as if he were writing, not space fantasy, but Western formula fiction. Then, with a hint of Indian or pre-Indian magic, his hero, John Carter, is seized by an unknown force, lifted out of his earthly body, and transported, in an instant, to Mars. There he finds dry, ancient-looking scenery, relieved by small flowers and succulent plants; wild animals well suited for riding; tribes of fierce fighting men; ruined cities of barbaric splendor—in other words, he finds a dream or fantasy version of the American Southwest.

The landscape of Mars is clearly analogous to that where his journey begins. Just before his translation to the Other World, Carter muses on the scene before him in magical, atmospheric terms, like those used by Irving and Hawthorne for the very different scenery of the Northeast:

> Few western wonders are more inspiring than the beauties of an Arizona moonlit landscape; the silvered mountains in the distance, the strange lights and shadows upon hogback and arroyo, and the grotesque details of the stiff, yet beautiful cacti form a picture at once enchanting and inspiring; as though one were catching for the first time a glimpse of some dead and forgotten world, so different is it from the aspect of any other spot upon our earth.[4]

Out of this insight into the strangeness of the familiar (to Burroughs) landscape comes the overall inspiration for his conception of Mars. Other elements enter into it as well. By Burroughs' time, astronomical observations of Mars had swirled together in the popular imagination to produce an image of arid wastes, interlocking canals, and cool, fertile bands around the polar caps. Burroughs found it easy to marry his knowledge of the West to the popular conception of Mars: the poles were like glaciers, the broad expanses were plateaus and dry sea beds, and the canals were a great, tree-lined irrigation system, like those he was familiar with in Utah and Idaho.

Here is our first glimpse of Martian scenery:

> I found myself lying prone upon a bed of yellowish, moss-like vegetation which stretched around me in all directions for interminable miles. I seemed to be lying in a deep, circular basin, along the outer verge of which I could distinguish the irregularities of low hills.
>
> It was midday, the sun was shining full upon me and the heat of it was rather intense upon my naked body, yet no greater than would have been true under similar conditions on an Arizona desert. Here and there were slight outcroppings of quartz-bearing rock which glistened in the sunlight; and a little to my left, perhaps a hundred yards, appeared a low, walled enclosure about four feet in height. (pp. 20-21)

Even the rocks carry the message that this new land is somehow an extension of the old; that certain of the rules (like gravitation) may be altered, but that most knowledge learned in the old world will relate to the new, and vice versa.

Burroughs had a facility for inventing fauna as required by twists of his plot; otherwise his worlds are rather empty. On Mars, there are two types of animals: those which threaten the main characters and those which get them out of scrapes. Both kinds are grotesque in appearance—Mars seems to favor extra legs, tusks, bulging eyes, and gaping, froglike mouths—but Burroughs gives the game away by assigning each monstrosity an earth analog. The *calot* is a Martian dog, the *thoat* a Martian horse, the *sorak* a Martian cat, the *banth* a Martian lion, and so on. Once we know the analog we can pretty much forget the animal's description: its character and function are set. Pat a calot and he will smile like a collie.[5]

Of Martian flora we hear very little. There is an ubiquitous carpet of ochre moss, reminiscent of Arctic moss and appropriate to the general starkness of the Martian scene. There is a milk-producing plant that might be inspired by Southwestern succulents like cactus and agave. Mostly there are generalized trees and flowers, of interest only as shade or shelter or fodder.

The physical appearance of Burroughs' Mars, in its contours and life forms, is weird and alien but at the same time strongly reminiscent of and derived from a part of the known earth. It is a consistent place. The animals, as I have said, all fit into a general mold. Burroughs is careful to keep in mind the low gravitation, thin air, and lack of water that are the prime considerations for the preservation of life on Mars. Likewise, after making one break with known reality, such as the so-called ninth ray that opposes gravitation, he is conservative in compounding the violation, so that the unknown operates within a stable, predictable framework. There are airships, yes, but they frequently break down, just like automobiles. There is telepathy, but it seems to be of limited use: primarily it helps in managing one's animals or in judging other people's reactions. This way of bounding the impossible, of keeping it within believable limits, is common to both fantasy and science fiction. Indeed, to judge from John Carter's adventures on the planet Mars alone, the Mars books might better be classed with the latter, where telepathy, antigravity, radium guns, and so on are more familiar than they are in traditional fairy tale and legend.

Nevertheless, I do think these stories at least lap over into the realm of fantasy, and that the Other World, here called Mars, is to be understood as a fantasy world; not accessible from our own through space and time and the extension of knowledge, but discontinuous with it, to be found only through some back door of the mind. The major indicator of its fantastic nature is John Carter's journey, or, rather than journey, his advent on Mars, as Burroughs calls it. The ingredients of this celestial voyage are clearly magical: a hidden cave, an ancient Indian witch, a binding spell, a compulsion from the heavens, and a threshold of cold and darkness. These are not the accouterments of a scientific space journey but of a voyage to heaven or hell or their buffer state, fairyland; and that last I believe Mars, on a symbolic and functional level, to be.

The plot that winds through Burroughs' half-scientific, half-fantastic fairyland is a rambling one that is extended and compounded through another ten books. The broad framework of *A Princess of Mars* could, if one wished, be made to fit Propp's morphology of the folktale with a bit of tailoring—the essential boy-gets-girl-and-kingdom movement is there— but there is a more accurate forecast of Burroughs' tale in the popular romances of Bulwer-Lytton, Conan Doyle, and especially H. Rider Haggard. Here is an approximate "morphology" of these tales:

First function: the hero sets out from society. He is generally rich, handsome, and successful in the civilized world, but something calls him into parts unknown and wilds uncharted.

Second function: a mysterious messenger appears. He picks out the hero from among his companions and hints to him of a lost civilization to be found in the wilds of Africa, South America, or outer space.

Third function: the journey. Preferably tropical, but the arctic will do. Must be arduous.

Fourth function: capture by strange warriors. They are the outlying guards of the hidden kingdom.

Fifth function: protection of the hero by a young girl. This girl may or may not be attractive. She is not the heroine, and may even be opposed to the heroine, but she loves the hero with a doglike faithfulness and nurses, protects, and instructs him with no thought of reward.

Sixth function: appearance of the queen. This is the true heroine. She may be either good or evil, but must possess an exotic, almost divine beauty. The men of the lost kingdom worship her as a goddess. The other women of the kingdom do not count.

Seventh function: lovemaking. Usually interrupted by eighth function.

Eighth function: battle. Sometimes the lost kingdom rebels against its priestess-queen; other times it is attacked by the less civilized tribes around it. At this point the hero goes native and shows himself to be a Roman gladiator under the skin.

Ninth function: consummation. The story may end in marriage or a Wagnerian love–death. Both are equally satisfying, since both imply a complete break with the outer world. This conclusion is in contrast with the fairy tale ending, which usually involves a return to the opening milieu and a setting of it to rights.

Probably the finest story conforming to this outline, the one that determines the type, is Haggard's *She*. More writers than Burroughs have followed his example, in England and in America. Burroughs, though, was the first successful bearer of the Haggard tradition in this country, and most American lost world inventors are stamped with his influence, as well as with Haggard's.[6]

As Burroughs develops the outline, the hero, "a Southerner of the highest type," is already on his way into the wilds of Arizona.[7] The messenger, who is to foretell the new land, might be either the first Indian who follows the hero into the magical cave and reacts to its eeriness or, more likely, the witch-woman whose potions bring about his translation to Mars. This woman is not seen until the end of the book. After its ten-year span Carter finds only "the dead and mummified remains of a little old woman with long black hair," leaning over "a round copper vessel containing a small quantity of greenish powder" (*Princess*. p. 158). We never know if this sorceress is an Indian medicine worker or if she is somehow connected with the Indian-like red Martians. Her message is an inarticulate one—just a moan and a puff of vapor that launches John Carter on an astral journey. The inference is that Indian magic, with its smoke and its trips down the peyote road, is a link between the two worlds.

The third function, the journey, is not so tedious as a trek across a tropical desert, but it is far longer, and seems to be spiritually, if not physically, arduous. Function four, capture, is immediate upon John Carter's appearance on Mars. Function five follows not long after, when Sola, a young girl of the green Martian tribe that has captured him, feeds and shelters him and teaches him the Martian language. She is obviously a helper and not a romantic possibility: "My fair companion was about eight feet tall, having just arrived at maturity, but not yet to her full height. She was of a light olive-green color, with a smooth, glossy hide" (*Princess*, p. 30).

The green warriors also bring about function six, the appearance of the goddess-queen, by capturing Dejah Thoris, Princess of Helium. She is the standard pagan beauty, but not, interestingly enough, a lone Caucasian among the lesser breeds, as is so often the case with these chauvinistic hero tales. Dejah Thoris is a red Martian:

> Her face was oval and beautiful in the extreme, her every feature was finely chiseled and exquisite, her eyes black and lustrous and her head surmounted by a mass of coal black, waving hair, caught loosely into a strange yet becoming coiffure. Her skin was of a light reddish copper color, against which the crimson glow of her cheeks and the ruby of her beautifully molded lips shone with a strangely enhancing effect. (p. 46)

In this passage Burroughs plays his full hand in the matter of describing heroines. There are only so many ways to say "beautiful and strange," at least for a prosaic writer like Burroughs. His later descriptions of Dejah Thoris grow more effusive but add nothing to our conception of her, and all his other princesses of Mars and elsewhere follow the same model. By the time we have met the strangely beautiful Thuvia and the strangely beautiful Phaidor in the second volume—to say nothing of the dozens more that twine exotically through Venus and Pellucidar—we begin to feel a powerful sense of *Dejahvu*.

Lovemaking in Burroughs is always brief and usually comic. John Carter and his princess fall in love instantly, but run afoul of their differing cultural patterns. Burroughs takes delight in portraying the otherwise flawless hero as a bumbler at love. The lovers' exchanges do not bear repeating here; the humor in them is as embarrassing as the sentiment. If there is anything Burroughs is less adept at than portraying women, it is showing men and women together. Luckily, the lovemaking is soon cut short by a "duel to the death" (p. 73), neither the first nor by any means the last of John Carter's battles.

Battle is supposed to follow lovemaking in the morphology, and so it does here, but Burroughs has compounded and recompounded this eighth function so that it punctuates virtually every other movement in the book. Is John Carter entering a city? He fights his way in. Is he leaving? He fights his way out. Has he met a friend? He engages in combat by his side. An enemy? He bests him in battle.

The final function, consummation, takes its happier form in *A Princess of Mars*. John Carter, the interloper, rescues his heroine, weds her, and takes his place as prince of Helium, living happily with her for ten years. Burroughs always had a taste for planting the seeds of a sequel, however, so the final pages of the book find Carter transported back to earth against his will. Then, in *The Gods of Mars* and *The Warlord of Mars*, he fights his way through another series of trials to win Dejah Thoris once again and be awarded the grander title of war-chieftain of all Barsoom. The plot in these two novels is a reworking of the first plot. They are really excuses for following the hero on a voyage of discovery around the new planet, literally from pole to pole.

John Carter himself is as strictly defined by the lost world mode as is the plot he fights his way through. The hero of such a novel is significantly different from that of a traditional wonder tale. The fairy tale hero commonly has a home and family, but no distinction. He is just Jack, the woodcutter's son, or at best the disinherited third son of a minor king. The hero of a Burroughsian adventure, however, must be rootless and yet, paradoxically, of the noblest lineage. Carter is a wandering orphan of indeterminate age, a combination of Melville's Ishmael and the Wandering Jew of European legend: "I am a very old man," the story begins, "how old I do not know. Possibly I am a hundred, possibly more; but I cannot tell because I have never aged as other men, nor do I remember any childhood" (p. 11).

Yet this ageless outsider is, at the same time, heir to the nearest thing to an aristocratic tradition in America: landed Southern wealth. Burroughs precedes the narrative with a foreword, in his own name but not his own character, in which he expands the statement on John Carter that opened the first magazine version:

> He was a splendid specimen of manhood, standing a good two inches over six feet, broad of shoulder and narrow of hip, with the carriage of the trained fighting man. His features were regular and clear cut, his hair black and closely cropped, while his eyes were of a steel gray, reflecting a strong and loyal character, filled with fire and initiative. His manners were perfect, and his courtliness was that of a typical southern gentleman of the highest type. (p. v)

Throughout the books, Carter justifies his own behavior by repeating his claim of being a Virginia gentleman. Generally, whatever it is that a

Virginia gentleman will or will not do turns out to be the custom on Mars as well.

Carter's Southernness is a prop. The Southerner's belief in his own gentility provides a convenient shorthand for saying that Carter is superior innately, by inheritance. Tarzan, similarly, is not just any child raised by animals, but an English lord, whose attributes shine through all barriers of circumstance. What Burroughs is proposing in these and others of his heroes is a theory of natural aristocracy coinciding exactly with social position. If Burroughs were, as he intimates in his foreword, a distant nephew of John Carter's, equally blue-blooded, we should have to call him a fearful snob. In reality, he came of ordinary Midwestern parentage and was physically undistinguished, just another mortal daydreaming of superman.

Burroughs' Martians fit into various categories. Most are essentially human—lesser versions of the hero. Among these, there is an interesting hierarchy by race. Red men, analogous, as I have said, to American Indians, are the highest in morals and prowess. Black men are next, noble but misled by a false goddess. Yellow men are a little less impressive than black, and white men are least admirable, being spiteful, treacherous, and totally bald.

Women of all four races are mysterious, unpredictable, and alien. Any of them may unexpectedly demonstrate paranormal powers, as when Thuvia exercises control over a lair of vicious "banths." It is a woman who deludes the black men of Mars into thinking her a goddess, and it is a woman who sends John Carter to Barsoom. Actually, Burroughs places Barsoomian and earth women in the same alien class. They are all half-witch, half-goddess: the only really supernatural figures in the books. Burroughs, who is uncomfortable with women characters, generally keeps them offstage, lost or in enemy hands until the final stages of the book, leaving only fightable and therefore understandable aliens to deal with.

The green men of Mars are wonderfully fightable. Savage, grotesque giants with no trace of sentiment, they are the perfect foils for a fighting hero, either as enemies or as companions. They may have folk roots; there are many giants in European tradition, even green ones. Tars Tarkas, the giant chieftain, is a variation on the Green Knight fought by Sir Gawain. The green men are appealing in their irresponsible, innocent violence. They provide relief from the gentlemanly code of Carter and the red Martians. Freudians might call them personifications of the id.

Green and red Barsoomians, who are similar in culture, may also represent the two divisions of Indians as seen by white settlers. The red are the "good Indians," who cooperated with whites, and the green are the "bad

Indians," who fought back. It is the uncooperative Indians, like Sitting Bull or Cochise, whom we secretly admire, whose role we take in childhood games. That might explain why John Carter's closest friend is not a red Martian but green Tars Tarkas.

More strange creatures appear in later Burroughs books, but none rank about mankind. The Mars stories are tales of conquest, of Western man expanding his territory across another world as he has this one, though Carter plays at being a red Barsoomian. No creature may be greater or wiser than he, because that might stop his advance. That is one of the meanings of the Mars series, as expressed in the very fabric of its invention: that man—white, male, American man—is the measure of all things.

What other meanings may be inferred from Burroughs' system of fantasy? One hesitates to dig too far below the level of pure entertainment for fear of finding, as Hans Joachim Alpers claims to have found, that such stories are nothing less than Fascism in fable form, preaching a philosophy that is mystical, violent, fatalistic, power oriented, sexist, racist, imperialistic, anti-intellectual, and conducive to leader worship.[8] Alpers ignores the difference between writing about a thing and advocating it, but he has pinpointed a fundamental limitation in Burroughs and the subgenre that springs from him: insofar as Burroughs touches on ideas he does so immaturely, in a fashion which does suggest embryonic Fascism. But Burroughs had neither the insight nor the inclination to direct his fantasy toward dogmatic ends, and so any philosophical pitfalls beneath the surface of his adventures are so deeply buried as to be of danger to no one.

Edgar Rice Burroughs was neither more nor less than a good storyteller, with as much power—and finesse—as a bulldozer. A measure of his strength is the frequency with which he is imitated. Burroughsian science fiction and fantasy filled the popular magazines, usually called pulps, of the thirties and forties. E. E. "Doc" Smith, Robert E. Howard, Abraham Merritt, and many others turned aspects of his fiction into books and series of their own. In recent years, the Burroughsian line has hardened into a fixed formula often referred to as "swords-and-sorcery." In this case, imitation has gone beyond flattery and become a strait jacket, but some of the practitioners of swords-and-sorcery may yet break loose and produce fantasy that is derived from Burroughs and yet greater than its source.

The second important fantasist of the early decades of this century is James Branch Cabell, and in many ways he is directly opposite to Burroughs. Whereas Burroughs became a literary man by accident late in life, Cabell began writing early and never seriously considered any other career except for a fling at journalism. Burroughs poured out his stories for the popular magazines, while Cabell published in elite journals like *Harper's*.

Burroughs was a problem student, though apt enough when he cared to be, and quit after high school; Cabell graduated from William and Mary at the age of nineteen. Cabell had the Southern aristocratic lineage that Burroughs only dreamed of and moved in circles far removed from Burroughs' world of offices and sales.

Still, there is something that links them, despite vast differences in background and, as we will see, style of writing. In an informal essay in *The Hudson Review*, George P. Elliott lists those stories which aided him, in his youth, in "getting away from the chickens": that is, in escaping from the limitations of his daily life and the frame of mind it threatened to impose. "Gradually," he says, "it occurred to me that pimps and drunks and hot jazz addicts were no more real than anybody else and that books about The People, who grimly did not think, were like bad dreams."[9] There were better dreams available, and among them he includes Burroughs' Mars and Cabell's Poictesme (p. 388).

Burroughs might be passed off as a writer for children or at best adolescents, who only seemed to be writing for adults, but in Cabell we have someone complexly and self-consciously proposing to create a fairy world for mature Americans. That is not to say that America had entirely given up its hard-edged rationalism in favor of symbols and enchantments. Readers like Elliott and writers like Cabell were still in the minority, but it had become a substantial minority, and its readers and writers had found one another. Now they could afford to scoff at those who wore their common sense like blinders over the imagination. Here is Cabell's assessment of his well-known contemporaries:

> ...we were, at just that time, being edified rather remorselessly. Sinclair Lewis had, via the book to which I have but now referred [*Main Street*], detected several flaws in the cultural life of the Middle West; John Dos Passos had discovered that the Wilson War had been conducted not altogether as a pleasure trip for the private soldier; and Upton Sinclair was in his customary low spirits.[10]

Cabell goes on to say that of course life is grim—we have known that since *Ecclesiastes*. It is one's duty as an artist to think up something superior to life. Then we can change things for the better, or at the least give people a respite.[11]

Burroughs, one might say, was shallowly disillusioned with the American dream. Once his books started selling he returned to the faith, and his inspiration for fantasy began slowly to leak away. Cabell was deeply disillusioned. To him, American optimism was a foreign thing. There was another philosophy closer by that must have seemed to him more honest, more insightful into human nature. That was the Southern creed, which stated from experience that man is a fallen creature who enslaves his fellow and makes war upon his neighbor. With this philosophy in mind, Cabell turned to fantasy, in which things-as-they-are can be turned into things-as-they-ought-to-be and in which man and the universe can be called into account for their treatment of one another without dwelling on the banalities of violence and social injustice.

In so doing, he incurred the outrage of those whose wagons were still hitched to the star of American perfection and who viewed literature as a tool for reform. Granville Hicks excluded him from *The Great Tradition* (of realistic fiction) with the kind of distaste with which one picks a slug off a rosebush:

> He is a sleek, smug egoist, whose desire to be a gentleman of the old school breeds dissatisfaction with the existing order, but who has not enough imaginative vigor to create a robust world in which deeds of chivalry and gallantry are performed. Instead, he has written wild little fantasies, carefully baited with obscenities. His whole work is a structure of lies, from his tinselled style to his theorizing on life and literature.[12]

On the other side, Cabell's supporters founds in his work a richness of meaning and a brilliance of invention new in American prose, or at least latent since the days of Hawthorne and the recently rediscovered Melville. Referring to Cabell's best-known book, *Jurgen*, H. L. Mencken asked in 1927, "where is there another American book so beautifully contrived, so genuinely a masterpiece?"[13] In 1932, Carl Van Doren wrote:

> His universe in various fashions resembles that of *The Faerie Queene*, wherein geographical and chronological boundaries melt and flow, wherein fable encroaches upon history, and the creative mood of the poet re-cuts his shining fabrics as if they were whole cloth intended solely for his purposes.[14]

Yet Cabell did not at first intend to write works that could be hailed as masterpieces or damned as pernicious falsifications. Like Burroughs, he wanted to entertain, and like him, he started out by appropriating the manner of those books that entertained him. In this case, those were the dashing and improbable melodramas set in Graustark or Ruritania or some other romantic never-never land on the far edge of plausibility. In an imaginary encounter in his retrospective *Straws and Prayer-Books*, Cabell puts the following speech into the mouth of his younger self, who finds he does not quite approve of the products of his maturity:

> For I would like to write the very nicest sort of books,—like Henry Harland's and Justus Forman's and Anthony Hope's. They would be about

beautiful fine girls and really splendid young men, and everything would come out all right in the end.... [15]

And the younger Cabell did write a few of those stories, and set them in a be-julepped South or in an improbable Olde England. They offended no one and provided an excellent excuse for many graceful illustrations by Howard Pyle.

Soon, however, Cabell outgrew simple imitation and a certain flavor of his own crept in. He describes the growing aspiration which cut short his career as another Anthony Hope, his "daemon," as he calls it, as "the desire to write perfectly of beautiful happenings," but that is authorial misdirection.[16] What set him apart from the creators of Zenda and Graustark was his tone. Cabell was too sophisticated to write breathlessly of pure maidens and swashbuckling adventures, so he began to undercut them with irony. The bold young hero started to seem just a bit vain, the lovely heroine revealed herself to be none too bright, and the happy ending took on the look of doom. Most particularly, the action and characters of Cabell's stories remained archaic and conventional, but the reporting of them grew increasingly stark and modern, like floodlights on a medieval garden.

It is worthwhile looking at the relationship between Cabell and Pyle, who did so much to bring European traditions of wonder into American children's literature. Pyle's strengths are a direct, unsentimental style and a profound sympathy with the time and place he is recreating in text and drawings. If Cabell had absorbed those two attributes from his illustrator, he might not have fallen so strongly under the influence of shallow popular romance, nor might his later reaction against the illusions engendered thereby have been so caustic. When he did begin to infuse his stories with modern irony, Pyle refused to illustrate any more of them because he felt them to be "neither exactly true to history nor exactly fanciful."[17] One or the other he understood, but not a sensibility that played hob with what was known and then sabotaged its own flights of imagination.

No doubt Cabell considered Pyle naively out-of-date. When he reworked an early volume, Louis Untermeyer commended him for ridding it of "Pylishness."[18] No doubt, too, he was jealous of his illustrator, who was more popular than he. Reviews of his stories were not overwhelmingly favorable, but it was always pointed out that they were "beautifully illustrated by Howard Pyle."[19] For both reasons it was necessary for Cabell to assert his independence from Pyle and the values he represented. Rather than raising Pyle's type of story to adult complexity, he took off in the opposite direction, eventually making virtues of a sort out of indirection and mistrust of the very world he was writing about.

Despite Pyle's refusal to continue as Cabell's illustrator, *The Soul of Melicent* was published in 1913 with an especially fine set of drawings by him.[20] In this case, however, the collaboration was of a different sort. Here is Cabell's account:

> ... I confess to an old-fashioned liking for the Pyle pictures. Certainly he did not fail me in the *Melicent* pictures; for he made them to illustrate quite another text, in stories written by I forget whom. I cut the pictures from ancient numbers of *Harper's*, saved them, and in due course made up a story about them.[21]

Not surprisingly, *The Soul of Melicent* is unlike any other of Cabell's books. In style and spirit it is closer to authentic medieval romance, with characters who for once behave as handsomely as Pyle pictured them.

The truly typical Cabell fantasies began to appear around the time of World War I, an event which may have contributed to his undercurrents of bitterness and disillusion. Cabell belongs with the so-called lost generation of American writers; though he never went off to carouse with them in Paris, his outlook matches theirs. The works on which his reputation primarily rests begin with *The Cream of the Jest* (1917, revised 1922) and end with *Something About Eve* (1927). Both novels, and indeed every book Cabell wrote up to 1930, are included in what he called *The Biography of Manuel* and considered to be a single work in eighteen volumes. The *Biography* consists of short stories, essays, and novels, ranging from Europe to America, from the medieval era to Cabell's present day, and from drawing room satire to mock epic. It is united by a complex set of personal relationships—all of the principal characters ulitimately derive from one Dom Manuel of Poictesme—and by a set of insistent themes that imply that every actor in every generation is merely echoing the drama played out by Manuel. Hence a "biography" that spans centuries and continents.

When I discussed Edgar Rice Burroughs, I was able to let one or two volumes stand for the whole body of work. Anything worth finding in Burroughs can probably be found in *A Princess of Mars* or *Tarzan*. With Cabell it is not so easy to choose a representative sample. Each of his novels presents some particular facet of a greater statement, each subtly different from the one before. However, since *Jurgen*, of all Cabell's books, has attracted the most attention, I will concentrate my analysis on it and bring in other works as needed to qualify a point.

The world of *Jurgen* is a particularly broad one, embracing heaven, hell, Philistia, and Cockaigne. The book begins, however, in Cabell's imaginary princedom of Poictesme, which is a province of France roughly equivalent, in the nonfictional world, to the district of Gard, west of Provence.[22] Poictesme is distinguished from its earthly analog in having within its borders several gateways into the lands of mythology, and, especially in the early days, divine or magical forces play an important part in its history.

Poictesme is no fairyland, but it is Cabell's revival of an older earth that was, in belief and story, at the border of fairyland. In *The Cream of the Jest*, he refers to it (quoting from one of his alter egos, Felix Kennaston) as "that 'happy, harmless Fable-land' which is bounded by Avalon and Phaeacia and Sea-coast Bohemia, and the contiguous forests of Arden and Broceliande, and on the west of course by the Hesperides."[23] As evidenced by the names he gives his various neighboring lands of enchantment, Poictesme retains always a bookish quality. Part of its essential nature is that it was invented by a man of twentieth-century America who has read much in old romances and to whom it does not matter greatly whether one sets out from Poictesme toward Avalon or toward an equally foreign Paris—or even toward contemporary Virginia, for that, too, becomes a province of literary imagination when Horvendile of Storisende steps into the body of Felix Kennaston of Litchfield in *The Cream of the Jest*. Horvendile points out as one of many creams of many jests the fact that neither place, Litchfield or Storisende, is more real than the other (p. 28). Both exist, for the purposes of the story, only *in* the story. And that all-encompassing disclaimer which reduces all realms that have or have not existed to the same metaphysical level, is the springboard to Cabell's kind of fantasy.

The physical characteristics of Poictesme vary according to the needs of its creator. In *Jurgen* it is a prosaic place, a comfortable, prosperous, out-of-the-way corner of Europe where the hero, Jurgen, makes his living as a pawnbroker. Such ordinariness is required to underline Jurgen's extraordinary travels in the body of the book. Even in *Jurgen*, however, Poictesme differs from unmediated reality. It is less cluttered and more leisurely than the contemporary world, and its inhabitants are unusually eloquent. Cabell comments in *The Cream of the Jest*:

> Undoubtedly, it was a land, as Horvendile whimsically reflected, wherein human nature kept its first dignity and strength; and wherein human passions were never in a poor way to find expression with adequate speech and action. (p. 13)

Notice that Cabell comments only on human nature, not on the world of field and forest outside his towns of Storisende and Bellegarde. That larger world is never his concern. Cabell's sensibility regarding nature falls somewhere between the twelfth and eighteenth centuries: that is, long after the elements had ceased to be the objects of continual fear and worship and before the romantic revolution had reaffirmed mankind's ties with the wild. And so all we see of natural Poictesme are stage settings, called, for variety, Amneran Heath or the Forest of Acaire, but no more individualized than the green backgrounds of tapestry. Cabell was more interested in recording spiritual states and human interactions than in sketching the world around his characters.

Therefore, Jurgen travels from Poictesme to heaven and hell without any noticeable change in scenery—or even climate. What we do notice is the change in Jurgen.

It is not for nothing that the book of Jurgen's adventures is named for its protagonist. He stands out much more clearly than anyone he meets or any act he performs. He is arrogant, restless, verbose, amorous, and irreverent. He is, as he maintains throughout the book, "a monstrous clever fellow," and it is unclear whether the monstrosity is ascribed to his cleverness or to himself.[24]

He is engaged in a threefold quest, for his vanished wife, Lisa, for his lost youth, and for justice. Dame Lisa he regains, at the very end of the book (he was in no hurry about it). His youth returns, or at least the appearance of it, but he finds it a burdensome thing and reverts to middle age. Justice he finds nowhere in the universe, though he is offered everything his heart desires. It seems that his idea of justice is not merely to reap the rewards of the earth, but to understand its workings as well, and that Koshchei the Deathless, "who made things as they are" (p. 15 and elsewhere), does not allow.

Who does Jurgen remind us of? First of all, he is clever Hans or Jack or any other undaunted hero of folktale. Not a warrior, nor burdened with a rigidly noble code of behavior, he relies on his wits and on the aid of others to solve his problems. He is a masterful liar and a prudent evader of danger, and his primary business is to arrive at the next chapter unscathed. His more literary ancestors include such rogues as Odysseus and Huck Finn.

Second, Jurgen is a wit and a gallant. Though it is appropriate to his role as trickster, his humble trade hides the fact that he has also traveled much in court circles and knows the rules of public decorum and private flirtation. This aspect of Jurgen was the original focus of the book, which Cabell then called "Some Ladies and Jurgen."[25] In his role as ladies' man, Jurgen is reminiscent of the cuckolding protagonists of Restoration comedy. Like Horner, in Wycherley's *The Country Wife*, he makes a game of seduction, commenting all the while in double entendres on his success. It was Jurgen's Restoration tendencies which got the book banned, and thus launched it onto the best-seller lists, but his most important role moves him well outside the range of the drawing room manners of a bygone age.

Third, and most importantly, Jurgen is the fictional representative of Cabell himself. It is dangerous to equate an author with any one of his characters, but Cabell's heroes are so consistent in certain respects that they seem to represent fairly the concerns, at least, of their inventor. All of them, including Jurgen, are idealists in youth, filled with deathless love and a burning urge to create. Nearly all are disappointed, first in love and then in their own creations. Jurgen's true love, Dorothy la Désirée, marries another, and his poetry pleases only himself. Manuel marries his love, but she proves as humanly fallible as he, and the being he shaped out of clay as his *magnum opus* becomes a limping and evil god. Freed from their first illusions, Cabell's heroes then turn to questioning the acts of the gods. In their wry way, they challenge heaven, and are ambiguously rewarded. Often the gods return them to the beginnings of their own stories. Jurgen's adventures end at the same moment they began; his life is unchanged and his questions are unanswered, except as they may be puzzled out of mute experience.

It is this third role of Jurgen's which reveals most clearly the time and place of Cabell's writing. Tricksters and rakes may be found in almost any literature, but the particular flavor of Jurgen's loneliness, his iconoclasm, his rootlessness, and his yearning after beauty and meaning mark him unmistakably as a product of twentieth-century America. Despite the difference in their surroundings, Jurgen and Babbitt are kin. Dom Manuel, who rises from obscurity to wealth and power without ever being satisfied, is spiritual cousin to Jay Gatsby. H. L. Mencken found Jurgen to be the perfect personification of a triumphant but hollow America at the close of World War I.[26]

American disillusion took as its characteristic form in the 1920s an air of disaffection that was intended not to hide one's emotions, but to make them seem unimportant. One was supposed to laugh at oneself for hurting. "Irony and pity," was Hemingway's description of the popular tone.[27] Jurgen carries this attitude, of (self) pity artfully revealed through irony, as through a veil of lace, into his every encounter, romantic or spiritual. When, for instance, he is tempted by Queen Anaïtis, a love goddess older and earthier than Aphrodite, he says to her:

> Sweetheart, ... you paint a glowing picture: but you are shrewd enough to borrow your pigments from the daydreams of inexperience. What you prattle about is not at all as you describe it. You forget you are talking to a widely married man of varied experience. Moreover, I shudder to think of what might happen if Lisa were to walk in unexpectedly. (pp. 342–43)

Jurgen's ironic irreverence permeates not only his own statements but the narrative as well, and to my mind its continual juxtaposition with old and solemn myth or legend is unpleasantly jarring. What may have been fresh and bracing when the book first appeared now seems archaic and artificial as only outdated sophistication can seem. The most miraculous event seen through Jurgen's eyes grows tedious, and for all of Cabell's facility with words and his familiarity with things magical and mysterious, none of his books stir as much wonder as Burroughs' adolescent adventures.

Cabell is certainly the most knowledgeable of all the authors discussed so far as to sources for fantasy. His story lines derive from myth, fable, legend, and *Märchen*, intertwined with a deft hand. *Jurgen*, for instance, has several incidents drawn directly from some of the Russian tales analyzed by Vladimir Propp in producing his *Morphology of the Folk Tale*.[28] Cabell, however, subverts the happy endings of the tales, burlesquing them or introducing into them incongruous results, like the disappointments noted above.

For nonhuman characters, as well as for plots, Cabell drew on his encyclopedic knowledge of folklore and romance literature. Any god or beast known to man is likely to pop into one of his stories. Paul Brewster notes:

> In *Jurgen* and *Figures of Earth*, Cabell has drawn upon the following works, among others: Baring-Gould, *Curious Myths of the Middle Ages* and *Legends of the Old Testament Characters*; Malory, *Morte d'Arthur*; Keightley, *The Fairy Mythology*; Balzac, *Contes Drolatiques*; Suetonius, *De Vita Caesarum (Lives of the Twelve Caesars); The Famous History of Dr. Faustus*; Brand, *Popular Antiquities of Great Britain*; Middleton's *The Witch*; *The Mabinogion*; Lewis, *Francois Villon*; Tooke, *The Pantheon of Heathen Gods*; Ralston, *Russian Fairy Tales*; Andersen, *Fairy Tales*; Flaubert, *The Temptation of St. Anthony*; Pliny, *Historia Naturalis*; Edwardes and Spence, *A Dictionary of Non-Classical Mythology*; Burton, *Anatomy of Melancholy*; Spenser's *The Fairie Queene*; *The Prose Edda*; Strickland, *Lives of the Queens of England*; the Grimm Kinder u. Hausmärchen; and *Locrine*, of the Shakespeare *Apocrypha*. In addition, there may be some slight indebtedness also to Davenant's *Gondibert*, the *Idylls* of Theocritus, and Rabelais.[29]

Cabell's books remind one of the great but unselective compendia of mythology that appeared just before the turn of the century, like Frazer's *The Golden Bough*. Like Frazer, he is operating from the idea that all such beliefs are equivalent and interchangeable, whether gathered from Russian peasants, Tahitian tribesmen, or Celtic poets. Myth seems to represent, to both Frazer and Cabell, a set of untruths so beautiful that they cannot but regret their unbelief. This is the attitude of one who has never seen myth at work in society, but only as extracted in books. In Cabell's case, poetic rendering does not make up for lack of conviction, for no one of his gods or heraldic beasts appears as more than a curiosity, or an element in an obscure allegory.

All of Cabell's books lend themselves to allegorical interpretation, though the meaning of certain signs is ambiguous. Cabell affixes to his story two comments which warn off prospective allegorizers. As "E. Noel Codman," he states that:

> A fixed construction is very idle. If readers of The High History of Jurgen do not meddle with the allegory, the allegory will not meddle with them. Without minding it at all, the whole is as plain as a pikestaff. It might as well be pretended that we cannot see Poussin's pictures without first being told the allegory, as that the allegory aids us in understanding *Jurgen*. (facing table of contents)

Again, as "John Frederick Lewistam," he advances a subtler argument against forced extraction of meaning:

> Too urbane to advocate delusion, too hale for the bitterness of irony[!], this fable of Jurgen is, as the world itself, a book wherein each man will find what his nature enables him to see; which gives us back each his own image; and which teaches us each the lesson that each of us desires to learn. (facing table of contents)

Nevertheless, a book whose form, as spiritual journey, corresponds closely with that of *Pilgrim's Progress*, which calls one of its realms Philistia and another Pseudopolis, which pictures hell as a jingoistic democracy and heaven as the invention of a stubborn old woman, and whose motive force is a black god "who made things as they are," must be suspected of carrying at least some of its freight on allegorical vehicles. Simple allegory it is not, certainly, but one cannot fairly read the book without making some attempt to assign approximate values to Koshchei, the shirt of Nessus, Mother Sereda who bleaches all things, and the garden between dawn and sunrise where all lovers walk briefly. These things are consciously selected, and they are consciously perceived through the rational act of allegorizing. Most traditional fantasy, on the other hand, operates through symbols which can penetrate to the unconscious mind whether or not we consciously apprehend their import.

As a way of distinguishing more clearly between the two modes, we might note that a symbol can be pondered at length without exhausting its significance. Any amount of interpretation simply deepens the mystery, as with Melville's white whale or Mark Twain's Mississippi. Elements in an allegory, on the contrary, do not bear too close inspection, or else they begin to outgrow their original purpose. For this reason, Cabell minimizes the actual magic in his stories, for magic is closely allied with symbolism. Where another writer might dwell on Jurgen's transformation to a young man and find therein matter for wondering and pondering, Cabell hastens us past it with "Then Jurgen set about that which Mother Sereda said was necessary" (p. 46). This is one of Cabell's most common and most irritating devices.

In studying Cabell, we find that the more diligently we search out his meanings, the farther we wander from the actual mechanisms of fantasy in his work. Those two elements, meaning and magic, which should be most inextricably linked, are simply unrelated. Since I am primarily interested in Cabell as a fantasist, I will not take the time to explore what he has made into an independent dimension of his novels. Cabell was, however, an intelligent writer, and those who are interested in piecing together his philosophy would do well to consult two works which deal with it at length, Desmond Tarrant's *James Branch Cabell: The Dream and the Reality* and Arvin Well's *Jesting Moses*.

The third major fantasist of this era falls somewhere between the first two, less naive than Burroughs but not so cooly artificial as Cabell. H. P. Lovecraft shares with the others a deep aversion to the everyday world and a powerful inclination toward relics of the past, especially the institution of aristocracy. (I have wondered if that is the reason for the stress on ancestral middle names—why not just Ed Burroughs, James Cabell, and Howard Lovecraft?) Lovecraft's revulsion from the modern world was so extreme that he avoided learning any trade, spent much of his life as a semirecluse in the oldest sections of Providence, Rhode Island, insisted on singing "God Save the King" and "Anacreon in Heaven" when others sang "America" and "The Star-Spangled Banner," and did his early writing in eighteenth-century heroic couplets.[30]

Lovecraft obligingly detailed many of his literary sources for us in a long essay on *Supernatural Horror in Literature*.[31] Among American writers he cites Gothicists Charles Brockden Brown, Nathaniel Hawthorne, Ambrose Bierce, Henry James, Robert W. Chambers, Mary E. Wilkins, and of course Edgar Allan Poe. From all of these he learned how to infuse American scenes with brooding apprehension. From Poe in particular he took an extravagant diction and a literary theory based on psychological effect.

Among Lovecraft's British sources we find especially the writers of decadent horror fantasy from around the turn of the century. He praises Oscar Wilde, M. P. Shiel, Bram Stoker, Clemence Houseman, Walter de la

Mare, William Hope Hodgson, Arthur Machen, Lord Dunsany, and Algernon Blackwood. From these writers, Lovecraft borrowed the theme of a malevolent universe, sunny on the surface but filled with pockets of dormant evil. Machen in particular portrays meetings between unwary men and ancient gods better left undisturbed. Cabell, also, was a reader of Machen and may have imbibed from him some of the same sense of cosmic horror.[32]

Cosmic horror was not new in American writing—it underlies Poe's *Arthur Gordon Pym*, some of *Moby-Dick*, and much of Puritanism—but it took rather a new form under the influence of twentieth-century scientific exploration. Discoveries in astronomy and physic made the earth seem small and terribly vulnerable to physical forces or (if one had a good imagination) alien invasion. Advances in biology increased our awareness of grotesque life forms here on earth and led to speculation about hitherto inconceivable monstrosities elsewhere. Earth-based religions lost some of their power to comfort us, while speculation along parapsychological lines suggested possibilities of physic powers neither benign nor humanly comprehensible.

Lovecraft's fiction is based upon an awareness of all of these trends. Much of it verges, as does Burroughs' writing, on science fiction, for science had rebaptized the old night terrors and given them a new rationale. Lovecraft read Burroughs in his youth, though he later repudiated him, and he might have seen in him the advantages of an interplanetary setting.[33] Much of Lovecraft's later writing involves gruesome entities from outer space, whose powers approach the deific. These stories, which have been grouped by Lovecraft's followers under the rubric of the "Cthulhu mythos," lie just outside the field of fantasy proper. They may be better discussed with works of pure science fiction or in a category of their own. They take place, not in a fantasy world, but in what we must secondarily believe is our own familiar planet: that is precisely the source of the horror. Horror, not wonder, is their primary effect, and indeed is the single aim of many of them. They do not follow fairy tale structure, but rather have their own distinctive form, gradually spiraling in on unspeakable revelations.[34]

There are, however, stories by Lovecraft in which wonder and horror are both evoked and which clearly belong to the realm of fantasy. Primary among these are the stories of Randolph Carter, the most ambitious of which is *The Dream-Quest of Unknown Kadath*.[35]

The *Dream-Quest* is a derivative work. Its language and the manner of its inventions are modeled closely on the fantasies of Edward Drax Plunkett, Lord Dunsany, which in turn are a blend of Oriental extravagance and Celtic twilight, half George MacDonald and half Omar Khayam.

Lovecraft takes over entirely the barbaric kingdoms and jeweled towers, the allusions without referent and the unpronounceable names that fill Dunsany's tales. He does, nonetheless, add elements of his own, and they are worth taking note of.

First of all, the world of *The Dream-Quest* is a dream world, but a dream world like none we have seen before. Whereas for most writers, dream is used as a way of illuminating waking life, Lovecraft sets up dream as an independent universe, as real as and possibly more important than waking life. It has a geography all its own, topologically unlike that of any earthly place. It has a front door to the waking world and several back doors. The front door is the normal and proper point of entry, with a protective accompanying ritual: first one descends the "seventy steps to the cavern of flame," where one meets "the bearded priests Nasht and Kaman-Thah." Then, if one is bold, one takes the "seven hundred steps to the Gate of Deeper Slumber" and arives at the "Enchanted Wood" (pp. 291-92). The back doors lack this defense of ritual; one of them leads through an underworld of ghouls and gravestones and another gapes in the abysses of the sky.

Within the world of dream there are seas and deserts and immense mountain ranges, and huddled at the boundaries of these are the settlements of men, half-men, and gods. It is an inhospitable but sometimes awesomely beautiful world. It is, even with its horrors, an antidote to the bland terrors of daily life, like automobiles, telephones, and editors. Lovecraft insists on its independence from the lesser realities of daytime. In a related short story, "Celephais," a dying Englishman takes up permanent residence in a city of his own imagining:

> And Kuranes reigned thereafter over Ooth-Nargai and all the neighboring regions of dream, and held his court alternately in Celephais and in the cloud fashioned Serannian. He reigns there still, and will reign happily for ever, though below the cliffs at Innsmouth the channel tides played mockingly with the body of a tramp who had stumbled through the half-deserted village at dawn....[36]

That is not to say that the world of dream is a complete universe in itself; rather it is the dark, exotic half of life, with its own rules and rewards, though most people discount it or are unaware of the time they spend there. The above-mentioned Kuranes finds that it is not so blissful after all to have sealed himself off in the dream world. In *The Dream-Quest*, he admits to Randolph Carter that "he could no more find content in those places, but had formed a mighty longing for the English cliffs and downlands of his boyhood; where in little dreaming villages England's old songs hover at evening behind lattice windows, and where grey church towers peep lovely through the verdure of distant valleys" (p. 336).

Nor is it good to find oneself permanently outside the nighttime universe, as Carter does for a time in "The Silver Key."[37] To come and go as one wishes, to balance the two halves of existence, that is the ideal. Neither Carter nor Lovecraft himself might be said to have fully mastered waking life, but both were true champions of dream. Here Carter differs from most of Lovecraft's heroes, who are victimized by the things they call up from the past or the unconscious. Carter is a little closer to the fairy tale hero, though he lacks the common sense universality of most.

Most of *The Dream-Quest*, like many others of Lovecraft's stories, may have arisen from actual dreams.[38] One of the most striking conceptions in the tale came directly from a recurring dream of Lovecraft's childhood:

When I was 6 or 7 I used to be tormented constantly with a peculiar type of recurrent nightmare in which a monstrous race of entities (called by me "Night-Gaunts"—I don't know where I got hold of the name) used to snatch me up by the stomach & carry me off through infinite leagues of black air over the towers of dead & horrible cities. They would finally get me into a grey void where I could see the needle-like pinnacles of enormous mountains miles below. Then they would let me drop—& as I gained momentum in my Icarus-like plunge I would start awake in such a panic that I hated to think of sleeping again. The "night-gaunts" were black, lean, rubbery things with horns, barbed tails, bat-wings, and *no faces at all*. Undoubtedly I derived the image from the jumbled memory of Doré drawings (largely the illustrations to "Paradise Lost") which fascinated me in waking hours. They had no voices & their only form of real torture was their habit of tickling my stomach before snatching me up & swooping away with me. I somehow had the vague notion that they lived in the black burrows honeycombing the pinnacle of some incredibly high mountain somewhere. They seemed to come in flocks of 25 or 50, & would sometimes fling me one to the other.[39]

These night-gaunts, as he describes them here and within the story, are perfect fantasy creatures. They are unlike any known living beast, but there is enough similarity to things we have seen or to traditional monsters to strike a response. They are treated as independent entities with whom the hero comes in contact, rather than as mere impediments or embellishments to the story. They are described with quiet conviction; one has the feeling that Lovecraft could go on with their appearance and habits as long as he wished. They cannot be assigned any strict allegorical significance, but within the story one senses they do indicate some kind of meaning, something about the nature of darkness itself, perhaps, and the ways we try to combat it.

Burroughs never lingered long enough on any single invention to bring it to such life, and Cabell—well, to Cabell, no mere being merited the kind of care he reserved for ideals and abstractions. Lovecraft invents dozens of such creatures with equal or nearly equal success: fluttery Zoogs; toadlike and tentacled merchants from the moon; vast, unseen dholes; ghouls "meeping" and "glibbering" in the mould; and dark gods like "the crawling chaos Nyarlathotep" (p. 376). Not an agreeable group, but a vivid one. If Lovecraft errs in his inventions, it is in the direction of overconcreteness, as in some of his horror stories. I find his oozier inventions pedestrian in comparison to the elusive night-gaunts, though Barton St. Armand makes a good case for a symbolic dimension to the slime of corruption in horror fiction.[40] Many readers and critics, indeed, find considerable psychological significance in the most macabre tales and dismiss brighter fantasies as shallow, though my feeling runs quite the opposite. At any rate, in *The Dream-Quest*, Lovecraft does keep his tactile imagination under control and thereby satisfies both sides.

The story structure of *The Dream-Quest* is loose. Most of Lovecraft's writing is in the strict short story form developed by Poe, which is admirably suited for the conveyance of a single psychological effect. In dealing with a larger stage and a broader play of sensations, Lovecraft occasionally loses his way. The basic outline is as follows: Randolph Carter catches a glimpse, in his dreams, of a golden city, but is denied access by the gods. He sets out to find the home of the gods and to demand admission to the unknown city. After many adventures he reaches the gods' abode, in faraway Kadath, and finds them gone and the sinister Other Gods of outer space in their place. He is taunted by a vision of his city, which is revealed to be a dream-transformation of his native Boston, and sent through the cosmos to his destruction. But having discovered the nature of his goal, he possesses the key to it, and can escape by plunging through nightmare into wakefulness. The quest archetype underlies this story pattern, as it does the fairy tale, the lost-world fantasy, and the picaresque odyssey. Indeed, this story combines elements from all of those types.

The story's ending is plagued by a weakness built into the dream framework: the hero must eventually wake up. In this case, our disappointment is tempered by three considerations: first, the dream world remains to be revisited; second, Carter has escaped with a valuable piece of knowledge; and third, that knowledge pertains to both sides of his life. He has learned that his home city has a magical double, and that the beauty of the dream city reflects back on its earthly twin: "For through the unknown ultimate cycle had lived a thought and a vision of a dreamer's boyhood, and now there were re-made a waking world and an old cherished city to body and justify these things" (p. 385).

For all its flaws, among which I would count repetitiveness, minimal characterization, and prose that occasionally goes right past purple into the ultraviolet range, *The Dream-Quest of Unknown Kadath* is a tolerable fantasy. It is inventive, its author takes it seriously enough to lend it substance, and its ideas are developed naturally through the unforced play of event. Lovecraft did not try to give us his conclusions on childhood and death and dream; rather he set those things together on an appropriate stage and let them fall into narrative patterns, from which we may draw our own lessons. The book attempts, too, to incorporate something of American life and landscape into its fantasy world, though I do not find the mythologizing of Boston entirely successful, not, certainly, on the order of Baum's recreation of the prairies in Oz. Lovecraft dealt better with the American scene in his tales of horror, some of which incorporate authentic bits of New England folklore.[41]

It remained for Lovecraft's imitators—and he had nearly as many as Burroughs—to begin to draw together the shadowed America of his gothic tales and the Other World of his fantasies. The best of these, a writer who took inspiration not only from Lovecraft, but also from Burroughs, Baum, and practically the whole growing tradition of American fantasy, is Ray Bradbury, the opening subject of the next chapter.

SEVEN

The Baum Tradition

THE WRITERS discussed in this chapter share the important trait of having read some or all of the Oz books. They are not alone in this regard. Few bookish youngsters from 1900 on could have missed poring over at least *The Wizard*, nor failed to comprehend its significance: there was at last a fairyland reserved for American children (and carefully selected grown-ups). We might expect, therefore, to look to the generation after Burroughs, Cabell, and Lovecraft for an entirely different approach to fantasy from their anxious one. The younger writers should by rights share some of Baum's easy, humorous confidence in dealing with the impossible. They should understand his methods of tailoring native homespun into fairy garments.

Again I have chosen three representative authors. Besides forming the traditional magic sum, these three illustrate the best and clearest results of Baumian influence. Other writers have paid homage to the first unabashed American fantasist, but their own work is primarily along other lines.[1] These three are in the direct line, although, as we will see, many streams of tradition converge in the work of each.

One of the three, Edward Eager, wrote for children, as Baum did. The others, Ray Bradbury and James Thurber, are known primarily as writers for adults—but the works I will discuss are found, rightly enough, in many a children's library. It seems that once fantasy was established as a legitimate mode for children's fiction and for adult, the distinctions between the two began to break down. Once again it became a genre—perhaps the only genre—with an audience of all ages, as it had been in its original oral form.

Good fantasy can please the simplest minds with its bold inventions and its highly structured story line, but it reserves a part of its meaning to challenge the most sophisticated reader. One never feels one is penetrating more than a single additional layer with each rereading of, say, *The Princess and the Goblin*. For this reason it becomes an arbitrary task to sort out the children's writings of a writer like Ray Bradbury from the rest of his work. It is all of a piece in that respect, accessible to some readers at any age, and to others at none.

In matters of style and subject, however, there are several different strains of Bradbury's fiction. First of all there are the Lovecraftian "creepy-crawly" stories. Bradbury was schooled in fiction writing in the same amateur and pulp magazines that published Lovecraft's work. Indeed, an early collection of Bradbury's short stories was published by Arkham House, the company that exhumed H. P. Lovecraft, so to speak, from the amateur publications where his work lay undiscovered.[2]

That collection includes stories of a murderous infant, a man obsessed by his own skeleton, a little girl drowned but not dead, and a ghostly crowd that gathers at nighttime accidents. In contrast to Lovecraft, with his ancient mysteries and sinister cults, Bradbury is more interested in finding the horrific side of the familiar. In his stories he invests such small, unnoticed things as a sand castle, a doll, or the dirt on a dog's paws with intense emotion, making full use of the rhetoric of horror that goes back from Lovecraft to Poe:

> It was a smell of strange earth. It was a smell of night within night, the smell of digging down deep in shadow through earth that had lain cheek by jowl with things that were long hidden and decayed. A stinking and rancid soil fell away in clods of dissolution from Dog's muzzle and paws. He had dug deep. He had dug very deep indeed. That *was* it, wasn't it? wasn't it? *wasn't* it![3]

This kind of breathy overemphasis becomes distracting when it carries over into Bradbury's more sophisticated work, but it is evidently an inseparable part of his style.

Another variety of Bradbury's fiction is lyrical, elegiac, exotic, reminiscent of Lord Dunsany and of Lovecraft's Dunsanian tales. The best stories in this vein are *The Martian Chronicles*, in which the requisite crystalline towers and forgotten civilizations are found within a half science fictional framework.[4] Set on a Mars which freely mixes rocket ships and magic, the *Chronicles* also suggest a second important influence on Bradbury's imagination, Edgar Rice Burroughs.

In an introduction to Irwin Porges' biography of Burroughs, Bradbury praises him as a writer made great by his impulses.[5] Burroughs' naive, uninhibited style provided an ideal school for a young imagination. When Bradbury was a child, he says, he read, played, and quoted Burroughs (p. xvii). It is not surprising, then, that his Mars has a strong hint of Burroughs'. Like his predecessor, he invents a second world from pieces of his own. Mars, as a truly new world, becomes a symbol for America. It has its explorers—tall, handsome, military men like John Carter, but treated with a great deal less admiration—and its settlers, including a Martian Johnny Appleseed. There are Martian natives, and again they are clearly analogous to American Indians. Bradbury, however, writing decades after Burroughs, writes not of great tribes of fighting red men but of a vanishing race of gentle, golden-eyed, mystical people.

A third and predominant strain of Bradbury's fiction takes in elements of the first two—the highly charged horror story and the autumnal otherworld tale—but its primary impulse is toward recapturing the calm, openeyed wonder of childhood, and the model for that endeavor, as might be expected from the title of this chapter, is L. Frank Baum.

In a little parable called "The Exiles," Bradbury described the death of the imagination and also cataloged some of his own favorite romancers and fantasists: Shakespeare, Poe, Carroll, Irving, Lovecraft, Dickens, and many more. In the story, long-dead authors assemble on Mars to preserve their creations, which have been eliminated from a mechanized Earth. As they are defeated, their imagined worlds crumble around them, and the last thing to fall, and the saddest, is the Emerald City of Oz.[6] Much the same sense of respect for Baum's Other World is shown in a preface written for Raylin Moore's *Wonderful Wizard Marvelous Land*, in which Bradbury extols both Baum and Burroughs. The latter he praises for having opened up the reaches of space, and the former for discovering a world of marvels right in America. It was Baum, he says, who "grew boys inward . . . kept them home, and romanced them with wonders between their ears."[7]

And in two of his novels, *Dandelion Wine* and *Something Wicked This Way Comes*, he set about transforming his own remembered childhood world into fantasy. Whereas Baum made a rectangular map of his travels east and west, drew a deadly desert around it, and called it a fairyland, Bradbury selected a single spot, which he calls Green Town, Illinois, and made it into a crossroads of reality and magic.

Green Town, based on Bradbury's hometown of Waukegan, is shown in two different lights in the two stories. *Dandelion Wine* is a summer book, a daylight book. It is not a fantasy, but much that happens in it borders on the fantastic. *Something Wicked* is an autumn, nighttime book. It is clearly fantastic, but, as in Bradbury's horror stories, great value is placed on common, seemingly unmagical things. *Dandelion Wine* came first: it was written in pieces from 1946 to 1957, when it appeared in novel form.[8] Then, having explored the territory, learned its secrets, and located its lurking mysteries, Bradbury wrote *Something Wicked This Way Comes*, first published in 1962.[9]

In the daytime, Green Town is a small, friendly, quiet town, full of family and friends. It is happily preoccupied with the business of life: planting, harvesting, growing up, and growing old. At night it is a beleaguered fort, full of isolated, unsure people trying to fight off the invasion of disrupting evils.[10] Both visions, one feels, are conditionally true, each incomplete without the other. Daytime is needed to prepare for the struggles of night, and those struggles are necessary to defend the peace of day.

The structures of the two stories are similarly complementary. Neither is couched in conventional fairy tale form. Rather, the first, *Dandelion Wine*, follows the pattern of Joyce's *Portrait of the Artist* or any other novel of coming-of-age. It begins with the discovery by the protagonist, Douglas Spaulding, that he is an individual, uniquely alive, and then gradually tempers the ecstasy of that insight with a growing awareness of death and loss and the mixed blessings of memory and responsibility.

Something Wicked starts out with an awareness of age and death— protagonist Will Halloway's father is old, while his best friend Jim Nightshade's father is dead and he himself is touched with a streak of morbidity. Then into this story comes the fear of age and death in concrete form. That is the way fantasy operates, by externalizing ideas and emotions and clothing them in appropriate imagery. In this case, fear is represented by Cooger & Dark's Pandemonium Shadow Show, a carnival that steals into town at three in the morning with a sound of funeral music on the calliope. As the story progresses, just as Douglas, in the other novel, learns bit by bit of the conditions limiting his life, Will, Jim, and Will's father gradually discover the inner resources, their own magic, to resist the dark carnival and finally to drive it away.

Sunrise leads to sunset; night slowly climbs its way back to dawn. These stories are not so much like fairy tales, with their orderly chains of functions, as like the sparer, more mysterious shapes of myth. *Dandelion Wine* and *Something Wicked* together describe the circle, the rise and fall and recurring rise that Joseph Campbell says underlies all myth.[11] By following its arc, the individual life mimics the motions of the universe.

So in the world of *Something Wicked* (I will hereafter concentrate on it alone, since it is the more fantastic of the two), we have the childlike, concrete, downright Americanness of Oz sustaining, for the first time, a self-consciously mythic structure. This breakthrough allows for a more serious tone and a broader range of implication than was available to any of the writers we have covered since Melville. Without shifting into the doubtings and double-dealings of romance, Bradbury has deepened the tradition of Baum into a form reminiscent of *Moby-Dick* or *The Confidence-Man*.

I use Melville, rather than Hawthorne, as a point of comparison here because Bradbury leaves us several clues indicating Melville as yet another major source of inspiration. As the author of a screenplay of *Moby-Dick*, used in John Huston's 1956 movie, Bradbury must have immersed himself in its depths and in companion works. I can find at least three instances of homage in *Something Wicked* alone. First, Will Halloway's father is an Ishmael, a wanderer and a questioner, torn by pantheistic elations and existential doubts. His job is that of caretaker in a library, where he spends nights exploring the stacks—a veritable sub-sub-librarian! Second, Cooger & Dark's circus is a microcosm of humanity that carries with it on its travels an example of every kind of human cowardice and selfishness. Its freaks and followers are bound to it by the promises of the management, who offer the illusion of certainty in the face of a threatening universe. The Pandemonium Shadow Show is analogous to the equally symbolic river-boat *Fidèle*, and Mr. Dark, the dazzling, ever-changing proprietor, is its Confidence-Man.

Third, the first harbinger of coming evil in the story, and the first not-quite-human character, is a lightning-rod salesman lifted intact and with fine effect from Melville's short story. Here is the lightning-rod man's warning to the boys:

> I'm on my way. Storm's coming. Don't wait, Jim boy. Otherwise—bamm! You'll be found, your nickels, dimes and Indian-heads fused by electroplating. Abe Lincolns melted into Miss Columbias, eagles plucked raw on the backs of quarters, all run to quicksilver in your jeans. More! Any boy hit by lightning, lift his lid and there on his eyeball, pretty as the Lord's Prayer on a pin, find the last scene the boy ever saw! A box-Brownie photo, by God, of that fire climbing down the sky to blow you like a penny whistle, suck your soul back up along the bright stair! Git, boy! Hammer it high or you're dead come dawn! (p. 9)

Bradbury reinforces the impact of his literary allusion with an overlay of folk expressions and beliefs: for example, the image in the eyes of a lightning-struck person. Like Washington Irving, he is good at finding the remnants of supernaturalism in our folklore and fusing them into stories of the marvelous. He looks out not for developed fairy tales or clearly imagined fantastic beings—those can more easily be found in the lore and literature of Europe and elsewhere—but for hints and phrases with which to tie the borrowed motifs to our landscape.

Many of those hints are found in superstitions. Mirrors, for instance, play an important part in the book's magic: in the carnival's mirror maze the past and future are revealed darkly in order to play on one's remembered and anticipated fears. Bradbury is simply making explicit our vague sense of the eeriness of reflections, as represented by the superstitious injunction against breaking a mirror.

As an example of a colloquial phrase developed into magic, he adopts a folk name for a dragonfly—the devil's darning needle—along with an old belief that the dragonfly can sew up the lips of the unwary. In a particularly effective passage, an old fortunetelling witch makes use of dragonflies in her spell:

> "Darning-needle dragonfly, sew up these mouths so they not speak!"
> Touch, sew, touch, sew her thumbnail stabbed, punched, drew, stabbed, punched, drew along their lower, upper lips until they were thread-pouch shut with invisible thread.
> "Darning needle-dragonfly, sew up these ears so they not hear!"
> Cold sand funneled Will's ears, burying her voice. Muffled, far away, fading, she chanted on with a rustle, tick, tickle, tap, flourish of caliper hands.
> Moss grew in Jim's ears, swiftly sealing him up.
> "Darning needle-dragonfly, sew up these eyes so they not see!"
> Her white-hot fingerprints rolled back their stricken eyeballs to throw the lids down with bangs like great tin doors slammed shut. (p. 165)

Many of the nonhuman characters in the book are, like the witch (who comes from a penny Tarot machine), supernaturalized elements from a carnival side show: freaks and hoaxes made real. A similar technique was used earlier by Charles G. Finney in his fantasy *The Circus of Dr. Lao*, [12] and again recently in Peter Beagle's *The Last Unicorn*.[13] Circuses and carnivals seem in this country to be like reservations or wildlife preserves where the unknown and the marvelous can be locked up for safe keeping, and peered at from time to time from behind bars. Finney, Beagle, and Bradbury generate considerable effect by opening the cages.

Mr. Dark, the Illustrated Man, is a blend of circus tattooed man, Melvillean confidence-man, and Lovecraftian demigod. There may also be a reference to Queequeg and his magical decorations. Dark and his partner are ancient, evil creatures, once human but transformed by illicit knowledge and unnatural desires: "The stuff of nightmare is their plain bread. They butter it with pain. They set their clocks by death-watch beetles, and thrive the centuries" (p. 147). The comparison with Lovecraft gives us another perspective for analyzing the story. It follows the upward curve of myth, the so-called night-sea journey, but more precisely it follows the basic outline of the horror story, as did Bradbury's early short pieces, altering only the outcome and implications.

The horror story postulates a normal world, a daylight world, which weird and frightening forces invade. Sometimes horrors enter from other spheres of existence, other times they have been there, dormant, all along and are waked by the foolhardy protagonist. Either way, once they enter they can never be expelled. The protagonist is powerless against them, and so he meets his doom, his dark epiphany. If he escapes it is only to tell his story and initiate others into the horrible mysteries.

But, as Bradbury must have noted, if we allow such freedom and power to the enemy, nothing but custom prevents us from appropriating a little magical power for the forces of good. The horror story depends on things remaining one sided, but fantasy demands both black magic and white. What Bradbury did, in *Something Wicked*, was use the conventions of gothic horror as a doorway to fantasy. All that needed to be done was to turn the fallible protagonist of horror fiction into a true fairy tale hero, someone the readers can root for and someone capable of striking back against dark gods, of stealing away a few of their prerogatives like the working of wonders.

One has the sense that the invasion of the dark carnival has results not intended by its owners. Its arrival throws things off balance, disturbs the established fabric of life. When the Tarot witch works her spells, when the carousel plays with time, they create a negative electric charge, as it were, like the charge the lightning-rod man senses building up in Jim Nightshade's house at the book's beginning. Because nature abhors imbalance, a corresponding charge begins to build in answer to the negative. The witch wakes inanimate objects to their potential power to do her bidding, but the waking proves contagious, spreading to objects that are not in her control. Evil gestures and incantations serve to bring out the magic in kindly acts and words. *Dandelion Wine* pointed out a great many of the rituals that develop in families and among friends: some of the same kinds of rituals reappear in *Something Wicked* with an added aura of the supernatural.

Will's father discovers that the carnival draws its strength from fear and sorrow, leaving it vulnerable to smiles and laughter. Those become the weapons of good, lent potency by the very evils they combat. A smile carved on a wax bullet kills the witch. The laughter of Will and his father brings Jim back from the edge, or beyond the edge, of death.

The book's happy ending, though not arrived at by the route followed in fairy tales, is appropriate to the characters involved, to the plot, and to the meanings carried on the plot. The greatest threat to the confidence-man, says Bradbury through his fantasy, is the confidence to resist his lures, and death is most terrible when we try hardest to deny it. High themes can grow from humble memories, if one has the trick of it. Bradbury's memories, with help from Lovecraft, Burroughs, Melville, and especially Baum, shape themselves into stories with the authority of archetypes.

Edward Eager, too, drew on a Midwestern boyhood to produce fantasy, but he did not trouble himself overmuch with myth. A fantasist has the choice of stressing his underlying message, as Bradbury does, or of subjugating it to the pleasures of fantastic invention. Some writers are exploiters of the marvelous, others merely explorers. In the extreme case, the former sort of writer turns to allegory, and the latter to absurdity. Both Bradbury and Eager lie closer to the golden mean than to these extremes, though the one does write a little too insistently at times and the other rather aimlessly.

Aimlessness is almost a virtue in Eager's work. A book like *Half Magic* is like a children's game played on an endless summer afternoon, a game that will incorporate any number of elements into its open-ended structure: a fire, a medieval tournament, a circus, ghosts, camels, and all the sights and sounds of Toledo, Ohio, in the 1920s. These things are presented in such amazing and delightful proximity that one can hardly quibble over the evident lack of cognitive direction, though, as we will see, even these playful stories have their share of meaning.

Eager was a lyricist and playwright for some time before he thought of writing a fantasy for children. What inspired him to do so was the experience of reading to children: he rediscovered books from his own childhood and found, as well, a hoard of undiscovered treasures.

"The best kind of book," says Barnaby at the beginning of Eager's *Seven-Day Magic*, "is a magic book."[14] And the best of all magic books, according to Eager, are those by L. Frank Baum and an English contemporary of his, E. (Edith) Nesbit. Nesbit ranks first, and probably rightly, for her books are superior to the Oz books in style and subtlety. Eager was a little apologetic about his enthusiasm for Baum—he was writing some years before the Oz revival of the sixties—but he did read the Oz books to his son: "I'm well aware that the best authorities on children's reading turn the other way when an Oz book goes by. But these were so much the favorites of my youth that I couldn't forbear trying them on Fritz."[15] Caught up in the magic worlds of Baum and Nesbit, Eager decided that there should be more books like theirs, and accordingly he set out to write some.

E. Nesbit's stories generally follow a formula that she derived from hints in Victorian fantasists like Mrs. Molesworth and F. Anstey. This formula concerns the leaking of magic into the known world and the consequences thereof—rather the reverse of Dorothy's invasion of Oz. The agent of magic may be an enchanted object—a ring, a flying carpet, a broken amulet—or a creature—phoenix, mermaid, psammead, or mouldi-warp. Nesbit describes the encounters between these magical agents and various groups of capable and unconventional children, leading the children from a state of boredom or unhappiness through a period of chaos to a happy reordering. Things are resolved only when they begin to understand the rules governing the magic: generally this involves acquiring a more mature perception of the world as well.

Eager summarized the formula in the chapter titles of *Seven-Day Magic*: Finding It, Using It, Taming It, Losing It, Thwarting It, Being Thwarted, Keeping It?, and Giving It Back. This formula has some advantages over the traditional fairy tale structure. It is more tightly organized, it adapts well to modern settings, it encourages sharper characterization since the characters need not be particularly heroic, and it allows for a rich play of humor within an essentially serious framework. Notice that some of these advantages—modern setting, characterization, and humor—were also sought by Baum in his reworking of the wonder tale.

Eager took the Nesbit formula and fleshed it out with Baumian characters and events. Nesbit's children are products of the English nursery: they are whimsical, close knit, and remarkably isolated from and ignorant of adult society. Eager's children, like Baum's, are in the more worldly American mold. They have a keen understanding of affairs cultural, financial, and social, and they view their elders with affectionate condescension. Any of the four children of *Half Magic* would be at home in Oz; indeed would immediately go about setting things to rights. As a matter of record, the children in the bookish *Seven-Day Magic* do find themselves in a country which may be Oz in its Dorothyless prehistory, and they handle themselves admirably.

Eager's capsule descriptions at the beginning of *Half Magic* are good examples of the pointed colloquial humor that sets him within the Baum tradition:

> Jane was the oldest and Mark the only boy, and between them they ran everything.
> Katharine was the middle girl, of docile disposition and a comfort to her mother. She knew she was a comfort and docile, because she'd heard her mother say so. And the others knew she was, too, by now, because ever since that day Katharine *would* keep boasting about what a comfort she was, and how docile, until Jane declared she would utter a piercing shriek and fall over dead if she heard another word about it. This will give you some idea of what Jane and Katharine were like.
> Martha was the youngest, and very difficult.[16]

Into the lives of these four comes an ancient talisman of magical powers. That is a highly unlikely event and would certainly place a severe strain on our secondary belief if it were not for a deft bit of legerdemain on Eager's part:

> It was fine weather, warm and blue-skied and full of possibilities, and the day began well, with a glint of something metal in a crack in the pavement.
> "Dibs on the nickel!" Jane said, and scooped it into her pocket with the rest of her allowance, still jingling there unspent. (p. 10)

There is the magic, scooped into Jane's pocket and into the story without our knowing it. From here on, no matter what we find out about the talisman's age, appearance, and powers, we still carry our first impression of it as a lucky nickel found on the sidewalk: an unusual one, to be sure, like an Indian head or a minting error. Like Bradbury, Eager picks an object already tied to superstition to carry the weight of his fantasy.

The coin's virtue turns out to be the granting of wishes, with a twist. Exactly half of one's wish is granted. That simple condition leads to a dizzying set of adventures and mishaps as the four children explore other times (King Arthur's), other places (the Sahara, on account of a half-granted wish about a desert island), and other lives (Jane's, if she had grown up in a very different household). The magic is rigorous in its logic, with no mercy on hasty or mathematically inept wishers. It is as perverse and literal minded as a computer.

Eager understood that, like the magic coin, a valid fantasy has to obey certain rules. Satisfying magic is never of the something-for-nothing sort; rather it has its own version of the laws of gravity or thermodynamics. The rules of magic are quite clearly demonstrated in E. Nesbit's fantasies. I might summarize them as follows:

Rule one: what is wished for must be paid for.

Rule two: every magical act sends ripples of consequence to the ends of the world.

Rule three: magic tends toward chaos unless restrained by patterns of word and number.

These rules are generally applicable to good fantasy: they seem to be as fundamental to magic as Frazer's laws of contagion and similarity.[17] But Eager deserves credit for being the first to apply them consciously to American fantasy. In the best of Eager's fantasies, the above laws shine through without undue emphasis and shape the story to its inevitable happy end. If there is a larger message in his works, it is that those same principles might govern more than magic; perhaps, one speculates, they underlie every operation in the universe.

A message like that cannot be presented with the intention of teaching us something new. There is nothing the least bit didactic about Eager's work, any more than there is in Baum's. If we are to accept the rules of magic at all, they must be self-evident once we see them demonstrated, like gravity. I suspect Eager wrote his stories in something of the same spirit that Galileo dropped his weights from the tower of Pisa, not to find anything out, but for the sheer pleasure of watching theory made visible.

Thus, instead of speculations on evil and mortality, we find in Eager only magical games or experiments. It was enough for him to study the elegant clockwork of a Nesbit story or an Oz book and put together working models of his own. Sometimes his tinkering shows, when an adventure gets too literary or a borrowed device fails to assimilate. The magical turtle of *Magic by the Lake* works; the cockney toad of *The Time Garden*, modeled too closely on Nesbit's mouldiwarp (a regional term for a mole), does not. Jane's removal, in *Half Magic*, to a home one block away is a more tremendous adventure than all the changes rung on *Ivanhoe* in *Knight's Castle*. Eager's most successful stories follow Baum in locating the marvelous in the familiar. *Half Magic* makes Toledo a gateway to fairyland, and that is no mean feat.

In James Thurber's works of fantasy are combined Eager's homely, humorous magic and Bradbury's open concern with truths about the self and the universe, together with a stylistic richness beyond theirs or Baum's. Thurber's reputation is not limited to special interest categories like children's literature or science fiction: he is a Major Author. His work is often said to be in the line of Twain, Henry James, or T. S. Eliot, and, indeed, he shares traits with all three. In view of his literary standing and the evident sophistication of his themes and techniques, it may seem presumptuous to squeeze such a figure into the Baum tradition. But there he belongs, as the fullest flowering of that tradition.

Most of Thurber's writing is not at all fantastic, in the sense we have been using. Far-fetched as the events in *My Life and Hard Times* may be, they remain firmly within the possible and even have a grain of autobiographical truth. Only a few clues, like the unexplained footsteps in "The Night the Ghost Got In" or Great-uncle Zenas dying of the chestnut blight, show how Thurber could have generated a true fantasy from his hometown setting. The results might not have been unlike Eager's *Half Magic*, which is set just a few years later and a few miles north. Taking up another line of Thurber's fiction, "The Secret Life of Walter Mitty" and all its lesser kin are *about* fantasy, in the psychological sense, but we are never encouraged to confuse Mitty's wanderings with the secondarily believable core of the story. Nor does Mitty himself dream up anything truly impossible: he reflects what C. S. Lewis said about the earthbound nature of escapism.[18]

Thurber was content, for many years, to write fictionalized accounts of his Ohio past and his Connecticut present, along with assorted parodies and word games. Anything he had to say about marriage, character, and the imagination—principal early themes—could be said within those limits. Nevertheless, he had already begun toying with the stuff of fantasy, like a man who unconsciously rubs flax straws into fiber but has not yet thought of spinning them into thread. His toying was along two related lines, one dependent upon the ear, the other upon the eye, and both upon a unique and lively imagination.

Thurber had the gift (and a very troublesome gift it was in his blind, hypersensitive last years) of hearing not only what was meant but also what was actually said. As an example, a real estate agent let loose a flock of terrors without knowing it when he told Thurber, regarding a vacant house, "It's a common lock. A skeleton will let you in."[19] Thurber says he always, as a child, visualized such strange constructions and newly encountered clichés, and more than half believed in his own creations:

> There were many other wonderful figures in the secret, surrealist landscapes of my youth: the old lady who was always up in the air, the husband who did not seem to be able to put his foot down, the man who lost his head during a fire but was still able to run out of the house yelling, the young lady who was, in reality, a soiled dove. It was a world that, of necessity, one had to keep to oneself and brood over in silence, because it would fall to pieces at the touch of words.[20]

Adding to his hoard of verbal magic were a succession of friends and acquaintances who systematically warped the English language. The most memorable of these was a Teutonic handyman named Barney Haller. Thurber could only express his wonder at this man's private tongue by wrapping him in lightnings like a god: "Here was a stolid man, smelling of hay and leather, who talked like somebody out of Charles Fort's books, or like a traveller back from Oz. And all the time the lightning was zigging and zagging around him."[21] What did this man say that put him into the realm of the enchanted, represented, of course, by Oz? Here is a sample:

> "Once I see dis boat come down de rock," he said. It is phenomena like that of which I stand in constant dread: boats coming down rocks, people being teleported, statues dripping blood, old regrets and dreams in the form of Luna moths fluttering against the windows at midnight. (p. 136)

Haller's statement is merely a garbled account of a lightning bolt coming down a rod. What is wondrous is Thurber's way of taking it up and placing it in juxtaposition with various gothic devices and psychic phenomena so that it becomes one with them. Similarly:

> "Bime by I go hunt grotches in de voods." If you are susceptible to such things, it is not difficult to visualize grotches. They fluttered into my mind: ugly little creatures, about the size of whippoorwills, only covered with blood and honey and the scrapings of church bells. (p. 137)

Thurber is able to follow up on the verbal oddity, to give it an equally odd existence. He is talking, in this sketch, about the kind of mind that hatches grotches (his own, that is, not Barney Haller's, who only laid the egg). If he were speaking instead about a kind of world where grotches were as real as "de voods" around them, then he would be writing a new, Thurberish sort of fantasy.

So much for the ear's contributon. What about the eye? Thurber's vision during his creative lifetime went from bad to nonexistent. One eye was shot out by an arrow when he was a child and the other began to go soon after. Despite the apparent aptness of his accident to Edmund Wilson's literary theories about the Wound and the Bow, Thurber's blindness did not make him into an artist. Artists are made by strength, not infirmity, and the strength of Thurber's imagination positively transcended his visual problems. He made himself see: when the eye failed, the mind took over.

Now, when you put together an eye that records a fraction of what is before it, and that imperfectly, with a mind that insists on complete and ordered sight, you get results as wild as Barney Haller's linguistic black magic. "The kingdom of the partly blind," says Thurber, "is a little like Oz, a little like Wonderland, a little like Poictesme."[22] Here is what happens when Thurber breaks his glasses: "I saw the Cuban flag flying over a national bank, I saw a gay old lady with a gray parasol walk right through the side of a truck, I saw a cat roll across the street in a small striped barrel, I saw bridges rise lazily into the air, like balloons."[23] More ingredients for fantasy, lacking only a suitable mold.

In the 1940s, Thurber, troubled by darkening vision and a world situation even darker, made a break with the rational frame that had hitherto held his fantastic imagination in check, limiting it to flights of fancy and figures of speech. I can think of two possible reasons for his departure from the ordinary: one artistic, the other personal. First, he had always depended on close visual observation for his stories and sketches, even when he exaggerated what he saw. His reputation as a comic artist nearly equals his fame as a writer, and, just as his cartoons are fully developed stories caught at the moment of truth, his early stories are like sequences of cartoons, dependent as much upon gesture and composition as on dialog and plot. When Thurber could no longer see his subjects, he could not manipulate them: except for *The Thurber Album*, which reworks the materials of *My Life and Hard Times*, his later conventional sketches become increasingly circumscribed and static.

A more personal reason for a change of form is that Thurber began to want to say more than he could say in a contemporary, naturalistic setting. He felt increasingly that the world was on the wrong track, and he wanted to tell it so. Rather like Melville after *Typee* and *Omoo*, he was tired of recounting his adventures and was plumed for a flight of the imagination. The inner landscape he had been preparing for years now became the only world that was both accessible and satisfying. His mind's eye could still see, and it showed him a fairyland in which, unlike the real world, problems could still be overcome.

Thurber the fantasist emerged at the same time as Thurber the Jeremiah: indeed, the two are neatly combined in the pictorial fable *The Last Flower* and in the *Fables for Our Time*, which according to Richard Tobias, launched Thurber into his "high middle period."[24] Those works led to the creation of his most sustained pieces of writing, *The White Deer* and *The 13 Clocks*, as well as to the slighter fairy tales *Many Moons, The Great Quillow*, and *The Wonderful O*.

In 1934, Thurber wrote an appreciation of L. Frank Baum called "The Wizard of Chit [t] enango." In it, he praises the Oz stories for being "fairy tales with a difference,"[25] the difference being that Baum's tales reflect not some long-ago peasant life but his own time and place. Thurber recognized Baum's remarkable achievement in not only inventing an American fairyland, but populating it as well: "Baum wrote 'The Wizard,' I am told, simply as a tour de force to see if he could animate, and make real, creatures never alive before on sea or land" (p. 141). Except for the later volumes, which, as he observed, sink from fantasy to whimsy, Thurber approved of Baum's storytelling, as well as his setting and characters. Regarding Baum's introduction to *The Wizard of Oz*, in which he announces his intention to avoid heartache and nightmare in his stories, Thurber says: "I am glad that, in spite of this high determination, Mr. Baum failed to keep them out. Children love a lot of nightmare and at least a little heartache in their books. And they get them in the Oz books" (p. 141).

Thurber first read *The Wizard of Oz* and *The Land of Oz* when he was ten. Forty years later their influence surfaced in the writing of *The White Deer*. It, too, along with *The 13 Clocks*, is a fairy tale "with a difference," a difference which extends to each of the five facets of fantasy.

First of all is the fantasy world. The worlds of both *The White Deer* and *The 13 Clocks* lie closer to traditional fairy tale settings than does Oz. We find castles, enchanted forests, dukes, and wizards, all much as we might find them in works of the literary followers of the brothers Grimm. Thurber was never particularly interested in landscape as such, not like Baum, who was an unconscious regionalist. He was content to let convention dictate his locale, up to a point. The level at which his world strikes out on its own is that of fine detail. The enchanted forest of *The White Deer* is a standard magical forest, dark and mysterious, full of wizards and eerie creatures. But a closer look shows the Thurberian imagination at work, altering a flower here, an animal there, to exploit the magical possibilities of its name or shape: "If you pluck one of the ten thousand toadstools that grow in the emerald grass at the edge of the wonderful woods, it will feel as heavy as a hammer in your hand, but if you let it go it will sail away over the trees like a tiny parachute, trailing black and purple stars."[26] One can detect here the same slant vision that sees cats in barrels and bridges in the sky.

Thurber's ear is at work, too, generating magic from linguistic device: "The white deer flashed through the green forest and the King and his sons followed, past the barking trees, across the musical mud, in and out of a flock of wingless birds" (p. 18). The tree is a pun, the mud alliteration, and the birds a classic oxymoron.

Between the time of *The White Deer* and that of *The 13 Clocks*, Thurber came to rely more on tricks of sound than on sight. Occasionally, as in this paragraph in the latter work, sound repetition alone creates the effect of an entangling spell:

> The brambles and the thorns grew thick and thicker in a ticking thicket of bickering crickets. Farther along and stronger, bonged the gongs of a throng of frogs, green and vivid on their lily pads. From the sky came the crying of flies, and the pilgrims leaped over a bleating sheep creeping knee-deep in a sleepy stream, in which swift and slippery snakes slid and slithered silkily, whispering sinful secrets.[27]

Buried in the prose of both tales are strings of rhymes and metric feet, as in this speech of King Clode's: " 'Yammer, yammer, yammer,' said the King. 'I've had my fill of yammering. We must advise this Princess she's a deer. Perhaps she'll have the grace to disappear' " (*The White Deer*, p. 48). Sometimes these regularities seem accidental, an eerie piling up of poetic coincidence. Other times they signify the formality of a spell or decree: "Love me truly, fail me never, woman will I be forever; but if love shall fail me thrice, I shall vanish in a trice," says the Princess. "So tells the tale, so runs the spell. Prince Jorn, do you love me well?" (p. 100).

The headiest verbal magic in *The White Deer* accompanies the labors of the three princes. In the first of these parallel episodes, Thurber turns toward Lewis Carroll, rather than Baum, as a guide. Prince Thag, like Alice in *Through the Looking Glass*, loses his name in a forest of confusion and meets a man with Humpty-Dumpty's disregard for lingustic norms:

> "I distrust this stickish thicky stuff—" The tall Prince bit his lip. "Hag's thad enough."
> "A lozy moon globbers in the pipe trees," said a voice in a tone which for one reason or another thaggravated Had. "I'm up here in the crouch of the tree," the voice continued. (pp. 50–51)

The second Prince, Gallow, finds a different kind of nonsense in the Forest of Willbe: the destruction of meaning brought about by wrenching language to economic ends. The following passage may be a reference to the placarded knights of Twain's *A Connecticut Yankee*:

> As he jingled along the path, Gallow stared in amazement at a kind of forest he had never seen before. The trees were hung with signs and legends... "Lost Babes Found." "Giants Killed While You Wait." "7 League Boots Now 6.98." "Let Us Waken Your Sleeping Beauty." "We Put You on an Urn, Men Put You on a Pedestal." "Consult Panting & Young." "Seek Grailo, Even Better Than the Holy Grail." "Coach Pie, Pumpkin Wheels, Horse Traps, Mice Shoes." (p. 63)

Prince Jorn's labor, on the other hand, moves from nonsense to sense. He finds the true witch's broom hidden in a clump of witches'-broom, solves a riddle, and, with help, discovers that counting a thousand thousands (part of his appointed task) is not the same as counting to a million.

The nonsensical lands encountered by the three Princes are not, as in Lewis Carroll, the whole fantastic universe. Rather they are isolated pockets of absurdity like the places Dorothy and her friends encounter in *The Emerald City of Oz*: Fuddle-cum-jig, Flutterbudget Center, and Rigmarole Town. They help, through contrast, to define the norm, which is an orderly realm despite its surprises and inversions. Prince Jorn says of the enchanted forest:

> What's black is white,
> What's red is blue,
> What's dark is light,
> What's true is true. (p. 15)

And, he might have added, everything will come out right in the end, for that is the kind of world we are dealing with. Thurber has not departed so far from old-style fairy tale as to change that essential feature.

Nor does he drastically alter the fairy tale structure which leads to such a happy conclusion. Each of the fairy tales, as Charles S. Holmes points out, has approximately the same pattern.[28] It begins with a problem—what Propp calls a lack or insufficiency—proceeds through several attempts at solution by false heroes, men of worldly importance; and ends with the true hero in triumph, with girl or kingdom or some more private reward, like the respect of his fellows.

The smaller movements within this overall scheme also derive from traditional *Märchen*. There are interdictions and violations of interdictions, announcements, departures, thresholds, deceptions, meetings with helpers, and confrontations with enemies, all in the prescribed sequence, though not every element occurs in every tale.

It seems that Thurber determined to follow the rules of his chosen form, just as he did with his fables. Like the fables, however, the fairy tales add something above and beyond the structure: a certain self-consciousness, a covert announcement that, yes, the form is antique, but the author has reasons for selecting it and no other. Those episodes mentioned earlier, the labors of the three princes, call attention to the fairy tale conventions by briefly violating them. Suddenly encountering the twentieth century in the middle of the story is a shock that makes us more aware of, and grateful for, the return of an older, quieter world. Other things direct our notice from the story to things outside of it: references to "tarcomed" and "nacilbuper" and the "Forest of Artanis" (read them backward), echoes of popular songs, caricatures of people like *New Yorker* editor Harold Ross, figures of speech just short of anachronism, and unexpected playful turns, like a villain who feeds his enemies, not to pigs or dogs or tigers, but to geese.

Because of this self-consciousness, one is always aware, in reading Thurber's fantasies, that the happy ending is a fragile thing that depends very much on our accepting the conventions of the genre. It is different from the inevitable falling into place of a true *Märchen*. We can accept the idea that a fairy tale Prince and Princess will live happily ever after, but we are all too aware that we tarcomeds and nacilbupers will not. What we can do is to retell their stories and take courage and comfort from them.

The hero of a Thurber fairy tale is, in addition to being the prince or plucky commoner of *Märchen*, an artist of some sort. Prince Jorn is a musician and versifier, as is the nearly identical Prince Zorn of *The 13 Clocks*. Other Thurber heroes are poets, toymakers, and jesters. The fairy tale hero is common man in romantic guise, but the Thurber hero is uncommon man, the man of imagination and sensibility. There is a reflection of culture in this difference. Oppressed peasant storytellers tell how a youngest son or a soldier—someone of relatively low rank—can attain maturity and the dignity of marriage and property. Thurber tells how an artist—someone whose rank seemed to him to be low and sinking lower in mid-century America—can restore an ailing land and indeed is the only one who can do so.

Because Thurber's heroes are more imaginative than those around them, they are more in touch with the marvels of the fantasy world. They understand the linguistic and sensory playfulness represented by magic; it is just the sort of thing they themselves strive for in their art. Perhaps this is the reason that Thurber portrays magic primarily as a beneficent force in league with Jorn or Zorn or the great Quillow. For every hostile magical creature there are two or more that aid the hero in his task. A wizard, a sphinx, and even a witch are friendly to Prince Jorn. The only inimical being is the witch who has enchanted princess Rosanore and her brother— and she, it turns out, is actually a neutral agent employed by a jealous mortal. The less familiar creatures of *The 13 Clocks* waver interestingly between good and evil, but generally choose good: "'I make mistakes, but I am on the side of Good,' the Golux said, 'by accident and happenchance. I had high hopes of being Evil when I was two, but in my youth I came upon a firefly burning in a spider's web. I saved the victim's life'" (p. 20).

The Golux is a little man of untrustworthy powers who, nevertheless, helps Zorn win his princess. Allied with Prince Zorn and the Golux against the evil Duke are Hagga, a woman who weeps jewels; Hark, whom the Duke believes to be his faithful spy; the ghosts of children killed by the Duke; and even, in a way, the loathsome Todal, which "looks like a blob of glup," "makes a sound like rabbits screaming," and "smells of old, unopened rooms" (p. 32). It is this monster that finally does the Duke in.

Golux, Hagga, Todal: all three are examples of Thurber's ability to invent memorable characters and creatures based on suggestive sounds.[29] In this case, all three names derive from a code used by the United States in World War I, when Thurber was a code clerk in Washington and Paris. "Golux" simply meant "period," which must have seemed a terrible waste of an evocative word.[30] The Golux is a fine, elusive character, "the only Golux in the world, and not a mere Device" (p. 19). He is reminiscent of other supernatural little men, like Rumpelstiltzkin, but he is very much his own being, a unique mixture of pride, carelessness, and wisdom.

I have already dropped several hints concerning the dimension of meaning in Thurber's fantasies. In them he was working out for himself questions of love and honor, time and mortality, and the role of the artist in modern society. He uses fantasy as a kind of algebra, or a special language, in which to evaluate and debate all sides of the case. In order for his conclusions to be fair and valid, however, he must treat the fantasy form with the respect due any artistic endeavor, as he was well aware:

I believe that narrative comes first in a fairy tale and I have found out that if you start out with a set philosophy in mind the story is likely to become stilted or even pretentious. All I did was to write a fairy tale whose plot, incidents, and characters interested me, as did the writing. I have no doubt that philosophy is inherent in such an approach and anyone is welcome to read what they want into the book.[31]

As simple and brief as Thurber's fairy tales are, they are as packed with philosophy as any we have examined, for philosophical inquiry pervades plot, characters (like the Golux, who could well stand as Thurber's own muse of comic fantasy), and even the very language of each story. They are the natural vehicles for Thurber's qualified reaffirmation of faith in his craft and in mankind.[32]

Since I have treated these three authors, Bradbury, Eager, and Thurber, as representatives of the growing fantasy tradition that derives in major part from L. Frank Baum, I think it would be appropriate now briefly to cite some of the other writers they might represent. First of all, Bradbury is by no means the only science fiction writer to try his hand at fantasy. Robert Heinlein, Robert Bloch, Anthony Boucher, Henry Kuttner, Fritz Leiber, and Theodore Sturgeon have all played around with magic as well as machinery. Fletcher Pratt and L. Sprague de Camp (author, incidentally, of H. P. Lovecraft's biography) each attempted large-scale fantasy novels on European themes, and, more satisfyingly, collaborated on several stories burlesquing the swords-and-sorcery school of formulaic fantasy. In the last two decades many science fiction writers have been lured into the field of fantasy by the enormous impact of Tolkien's *The Lord of the Rings*, but the story of that influence must be left for the final chapter.

Fantasies of all sorts are now an accepted part of children's reading, from picture books on up. I will mention only a selection that I believe deal in original and challenging ways with the American scene. An early work that has disappeared almost without a trace is *The Cat in Grandfather's House*, written in 1929 by critic Carl Grabo. A better-known story is Carolyn Sherwin Bailey's *Miss Hickory*, the winner of the 1947 Newberry Award for children's literature. Both books rely on the animation of household objects, a technique that was attempted a century ago by Edward Eggleston but only became successful when combined with the vivid characterization and full secondary belief of Baum. Archie Binns's *The Radio Imp* (1950) and Edward Fenton's *Once Upon a Saturday* (1958) are richly evocative of place—one transpires in New York City, the other in a small New England town—and use magic to bring out the fullest flavor of their settings. Edward Ormondroyd's *Time at the Top* (1963) and Eleanor

Cameron's *The Court of the Stone Children* (1973) are the most satisfying American time fantasies to date. Madeleine L'Engle's *A Wrinkle in Time* (1963, also a Newberry Award winner) and Randall Jarrell's *The Animal Family* (1965) are haunting, unusual tales of personal discovery, not at all alike in setting or style but equally arresting in conception. L'Engle's book appropriates several science fiction conventions, as does Eleanor Cameron's *The Wonderful Flight to the Mushroom Planet* (1954).

There are no stories exactly like Thurber's. Other popular satiric writers turned to fantasy, like Thorne Smith and Robert Nathan, but were unable to throw off their sophistication and capture any true sense of wonder. Perhaps for this reason, Smith's *Topper* (1933) and Nathan's *Portrait of Jennie* (1940) are better remembered as motion pictures than as novels.

Closer in spirit to Thurber's fairy tales are the quiet, magical stories of his friend, mentor, and *New Yorker* colleague E. B. White. *Stuart Little* (1945) is the story of a mouse born to human parents—no explanation is offered. *Charlotte's Web* (1952) is the story of a friendship between a spider and a pig and of the extraordinary efforts on Charlotte's part to save Wilbur from the butcher. *The Trumpet of the Swan* (1970) is a fable on talents and how they differ. These stories, like the majority of those discussed in this chapter, are published for children, but it should be obvious by now that anyone looking for stories of wonder can ignore such divisions.

The Baum tradition, as I have attempted to trace it, is only one aspect of Baum's influence. The direction of that influence, in children's literature, in adult literature, and in American culture as a whole, is toward a new freedom of the imagination. Never before have we been so willing to accept the irrational and the magical, not in place of, but alongside the rational and the mundane. Judging from the literature alone, the change has been a profoundly positive one. As James Thurber said in his foreword to *The 13 Clocks*, "Unless modern Man wanders down these byways occasionally, I do not see how he can hope to preserve his sanity."[33]

EIGHT

After Tolkien

THE PUBLICATION of J. R. R. Tolkien's *The Lord of the Rings* in the 1950s radically changed the position of fantasy in this country. Even before it became a best seller and the object of a cult, Tolkien's story was noted by critics sympathetic to the genre as the work they had been waiting for, the first extensive exploration of the possibilities of modern fantasy.[1] It seemed on the one hand to sum up the whole Western tradition of the marvelous, with its echoes of Homer, Dante, and Wagner and its outright borrowings from the *Kalevala*, the Scandinavian Eddas, *Beowulf,* the *Mabinogion*, George MacDonald, and William Morris. On the other hand, the trilogy was an integrated story with a perception and a point of view that many readers found appropriate to the contemporary world: that is, it was not only a culminating work but also a seminal one, a challenge to the reader to go out and create something equally grand and equally magical.

Other British writers have affected the course of American fantasy— Lewis Carroll, Andrew Lang, George MacDonald, Arthur Machen, and E. Nesbit all were imitated by writers on this side of the Atlantic. In each case it was possible after some amount of trial and error to apply the lesson learned to a native stock of characters and themes and thus move from imitation to real development, as one composer develops the melody of another. But in none of those cases was there such a solid mass of material to be absorbed into the native tradition. *The Lord of the Rings* fell like a great meteorite into the stream of American fantasy and almost blocked it off altogether.

One problem was that *The Lord of the Rings* provided many of its readers with an extraliterary experience. So powerfully did Tolkien evoke the sense of wonder in his fiction that one could almost forget that it was only fiction. It seemed, in some mystical way, to be true. Now, extraliterary experiences are not new with Tolkien, nor are they a bad thing. When a performance of *King Lear* wrings one's soul or when the death of King Arthur casts a gloom over the whole world, it is not simply because of Shakespeare or Malory's facility with plot and image. It is because of some movement within one's own mind, called up by the written or spoken words but not contained within them. The experience is extraliterary because it depends on the needs, expectations, and background of the reader. It defies analysis under any system of literary values. Some people get starry-eyed over the obscurities of Kahlil Gibran but find *Moby-Dick* deadly dull.

That is all very well: it is the reader's prerogative to be moved where and when he will. In the case of Tolkien, there is room for extraliterary transports and for appreciation on literary grounds as well. Too often, however, the extraliterary experience short-circuits the literary one, and that is a crime against any work of literature. *The Lord of the Rings* was, as Roger Sale says, "fearfully abused" by those who saw it only as an avenue of escape and were blind to its strengths and weaknesses as a work of art.[2] That is not an extraliterary experience but a subliterary one. And what kind of influence results from a source which was not adequately comprehended in the first place? Undigested meals produce nightmares, or ought to.

At any rate, undigested Tolkien has produced some literary nightmares of the first order. The worst offender to date is probably Terry Brooks's *The Sword of Shannara*.[3] With all respect to the author, who may have intended homage to Tolkien, this book and others like it are nothing more than throwbacks to the bad old days of "The Culprit Fay." They attempt to evoke wonder without engaging the mind or emotions, and they threaten to reduce Tolkien's artistic accomplishment to a bare formula. One finds in them nothing that was not in their model—*Shannara* is especially blatant in its point-for-point correspondence—but one most certainly does not find everything that *was* in the original. The solid homeyness of the Shire, the eerie aliveness of the forests, the brooding evil of Mordor, the despairing heroism of Frodo: all of these are lost, because they were rooted in Tolkien's own life and philosophy. His gold, like the fairies', turns to trash when it is stolen away.

To attempt to copy Tolkien is necessarily to misread, to mistake the mechanics of his tale for the substance. Roger Sale makes a good case for *The Lord of the Rings* as a study of "modern heroism," very much the product of two world wars and the upheavals of English urbanization.[4] Elves and rings and hobbits are part of Tolkien's way of confronting his life. But one finds no confrontation in the Tolkien imitations, only an engineered plot with characters that are unmotivated, unmemorable, and, God help us, cute.

Only a little better are the writers who think to recreate Tolkien by going to his sources. Without his scholarly understanding of and personal commitment to the English, Celtic, and Scandinavian epics, it is impossible to integrate them into a novelistic fantasy. One ends up simply retelling the exploits of Owain or Odin without adding to them. That is a valid literary activity but one more on the order of Hawthorne's *Tanglewood Tales* than of *The Lord of the Rings*. Sometimes the retelling is tied together with a modern story, especially in children's books: a group of children wander into the past or come across a relic from it. This kind of story is usually only as satisfying as its modern component. Gods and heroes move woodenly among the present-day characters like early experiments in combining live-action film with animation.

Despite my love of fantasy and of all the shining figures of myth and romance, I tire of meeting Arthur and Merlin and their Celtic forerunners in story after story. I would not grow weary, however, if these stories breathed new life into their heroes and wizards: if, like T. H. White in *The Once and Future King*, they boldly reinvented the whole Arthurian sequence. A step below White, certainly, but genuinely interesting are the children's fantasies by Lloyd Alexander known as the Chronicles of Prydain.

The Chronicles take place, not in an Arthurian setting, but in the mythological Wales that preceded Arthur, altered a bit to make it conform to the Tolkienian pattern. It has an Aragorn figure called Gwydion, a Gandalfish wizard called Dallben, a dwarf named Doli, a softened Gollum called Gurgi, and a boy hero, Taran, who is hobbitlike because of his comic innocence and small size. The first story, *The Book of Three*, is no more than a clever imitation of Tolkien, lighter in tone than its model and based primarily on Welsh myth, rather than on a combination of Northern motifs.[5] By the last two books, however, Taran has grown up, the land of Prydain has taken on a degree of solidity, and the author has found in his story an outlet for some real philosophical exploration.

Interestingly enough, the Chronicles of Prydain become most engaging when Taran reveals himself to be a hero in the American grain. In the fourth book, *Taran Wanderer*, he becomes, as the title indicates, a wanderer, an experimenter, a seeker after an identity that always seems to lie over the next hill.[6] In his metamorphoses and in his restlessness he resemble Hawthorne's Holgrave, Cooper's Leatherstocking, and that other orphan, Twain's Huckleberry Finn. And in the final volume, *The*

High King, which won the Newberry Award for 1968, Taran finds his identity, as Americans have throughout our literary tradition, in the future rather than the past.[7] Without ties or ancestry, and with a wife who renounces her own heritage, he becomes King of Prydain and leads it into a new, unmagical age. Like the nameless couple in Hawthorne's short story, "The Maypole of Merrymount," Taran and Eilonwy stand together at the end of the story, shorn of the trappings and enchantments of a lost age, ready to move together into a soberer world. It is a moving ending and an appropriate one, an ending which is the natural flowering of the cross between alien motifs and the author's own culture.

With Alexander we move into the category of modest or half-successes. These are works whose authors understand that they must bring something of their own to the borrowed materials, even though they may not be entirely sure how to do so. Often the authors of such stories have worked in modes other than fantasy, and what they add to Tolkien is some quality or technique found in their other works.

Andre Norton, for instance, is a writer of space adventure, in the line that goes back to Burroughs. Her stories are less violent and her heroes more sensitive, but her basic orientation approximates his. Both writers create half-scientific, half-magical worlds that fit their particular talents and desires. The story type that dominates Norton's fiction is that of the seemingly unimportant youth who attains superhuman powers: telepathy, psychokinesis, clairvoyance, or one of a great many ingenious Norton variations on these. When Norton came under the influence of Tolkien, the results were largely positive. His example reinforced her own interest in creating self-consistent worlds, it suggested ways to tighten her sometimes awkward plots, and it encouraged her to lean less heavily on science-fictional apparatus (never a strong point of hers) and more on fairy tale motifs.

A book like *Judgment on Janus* is clearly derivative of Tolkien, but it is also typical Norton.[8] In it a hero from her space-opera universe—like many of her characters he is a refugee from a great interstellar war, living in a ghetto called the Dipple—arrives on a world of magic. His identity becomes joined with that of a long-dead elflike warrier, and, combining the strengths of both personalities, he helps to quell an ancient evil. The story, also, has two personalities, two ways of looking at events. It works because the magical viewpoint and the scientific coincide on Norton's key issues: cooperation with nature and the individual's integration into a community. The resolution of the fantasy plot also solves the hero's problems within the science fiction framework. It is an answer to the devastation and displacement brought about by advanced technology.

In more recent Norton books, particularly the Witch World sequence, magic almost completely overwhelms science as a rationale for action. In the first few volumes of this series, some comparison is made between our rational universe where the hero, Simon Tregarth, originates and the magical universe into which he is translated, but as Simon recedes from importance within the stories the comparison is also dropped. Later books, like *The Jargoon Pard*, develop a consistent and fairly complex notion of magic that is similar to Tolkien's: there is color symbolism, for example, that associates blue and green with good, organic magic; brown with animal magic (compare Tolkien's brown wizard, Radagast); and livid grays with evil.[9] Norton's system has its unique elements, as well, extensions of many of the mystical and pseudoscientific ideas found in her earlier books. Norton deals well and confidently with magical discoveries, confrontations, and artifacts. She balances inventions and borrowings to create new and appealing worlds. She is not a great writer of fantasy: her stories are limited and repetitive, like Burroughs's, and her style is often as raw as his. But, if she is formulaic, she has at least evolved her own formula which expresses her dreams and not those of Tolkien or anybody else.

Though Norton is not a sophisticated writer, her lack of irony and displacement often pays for itself in commitment to the story being told. Other, more ambitious writers fail to match the firm secondary belief that holds her tales together. Three such doubting fantasists are Peter Beagle, Stephen Donaldson, and Roger Zelazny.

Peter Beagle is one of the great appreciators of Tolkien. His essay on "Tolkien's Magic Ring" expresses the delight that many of us felt on discovering *The Lord of the Rings*.[10] It points to Tolkien's own faith in his materials as a source of strength, and it describes the sense Tolkien conveys that his story and the world within it were found rather than invented. But it has little to say about *how* Tolkien makes his commitment infectious, and that should be the main concern of anyone who intends to follow in his footsteps.

Before Beagle attempted a fantasy he wrote a funny, offbeat ghost story called *A Fine and Private Place*.[11] The type of low-key satire found in it is completely foreign to Tolkien's fantasy: it is more likely to be found in the better grades of television situation comedy. When, in *The Last Unicorn*, Beagle attempted to express his appreciation for Tolkien in the form of a literary homage, he had to find some middle ground between the style he was accustomed to and the matter he was trying to incorpate. If there is any middle ground between wry comedy and high fantasy, it might just be the Thurber fairy tale, which is dazzling and funny and solemn, all at the same time. And the tone of *The Last Unicorn*, in its opening pages, is remarkably like that of *The White Deer*. Even little tricks like the anticlimatic catalogs that both mock the subject and endear it to us, are the same. Here is a sample, a description of the unicorn:

> She had pointed ears and thin legs, with feathers of white hair at the ankles; and the long horn above her eyes shone and shivered with its own seashell light even in the deepest midnight. She had killed dragons with it, and healed a king whose poisoned wound would not close, and knocked down ripe chestnuts for bear cubs. [12]

But as soon as Beagle tries to inflate his fairy tale to encompass a world and a vision, after the manner of Tolkien, the Thurberish deftness departs and he grows self-conscious. The graft fails to take, and the two components draw apart, the magic into sentimentality and the modern voice into embarrassed joking. He gives his wizard the deflating name of Schmendrick and lets him indulge in anachronisms at the expense of the story, unlike Thurber, whose anachronisms always reinforce the charm of the fairy tale world through contrast. The center of *The Last Unicorn* does not hold: its characters and imagery go flying off in all directions, without reference to the patterns of significance that should command. Parts of the story are memorable: the fraudulent magical circus that reminds one of Ray Bradbury's sinister carnival, the outwardly prosperous but inwardly barren town, the vision of unicorns floating like froth on the surf, the ponderous and fearsome Red Bull.

But Beagle does not gather these things into a satisfying whole because he lacks faith in them. He must lack faith, since he is always throwing pixy dust in our eyes to keep us from finding him out. This is pixy dust: "The witch's stagnant eyes blazed up so savagely bright that a ragged company of luna moths, off to a night's revel, fluttered straight into them and sizzled into snowy ashes" (p. 29). So is this: "Schmendrick lighted down to support her, and she clutched him with both hands as though he were a grapefruit hull" (p. 217). The first is uncalled-for, the second (grapefruit hull?) just silly. In neither case does the imagery advance the story, or even relate to what is going on. One feels like telling the author to play fair and let us see what he is about. Fantasy is not like parlor conjuring; its effects do not arise from misdirection and patter.

Stephen Donaldson does not try to fool the eye—or even to beguile it. The three volumes of his *Chronicles of Thomas Covenant the Unbeliever* plod along as straightforwardly as a horse with blinders. [13] But he shares Beagle's self-consciousness. As the title of his trilogy indicates, he has attempted to dramatize the very unbelief that mars so much American fantasy and to incorporate it into the world he is making. Into a landscape derived from Tolkien and a few other fantasy writers, he throws an unwilling, unlikeable, unbelieving hero named Thomas Covenant. Covenant is, in our own world, an author who contracts leprosy and is thereupon rejected by wife, friends, and society. When he is catapulted into the fantasy world, he carries over into it all the bitterness engendered by his disease, even though he is cured of it for the duration of his visit. By the end of the third volume he has rejected the land, betrayed most of his friends there, and pretty much alienated the reader; and then we find out that his skepticism is the secret weapon that will destroy the evil Lord Foul and bring happiness to everyone but himself. There is no explanation of why something that has brought nothing but grief can be the ultimate defense of good. Covenant returns to our world not too much different than when he left it, though supposedly cured of his resentment against humanity.

The concept is interesting but troublesome, for it seems to ask us to share Covenant's scorn for worlds of magic. The whole three-volume adventure is reduced to a sort of psychotherapy for its hero. Since he does not and, according to the plot, cannot commit himself to the imagined realm, he never establishes a relationship with anything outside of himself (making his name rather ironic), nor can the author stand outside his protagonist and demonstrate that his world is really a place of wonder and meaning, for that would verify our suspicion that Covenant is an idiot for holding himself aloof. Like Beagle, Donaldson fails to bridge the gap between his personal and cultural concerns and the adopted medium in which he is seeking to express them.

Roger Zelazny is primarily a writer of science fantasy. His work, like Andre Norton's, is a partial rationalization of magical motifs through the vocabulary and conventions of science fiction. Like Norton, he learned from Tolkien something about appropriating elements from various traditions, but he goes farther afield than does Tolkien. In one of his books, *This Immortal* (1966), he draws on modern Greek legend; in *Lord of Light* (1967) he plays off Hindu myth against Buddhist thought and both against American worship of technology; *Creatures of Light and Darkness* (1969) is loosely based on the Egyptian pantheon, but includes a Jehovah figure, a spirit-of-revolution called the Steel General (who comes with very little change out of L. Frank Baum's *The Enchanted Island of Yew*), and a wildly original cosmology. In *Isle of the Dead* (1969) and *To Die in Italbar* (1973), Zelazny goes farther still. He creates an alien race, the Pei'ans, and a mythology to go with them, and then weaves that mythology into his novels. All of these books reveal an awareness of the workings of myth that bodes well for Zelazny when he should undertake to leave science behind and write a fantasy.

And Zelazny has undertaken a fantasy: five volumes set in the fantasy world of Amber, which is, as might be expected, a striking, well-imagined, and unusual place. Zelazny develops his fantasy world in a way never attempted before, to my knowledge. The first book, *Nine Princes in Amber* (1970), carried its hero, Corwin, from Earth to Amber, where his siblings were carrying out a set of Machiavellian plots to gain the throne of their vanished father. Corwin has amnesia and only gradually begins to remember Amber and to take his part in the plotting. Amber, it seems, is the true center of existence, and all other worlds are shadows of it, called into being according to the interests of Corwin's superhuman family. In the second book, *The Guns of Avalon* (1972), the plot is carried a little further, but, more importantly, we learn an entirely new explanation for the events in the first volume. With the third and fourth volumes comes a little more action and still further revelations and revisions of what went before. What seemed simple comes to seem complex, mysterious, and dangerous. The series is put together like a set of transparent overlays: each one makes a new design by adding to what was already there. The final book, *The Courts of Chaos* (1978), is disappointing only in that it leaves the design less complex than earlier hints lead us to expect.

It is a good framework for fantasy, but there are weaknesses. First, most of the action of the story is stock adventure, out of *The Prisoner of Zenda* by way of Edgar Rice Burroughs. Second, there are not many characters, and not much variety among them. One of Zelazny's sources for the world of Amber and its residents is the Tarot deck; there is such a deck in the stories, with the faces of Corwin and his family for the greater trumps. Unfortunately, the family is as hard to tell apart as a set of playing cards: different colors and designs, but they all have the same value. A third problem is Corwin himself. We have seen him before, in almost every one of Zelazny's novels. His prototype is Humphrey Bogart—the tough guy with a tender heart who talks in slang and thinks in poetry. Here is a sample of Corwin's private-eye style:

> Some natural skepticism as to the purity of all human motives came and sat upon my chest. I'd been over-narcotized, I suddenly knew. No real reason for it, from the way I felt, and no reason for them to stop now, if they'd been paid to keep it up. So play it cool and stay dopey, said a voice which was my worst, if wiser, self.[14]

It is just this playing cool which throws the fantasy off. Zelazny cannot resist mocking the very influences, like Tolkien, that led him into fantasy. Here is testimony from another reader, talking about Zelazny and a similar writer, Fritz Leiber:

> When humor is intended the characters talk colloquial American Eng-
> lish, or even slang, and at earnest moments they revert to old formal usages.
> Readers indifferent to language do not mind this, but for others the strain is
> too great. I am one of the latter. I am jerked back and forth between Elfland
> and Poughkeepsie; the characters lose coherence in my mind, and I lose
> confidence in them.[15]

The same reader proposed a possible explanation for such stylistic incon-
cistency: it represents a deeper, a cognitive ambivalence:

> Sometimes I wonder if these two writers underestimate their own talents, if
> they lack confidence in themselves. Or it may be that, since fantasy is seldom
> taken seriously at this particular era in this country, they are afraid to take it
> seriously. They don't want to be caught believing in their own creations,
> getting all worked up about imaginary beings; and so their humor becomes
> self-mocking, self-destructive. Their gods and heroes keep turning aside to
> look out of the book at you and whisper, "See, we're really just plain folks."[16]

Is such self-doubt the necessary product of sophistication for an
American writer? It is not, for the writer of the above comments has herself
written the most challenging and richest American fantasy to date, with all
of Zelazny's self-awareness and all of Norton's or Baum's confidence in her
chosen medium. She—her name is Ursula K. Le Guin—has absorbed
Tolkien, comprehended him, and gone on in her own direction. Her
comments on Tolkien in the essay quoted above are appreciative but keenly
analytical, concentrating on his techniques of style and characterization,
the way one artist tends to read another.

Ursula Le Guin has given us a convenient guide to her career, at least
up to 1975, in her collection of short stories entitled *The Wind's Twelve
Quarters.*[17] The stories in this book span a dozen years and nearly as many
varieties of science fiction and fantasy. There is fairy tale, allegory, science
fantasy, hard or "wiring-diagram" science fiction (Le Guin's term, p. 129), a
surrealistic mode that Le Guin refers to as "psychomyth" (p. viii), and
essentially naturalistic narrative that takes place on another planet only
because the particular societal setting it requires does not exist on our own.

The first story in the collection is also the prolog to Le Guin's first
novel, *Rocannon's World.*[18] It is science fantasy, quite similar to that of
Andre Norton in tone and topic, but superior in technique. This blend of
magic and science has become a clearly defined subgenre of science fiction.
Among its distinctive elements are the juxtaposition of interstellar technology with tribal or feudal cultures (usually a matter of parallel development
or a lost colony); a reemergence of the magic arts, which are viewed by the
technological culture as parapsychological phenomena; a hero, usually a

stranger to the magic world, who undertakes to defend it from the encroachment of his own society; and a victory brought about by the hero's immersion in the rituals and mental disciplines of his adopted world. Although this story type has roots going back at least as far as Burroughs, it really differentiated itself from other science fiction in the early 1960s, as part of the romantic, primitivistic movement of that decade. Norton was one of the first to write science fantasy of this sort, and the best of her followers include Anne McCaffrey, Roger Zelazny, Marion Zimmer Bradley, and the early Le Guin.

Rocannon's World is, as I said, typical science fantasy, though with a more elegant style and sharper characterization than most. On the science side, it gives us space ships, galactic warfare, and a hero who is an ethnologist working for the League of All Worlds. On the fantasy side, it offers elves, dwarfs, winged tigers, wizardlike Ancient Ones, prophecies, curses, and perhaps an amulet. The real interest in the story is in watching representatives of each side attempt to understand the other and explain it in their own terms. In the prolog story, "Semley's Necklace," a woman of the feudal world travels by space ship to recover a family heirloom. Upon returning, she discovers that sixteen years have passed in what was, to her, a single night. Was it an evil spell brought on by her ambition or was it relativity? The answer is, seemingly, both. In the novel proper the scientist, Rocannon, becomes identified with a mythic figure called the Wanderer. Which is he? Again, both. The story will not let us reject either explanation.

Another term for science fantasy might be speculative romance. Like the earlier romances of Hawthorne and Poe, these are double stories, showing us one sober face and one fantastic one. They are built upon ambiguities that cannot be resolved. Instead of Gothic conventions and New England legends, they use the future as a gateway to the marvelous. In Le Guin's hands, speculative romance becomes as apt a tool for psychological probing as the older kind, and as appropriate a stage for dramatizing moral dilemma. After *Rocannon's World*, Le Guin went on to refine her sort of romance. *Planet of Exile* (1966), *City of Illusions* (1967), and above all *The Left Hand of Darkness* (1969) show a steady progress in her mastery of the form: the stories grow tighter, the issues more thought provoking, and the symbols at once more coherent and more elusive. The last book won the top honors in science fiction: the Hugo Award and the Nebula Award.

Again, it grew out of a short story. "Winter's King," also found in *The Wind's Twelve Quarters*, is a solid piece of what Robert Scholes calls structural fabulation.[19] It takes certain aspects of present-day life, extrapolates from them, and gives us a memorable system of characters and events through which we may grasp the significance of this altered reality to our own lives. In not very many pages, Le Guin creates a vivid impression of the planet Winter: cold, as its name tells us, but in some ways warm, for among the snow and ice we see solid, thick-walled buildings, large open fireplaces, furs, rich colors, and also passionate intrigues, loyalties, hopes. The story makes us aware of the impersonal interactions that go with our hotter climate, but, lest we judge too hastily, we discover that the passions of Winter have generated a tragedy that is averted only through the intervention of a cooler, blander society. The story's structural ambiguity is reinforced by a moral one, and both push the reader toward a more complex understanding of the events.

Many science fiction writers throw out worlds with abandon. One bold conception is excuse for a story, and a hasty narrative is enough of a hook to hang the idea on. Le Guin, on the other hand, seems reluctant to let a world go, once she has discovered it in her mind. "Semley's Necklace" intrigued her enough to do more exploration of Rocannon's World; a pair of brief tales, as we will see, led to three novels of the fantasy world Earthsea; and "Winter's King," though it completed the King's story, was only the first cursory mapping of the planet Winter, or Gethen. Looking more carefully at the world she had postulated, Le Guin found for it a natural history, a social order, two political systems, two corresponding religions, a body of myth and legend, and a fact which seems most notable of all to many readers—the people of Winter are all of the same sex, combining characteristics of male and female. And all of those things, from anatomy to mythology, are related. And, even more wondrously, all of this "background information" refuses to stay in the background: it shapes and is reshaped by the story at hand.

One senses that the full story could not be told without breaking, as Le Guin does, periodically into passages of history, anthropology, and, most importantly, myth. Those passages are as integral as conversations between characters, because the story is designed to make us feel the weight of certain truths. The truths Le Guin is interested in are like those of history or anthropology: not so much answers as questions that provoke and illuminate. They are even more like the truths of myth, that cannot be plucked out of their narrative setting but exist only in its movement. By showing us the myths of Winter, Le Guin shows us that her story, too, operates as myth. Once she has established a connection between event and myth, she is free to take up, along with novelistic subjects like character, emotion, and society, another kind of concern: one might say, for instance, that the whole book is about shadow, not as an image or a metaphor but as a category of existence. Shadows run through the book: physical shadows, as in the climatic journey across the ice fields, when the two principal

characters are disoriented by the lack of shadow; cultural shadows—
shifgrethor, meaning shadow, is the basis of Gethenian society; and spiritual shadows, like the darkness that surrounds the religious act of
"foretelling." We begin to understand that these are all one thing. Shadow
pervades the world. It is not death, or mystery, or night, though it may
resemble them at times. In the Gethenian song from which the book takes
its title, "Light is the left hand of darkness/ and darkness the right hand of
light."[20] Light and shadow move through the book like a pair of brother
gods, opposite but alike. That is one of the truths on which the story stands.

It is one thing to develop a sustained system of imagery throughout a
novel and let it suggest interpretations of the action, which is what Fitzgerald does so masterfully in *The Great Gatsby* and what Le Guin turned to
in her next major science fiction novel after *The Left Hand*. That technique
is one way of breaking the narrow bounds of naturalistic narrative, but it
can be dangerous if the imagery and story move in different directions, as
Samuel Delaney suggests happens in Le Guin's *The Dispossessed*.[21] Even
at its best the relationship between narrative and imagery is somewhat
arbitrary, and at worst one begins to feel preached at or imposed upon—
are all those symbolic walls or crosses or sunsets, one asks, really germane
to the story?

It is a very different thing to have the story itself grow out of a set of
images, not chosen arbitrarily but dictated by a recognizable myth.
Whether the myth is received or invented along traditional lines, it guaran-
tees that those images cannot be extraneous. When Le Guin tells us the
myth of two incestuous "brothers" of Winter, one of whom commits
suicide and is discovered by his living brother in a shadowless country
beyond the Northern ice, she establishes an analog for the novel as a whole.
All of the light we come across in the story exists in reference to the dead
brother, and all of the shadows echo the pain, courage, and love of the
living. Other embedded tales approach the relationship of light and dark in
other ways and give us other analogs. It is the resulting interplay of event
and symbol, wherein every detail is tied to a dozen different, but related,
mythic dramas, that gives *The Left Hand of Darkness* such compelling
density. The admirable *Dispossessed* seems arid to me in comparison; its
statements of meaning totter unbuttressed over the narrative ground.

Ursula Le Guin's three books of fantasy appeared interspersed with
her science fiction novels. The first, *A Wizard of Earthsea*, came out in
1968, a year before *The Left Hand of Darkness*. The second, *The Tombs of
Atuan*, was published in 1971, and the third, *The Farthest Shore*, in 1972,
preceding *The Dispossessed* by two years. It is not surprising, then, that her
fantasies share the same concerns as her science fiction novels and roman-

ces. Light and shadow, names, balance, communication across barriers: those are everpresent themes in Le Guin's fiction. But her approaches to the themes vary considerably. Her most striking works, *The Left Hand of Darkness, The Dispossessed*, and *The Farthest Shore* form a sort of triangle. At the apex is *The Left Hand*: it is the fullest treatment because it is both magical and real. To the left side of it is *The Dispossessed*, a detailed chronicle of realistic events, with a large cast of characters and a setting even more closely observed than that of *The Left Hand*. To the right of the apex is *The Farthest Shore*, a fantasy. It has few characters, and two of those take up nearly all of the book. It has a social setting, but the setting is abstract in comparison with her others, and much of the action transpires at sea, with no backdrop at all except water, sky, and a boat. *The Left Hand of Darkness* combines (future) history and myth, but the other two are respectively all history and all myth, or as close to those extremes as a work of fiction may safely come.

Leaving aside the relative standing of *The Farthest Shore* and the other two works, how does it rate as fantasy? In judging a work akin to myth, our major criterion should not be density of construction or wealth of detail, but the clarity and consistency with which it evokes our sense of the numinous, a sense compounded of equal parts of wonder and significance. Any work that aspires to mythicality should be outside our general frame of reference and yet have a profound effect on our perception of the world we know. And that is what I have been saying all along that a good fantasy should do. Fantasy is not myth, which is generally held to be ancient, anonymous, and traditional, but it is one of the many endeavors we have undertaken to continue the process of mythmaking into a literate, individualistic age—others are visionary poetry and some kinds of popular fiction—and the closest to the original in its narrative form.

In *The Wind's Twelve Quarters* Le Guin included two short stories which took place in a world, as yet unnamed, of islands, dragons, and wizardry. Using some of the techniques of science fiction world building and others learned from Tolkien, she showed us a few scenes, conjured up a few sensations, that suggested an entire Other World. Like Rocannon's World or Winter, this world is assigned a geography and a terrain, representative flora and fauna, and a pattern of human communities: all things a good science fiction writer knows he must portray quickly and sharply or his readers will get lost. Unlike a science fiction world, this world is not located in time or space—not Alpha Centauri VI, A. D. 6625. It is, like Middle Earth, a part of that universe called in fairy tales Once-upon-a-time. Our first indication that we are in the realm of fantasy is the presence of certain familiar, impossible beings. Tolkien demonstrated how a writer can select from the varied and confusing motifs of supernatural lore a few compatible traits and build from them a character like its folk ancestors but better defined and more amenable to manipulation through a sustained narrative. Tolkien's elves are as different from those of folk narrative as hybrid corn from maize, and as recognizably related. They let us know, first of all, that we are in a magical Other World, and, second, that it is not quite the same Other World as any we have heard of before. One might say they are archetypes, but in new dress.

Le Guin chooses to develop her own strains of wizard and dragon in "The Word of Unbinding" and "The Rule of Names." The former story also includes a troll, but that was, as Le Guin recognized, a mistake. The fewer the borrowings, the easier it is to convince the reader that they belong in the story, and besides, there is no sense competing with Tolkien, who has already given us wizards, trolls, dragons, dwarves, elves, bear-men, plant-men, half-men, and all the rest of his fabulous bestiary. Whatever he, or any fantasist, has already used successfully must be entirely reenvisioned. We must learn something new about wizards and dragons—which we do in Le Guin's stories—or the integrity of the fantasy world is breached and our attention called back to the stronger portrayal. There are no trolls in the final portrayal of Earthsea.

We know from its inhabitants, then, that Earthsea is a fantasy world. We also learn from the first two stories that it is composed of mountains, villages, forests of oak and alder, and a sea that cuts the world into a great archipelago of small to middle-sized islands: like Melville's Mardi, it is a world in fragments. That is about all the information we get, and it is enough for the two stories. Le Guin admits that in "The Word of Unbinding" she did not pay much attention to setting and that "The Rule of Names" was written for fun, so that Earthsea remains in both stories a vaguer place than does the planet Winter, even in its first appearance.[22] There is an experimental quality about both stories, an indication that an accomplished writer is moving into a new field and is keeping things as simple as possible to allow her to concentrate on the unfamiliar aspects of that field.

In this case, the unfamiliar is magic, which cannot be treated in the same way as science or pseudoscience. And we learn much more in these two stories about the workings of Earthsea's magic than we do about its appearance. It is based, first of all, on words and names. The two titles tell us that. Lest we forget it, they are put into capitals in "The Word of Unbinding"—the wizard Festin speaks Words and Names—and in "The Rule of Names" we are given a rather contrived lesson on names and their properties by a group of school children. The rules are, first, that everything has a secret name which expresses its essence, and, second, that knowledge of the name gives power over the thing. These rules continue to be the fundamental principles of magic in Earthsea, but in the three longer stories they are presented with more assurance and less fuss. Wizards, who have knowledge of true names and power to speak them effectively, can create illusions, summon faraway things, and transform themselves or anything else they choose. The true names of things, we learn in *A Wizard of Earthsea*, make up a language, which is the native tongue of dragons and the source of their wisdom, as it is the source of wizards' power. So the principles of magic, once Le Guin has established them, also help her define her magical beings and set them off from similar creations.

The fact that names are the vehicles of magic in Earthsea tells us two things. First, Le Guin is taking her concept of magic from a different source than Tolkien's. She has gone right past courtly romance and peasant lore to the universal beliefs of tribal societies. Hers is the magic of ritual name-bestowal, and singing to the hunted animal, and In the beginning was the Word. Her wizards are shamans, witch doctors. Like Claude Lévi-Strauss, she revives the ancient, magical view of the universe, the so-called savage mind, as an interesting alternative to our mechanistic, scientific view of the cosmos.[23] Second, since the essence of magic is language, her fantasy promises to offer a commentary on language and its artifact, literature. "The trilogy is, in one aspect, about the artist. The artist as magician. The Trickster. Prospero." So says Le Guin in her article on the writing of the Earthsea stories, entitled "Dreams Must Explain Themselves."[24] Her wizards are poets as well as shamans.

In "The Word of Unbinding" and "The Rule of Names," the world of Earthsea is only half finished. In the first book of the trilogy, *A Wizard of Earthsea*, its contours are filled out: shape and scale and features are fixed, though the symbolic range is not yet fully exploited. It has a map, not a geometric design like Baum's map of Oz but a detailed, believable map. It has a past. The story of Earthsea's past begins with its creation and continues with the acts of kings and wizards, expressed poetically in the songs that the people of Earthsea sing to remind themselves of their heritage and to guide their actions in the present. Some of the events in the trilogy itself, it says at the beginning, have entered the body of Earthsean lore as an epic, the *Deed of Ged*.

Earthsea has a society, too. The form of its society is determined largely by geography, by history, and by the existence of magic. The most evident determiner of Earthsea's culture is the sea that gives it its name. A world of islands must be fundamentally different from a world of solid land. Each community is, of necessity, isolated: to say that is just to reapply the metaphor to its root. Each is, therefore, stable, homogeneous, and self-absorbed. Very few of the islands are large enough to support cities or armies, so politics is an undeveloped art. Most people do not even think of themselves as belonging to nations. Those who travel will refer to themselves as residents of this or that island, or even by region: the East Reach, the Ninety Isles, or the central Archipelago, but their allegiance extends no further than the borders of their home villages. Villages are organized in a sort of tribal democracy. Larger towns seem to be aligned by craft or trade, with officials like Harbormaster or chief Dyer. A few of the largest islands have princes, and the Kargad Lands, far to the Northeast, have been consolidated into a Viking-like empire.

Running counter to the divisive influence of geography is a common heritage. Most of Earthsea speaks a single tongue, derived ultimately from the true, dragonish speech. Tales and legends pass freely from island to island, and the oldest are found from one end of the world to the other. Except in the Kargad Empire, where a savage religion has sprung up in support of the warrior culture, a consistent body of ritual links the farthest-flung peoples of the Reaches with those of the central isles. Chief among rituals is the Long Dance, which celebrates the summer solstice and recapitulates the story of the Creation of Éa and the raising of the islands above the sea. Associated with the common body of rite and song is the tradition of a single, appointed king who rules over all of Earthsea, making each island but a fragment of one great realm. At the time of *A Wizard of Earthsea*, there is no king. The idea of kinghood becomes more important in the later books, where it takes on its usual fairy tale association with the reaching of maturity.

The presence of magic makes a great deal of difference to the lives of Earthsea's people. They are faced every day with miracles and thus are made ever aware of the existence of natural forces and processes. If the wind blows at random, then there is nothing to be done about it, but if the wind can be turned to someone's will, then it becomes a bestowable boon or threat, and it behooves one to learn its operations and effects. More importantly, once one has the power to alter the world's wind, it becomes an act of will to let it go its own way. One must decide either to disturb the natural order or to be responsible for maintaining it. This is true not only of wizards, who have the power to impose their individual will upon the earth, but also of the rest of humanity, who have a collective influence perhaps greater than that of the wizards' specific talents. Most of Earthsea, guided by the inherited wisdom of legend and song, chooses to abide by the natural scheme and even to contribute to its essential balance and plenty by participating in rituals that reflect the cycles of nature—and we see clearly through Le Guin's descriptions how very rich and harmonious is life in Earthsea.

Again, as with the properties of names, we are back in the ancient, "primitive" view of the world from which our ideas of magic ultimately descend. Le Guin shows it to be a more complex and tenable philosophy than most early anthropologists, like Frazer or Malinowski, painted it.[25] At least in Earthsea, magic has more to do with taking part in the natural equilibrium than with wish fulfillment or mistaken science.

Magic, then, is responsible for the rituals of Earthsea. Religion, as such, does not enter in. There are no gods, except in the Kargish Empire, nor is there considered to be any order or plan beyond that evident in the natural world. There is no church or body of sanctioned scripture. There is believed to be wisdom in the old stories, but only such wisdom as can be tested by experience. Instead of priests there are wizards, and instead of a church, a school of wizardry. Wizards heal sickness and bless crops, as priests do in many cultures, but they rely on talent and technique rather than on divine favor. They gather together like monks on the Isle of Roke, but the purpose of their withdrawal is to develop skills and exchange knowledge, like a colony of artists and scientists. Out in the world, they are honored as professionals, but not necessarily revered as spiritual leaders. They have their way of approaching the mysteries of the earth, involving words and names, but other crafts have their own ways, equally valid.

One more thing Earthsea has, from the very first story. That is an underside, a darker half. A world of death lies parallel to the living world, and wizards, by virtue of their special gifts, can cross over to it at will and return, though, we are given to understand, it is a perilous venture and requires considerable strength of will. The imagery that portrays the world of death is particularly striking and disturbing. It is faintly reminiscent of the land beyond the blizzard in the Gethenian myth in *The Left Hand of Darkness*, but, whereas that was a place without shadow, this is a land without water. Ashes and cinders lie underfoot, unknown stars burn perpetually overhead, dry water courses cut the valley floors, and the dead walk unweeping through their silent towns. The atmosphere is eerie, but curiously tranquil. It is a place of resignation, of the peace that means an end to change.

This imagery comes from several sources. It suggests tombs in the deserts of Egypt, Ezekiel's Valley of Dry Bones, and the cave of Hades in the *Odyssey*. The ashes suggest the words of the Christian burial service, though there is no Christian resurrection there. The stars imply a transcendent order beyond life and death, but not necessarily one concerned with mankind. This dry landscape of death is reminiscent of the waste land portrayed in T. S. Eliot's poem of that name, and even more of his "The Hollow Men":

This is the dead land
This is cactus land
Here the stone images
Are raised, here they receive
The supplication of a dead man's hand
Under the twinkle of a fading star.[26]

There are almost certainly archetypal underpinnings for this vision of death. In "The Word of Unbinding," and *A Wizard of Earthsea*, Le Guin does not do much more than touch on the archetype: at some point in each tale she has need of a concrete sign for the idea of death, and death-as-country is more appropriate than death-as-person or death-as-weapon or any of the rest of our stock of symbols. In *The Farthest Shore*, however, the archetypal image is expanded and explored until it becomes almost as solid as the living side of Earthsea. At that point, Earthsea has grown into full maturity as a vehicle of artistic expression, as we will see.

What are the sources for the rest of Earthsea? Is there an actual model for the island world or any of its parts? Of course there is, but the models are so many and so well mixed that it is difficult to point them out. Physically, Earthsea most resembles the island groups between Asia and Australia, where, probably not by coincidence, some of the anthropological research that resulted in our present understanding of magic and myth was conducted. These islands show the same diversity within a common cultural framework as Earthsea, and the scale is similar. In climate, Earthsea more nearly resembles Europe or North America. Most of it is temperate, but the North is cold and the South nearly tropical. The animals and plants that cover the islands are a mixture of American and imaginary. Familiar American plants include alder, yarrow, rowan, apple, oak, and sage. We learn of them not only from description, but also from character names, which are taken from natural objects. Among these familiar terms we find invented ones—hurbah-trees, fourfoil, pendick, sparkweed, and corly—and it is difficult at times to remember which is which. One plant, kingsfoil, is included as a subtle tribute to Tolkien, who invented it. With animals it is much the same: cattle and goats graze the hillsides, and dragons prey upon them. The hero, Ged, makes a pet of an otak, a lemurlike wild creature.

The one spot in Earthsea we get to know best is the island of Atuan, the locale of nearly all of the second volume of the trilogy, *The Tombs of Atuan*. And Atuan, of all the islands, has the clearest referent in our world. It is Oregon, Le Guin's home state. The East is desert, not sand but scrub. On its broad plateaus grow sagebrush, bunch grasses, scrub junipers, and a few irrigated crops. Westward lie tawny mountains, then a dividing range,

then a strip of lush greenery, and finally the sea. Amid these vivid borrowings from life are things that set Atuan apart as an imaginary landscape:
gold-leafed temples, ancient monoliths, black-robed priestesses. In effect,
Le Guin has taken a part of our known environment and shown how wild
and exotic a beauty it possesses. It is a perfect example of fantasy's capacity
for estranging the familiar. Both strangeness and familiarity are evident in
this quietly convincing description:

> They sat by a tiny fire of sage on the hearth in the room behind the Godking's
> temple, Kossil's room. Outside the doorway, in the hall, Manan and Duby
> played a game with sticks and counters, tossing a bundle of sticks and
> catching as many as possible on the back of the hand. Manan and Arha still
> sometimes played that game, in secret, in the inner courtyard of the Small
> House. The rattle of dropped sticks, the husky mumbles of triumph and
> defeat, the small crackle of the fire, were the only sounds when the three
> priestesses fell silent. All around beyond the walls reached the profound
> silence of the desert night. From time to time came the patter of a sparse, hard
> shower of rain.[27]

The people of Earthsea vary according to the region they inhabit.
Those of the Kargad Lands are pale and fair haired, like the Vikings they
resemble. People in the East Reach are very dark skinned. Ged and most of
the people of the Archipelago are coppery brown, with black hair. Like the
Martians of Bradbury and Burroughs, they resemble American Indians. It
is often suggested that the Little People of Britain are a dim memory of
those who originally held the land, before the invasions of Celt, Roman,
and Saxon. American authors seem to be similarly mythologizing Indians,
portraying them as magical peoples allied with the forces of the earth.

The material culture of Earthsea is more medieval than anything else.
Costume is much like that in a story by Howard Pyle. Musical instruments
include lutes, pipes, flutes, and drums. Technology is minimal. There are
no power sources except wind, animals, and man. A higher grade of
technology is difficult to reconcile with fantasy, partly because the magical
folktale comes from a time before great machinery and partly because
technology overlaps magic in many of its operations: long-distance communication, rapid travel, illumination.

One danger in fantasy is that this necessary return to a premodern era
may become a sentimental retreat. Le Guin avoids this danger, as Tolkien
did, by giving the people in her fantasy problems which are appropriate to
their situation and also in some way analogous to our own troubles. All of
the turmoil brought about by England's industrial revolution is expressed
in the ravaging of the Shire, but on a hobbitish scale and within the limits of
Middle Earth industry. And it is impossible to read of the One Ring of
Sauron without being reminded obliquely of atomic instruments of de-

struction and intimidation. Likewise, magic in Earthsea invites comparison with American technological wizardry. Here the emphasis is not on physical damage caused by weapons and machinery but on the psychic cost of seemingly effortless meddling with the world. Without sacrificing fantasy's timelessness to a too obvious topicality, Le Guin lets her own concerns direct the unfolding of the imaginary world, making it another story of "modern heroism."

The kind of heroism Le Guin has in mind is the courage to understand and accept the universe. Each story of the trilogy takes a different approach to the basic problem, which becomes in each restatement more profound and more demanding.

A Wizard of Earthsea is the story of a sorcerer's apprentice. The motif of the rash young assistant who undertakes one of his master's spells and is overwhelmed by the force he has summoned is so obviously a good analog for modern technological man that it might seem almost a cliché. [28] But the story of this apprentice is never in danger of falling into cliché because its author lets nothing merely follow expectation, nor pass by without examination of its causes and implications. Ged, or Sparrowhawk, as he is usually called, since his true name is secret, is not simply the lazy assistant who can be rescued from his foolish conjuring by the returning master. Ged is a natural magic-worker of great power and greater pride. Son of an ordinary blacksmith on an island of goatherds, he wishes to prove himself to the other students at the wizards' school on Roke, and he wishes to make his mark on the world. The spell which proves his undoing is the same as Faust's temptation: he summons from death the spirit of a legendary beautiful woman. In doing so, he unintentionally releases into the world an evil, formless, nameless shadow. Being nameless, this shadow is beyond the control of even the Archmage of Roke, chief of all wizards in Earthsea. Unlike the Sorcerer of legend, the Archmage is unable to undo Ged's spell. He barely saves Ged's life, at the cost of his own. Ged is left, less than halfway through the book, masterless, disgraced, and in mortal danger from the thing he has summoned.

At this point Ged's story departs from the legend motif of "The Sorcerer's Apprentice" and begins to follow a direction more in line with Propp's morphology of the Russian fairy tale. Actually, the fairy tale aspects begin earlier, before Ged leaves his home isle of Gont to go to the school of wizardry. We can see the following correspondences with Propp's functions: first, there is the scene in which the wise, older protector leaves home and the young protagonist violates an interdiction in his absence, usually at the urging of a villain. In this case the young Ged is in the home of his first teacher Ogion. While out gathering herbs, Ged meets a girl his own age, daughter of a minor lord and a witch from a Northern island, and she goads him about his lack of power. Returning home he finds Ogion still out, so he makes bold to open his master's lore books and comes across the summoning spell that is later to be his undoing. We can see that the "Sorcerer's Apprentice" story is more or less an expansion of this segment of the full fairy tale morphology, but with slightly different emphases and without the optional tempter.[29] Ged's experience at the wizard school is a repetition or doubling of this initial movement, but with higher stakes, because Ged is older and more powerful and there is no master to return in time. This time the spell is recited and the damage done. And so we move into a new movement of the fairy tale.

The shadow of evil that Ged has called into the world becomes equivalent to the misfortune or lack faced by the fairy tale hero, who must, as Ged does, go on a quest to solve it. Ged is dispatched by the remaining Wardens of the school on Roke to seek out and confront the shadow. He travels to the part of the Archipelago called the Ninety Isles to be a village wizard. He does not stay there long, however, but sails westward to challenge the family of dragons who are menacing the Isles. Here his story begins to correspond with the fairy tale hero's meeting with the figure called a donor. This movement begins with the hero's testing by the donor, which can take, as one of many possible forms, that of combat with a hostile creature. Ged easily destroys several young dragons and holds his own against the old one, who offers him a bargain. The dragon offers to tell Ged the name of his shadow, but Ged has come to do a service for the islanders, and so he chooses instead to bind the dragon with an oath never to fly east of its ruined isle.

Now, a donor need not be in sympathy with the fairy tale hero. His testing can be malevolent and his gift unwillingly bestowed. So it is here. The dragon tests Ged physically and morally and proves Ged's power and honor. Ged seems to have gained nothing for himself, but he has actually received the magic gift needed to complete his quest. He now knows that the shadow, though it comes from a region of darkness and namelessness, has a name. All he has to do is figure out where it acquired a name, and he can overcome it. The dragon's unintentional tip is later reinforced by advice from Ged's old teacher, Ogion.

In a fairy tale, the final movement involves meeting and defeating the villain in direct combat. The closest thing to a villain we have seen so far in Ged's tale is the girl who tempted him to read the perilous spell. Now we meet that girl again: she is the wife of a lord on the barbaric island of Osskil, where Ged is lured by hints and omens. Osskil seems to be the appointed place of conflict with whatever agent has caused Ged's misfortunes. If this were truly a fairy tale, the witch girl would be the heroine, acting against her will upon the orders of her husband, the evil magician. Ged would overcome the magician and steal away the secret of his power, which turns out to be an ancient talisman called the Stone of Terrenon. He would escape with stone and girl, the villain would chase them unsuccessfully, and, with the stone's power, Ged would establish his kingdom.

Le Guin lets her story draw tantalizingly close to the expected pattern. The girl approaches Ged seductively and explains to him about the stone. She says it holds the secret of Ged's shadow and will help him defeat it. Her husband discovers her disloyalty and calls forth evil creatures to attack her and Ged. They change themselves into birds and flee.

But Ged has refused to draw on the power of the stone. It is a malignant thing that would turn him into a slave. The girl herself is cruel: she kills pursuing servants with a spell that runs hot lead in their bones. The magician really has nothing to do with Ged and his shadow, but is only serving the will of the stone. When Ged and the girl turn into birds, she is caught and killed, and he escapes but nearly loses his identity by remaining too long in bird form. The entire movement has been nothing more than a snare and a distraction from Ged's true quest. His problem cannot be solved within the framework of a fairy tale, any more than it was fully encompassed by the motif of the Sorcerer's Apprentice. Both parallels were apt, up to a point, because Ged's story is, first, about the uses and misuses of power, and, second, about coming of age. But Ged must find his own way to achieve power and maturity, and cannot rely, nor can the reader rely, on the comfortable certainties of traditional tale types.

In the end, Ged faces his true adversary, his shadow, and names it with his own name. He and the shadow merge. Its evil is not destroyed, but it is defused by becoming part of a greater whole that is neither all good nor all evil. Ged becomes a mature and moral individual by accepting the darkness that is a part of himself—accepting it without giving in to it. At the conclusion of the book we have moved away from folktale and into the same realm of symbolism that we saw in *The Left Hand of Darkness*. All of the other movements and conflicts were false steps, or rather object lessons that told Ged where to look for a solution by showing him where solution was not.

The other books of Earthsea do not wander into such byways of action and adventure but instead proceed directly according to the dictates of the symbolic content. On the most fundamental level, *The Tombs of Atuan* is a story of rescue, and *The Farthest Shore* a quest tale. In the former Ged makes his way to the Kargish Empire to recover a lost bracelet on which are inscribed runes of wisdom. He is first imprisoned by, and then aided by the young priestess Arha, from whose point of view the story is told. It turns out that Arha is the one truly imprisoned in a sterile existence. She does not even have a name: *Arha* means "the eaten one," the one whose life and identity are consumed by the "gods." Ged gives her back her name, Tenar. It is part of his power to be able to perceive the names of things. Together Ged and Tenar flee from the labyrinth under the temple of the Nameless Ones, who are akin to the spirit within the Stone of Terrenon: ancient evils who should never have been worshipped as gods.

The Farthest Shore begins with rumors that magic is failing in Earthsea. Ged and a young prince, Arren, set out to find out why. They go to the ends of the earth and beyond, into a realm of death, in search of the man who has upset the order of things. They find him, a renegade wizard who has defied the laws of life and death. This wizard has given up his true name in hope of living forever and has opened up a breach between the worlds of life and death. With a combination of their strengths, Ged and Arren defeat him and undo the spell that was draining magic and joy from Earthsea. Ged retires to the island of his birth and Arren becomes King, having fulfilled an obscure prophecy left by the last ruler of Earthsea.

These are simpler stories than *A Wizard of Earthsea*. They offer much less in the way of conventional plot. But they are stronger stories. They are based on the clash and resolution of qualities we think of as irreconcilable. *The Tombs* builds an overwhelming impression of isolation, darkness, perversity, all experienced directly by the priestess Arha as she learns her duties in service to the Nameless Ones. Isolation is expressed in the setting and in the lives of the priestesses. Darkness is in the looming monoliths that are the tombs of the title, in the dull black robes Arha wears, and in the maze of tunnels and caverns where the Nameless Ones rule as palpable presences. Perversity shows in the atheist priestess Kossil, in the wasting of young lives like Tenar's, in the neutering of temple slaves, and in the dedication of Kargish religion to age, fear, and death. Symbolic of all this wrongness is the Hall of the Throne, where Tenar's name is taken from her. Le Guin's description is patently a judgment, as description can rightfully be in a fantasy, though in an ostensibly naturalistic work one would feel called upon to object to such "loading" of meaning on a physical object:

> The throne on its high platform seemed to be curtained on each side with great webs of blackness dropping from the gloom of the roof; whether these were curtains, or only denser shadows, the eye could not make certain. The throne itself was black, with a dull glimmer of precious stones or gold on the arms and back, and it was huge. A man sitting in it would have been dwarfed; it was not of human dimensions. It was empty. Nothing sat in it but shadows. (p. 6)

Ged comes into the scene with a burst of light and life. He illuminates the heart of the darkness, the Undertomb, and shows it to be a marvel of crystal and filigree. To Tenar he brings, along with her name, an end to her long isolation. One might miss signs of the growing love between Ged and Tenar, but the symbolism in the joining of the two halves of the broken Ring of Erreth-Akbe, one half carried by Ged, the other locked away in Tenar's treasure chamber, is unmistakable. With Ged's help, Tenar renounces her authority over darkness and death and accepts light and a new birth.

The fundamental symbol of *The Farthest Shore* is the dead land. It is dry and dark and fearsome, but, unlike the tombs and tunnels of Atuan, it does not represent evil. The evil, says Le Guin, lies in our choosing darkness over light, or, for that matter, light over darkness, out of selfishness. One man in all of Earthsea refuses to die; he gives up his name and thus his identity to do so. By that one man's act a whole world is troubled. Others begin to desire eternal life. The first man, who is a man of power, appears to them in dreams and rumors promising an escape from death, and they give up power, love, responsibility, and dignity to follow him.

Symbolism has a logic. If there is a dry land there must be fountains somewhere else. If there is a traitor there must be a hero. If there is disorder there must be an underlying pattern. And these are not just simple polarities. The antithesis of every ill must also be its cure, and in order for that to be so the two terms must relate to one another not only as opposites but also as imperfect and perfect versions of the same thing. Tolkien understood this logic when he made orcs perverted elves and ringwraiths men with their substance eaten away by desire. Christian myth follows it by making Satan a fallen angel, and Christ an unfallen Adam. Bradbury made use of it in formulating his symbolic stories of night and day: the twisted amusements of the dark carnival undone by honest laughter. Le Guin lets the logic of symbol dictate virtually all the action in *The Farthest Shore*, and lets richness of symbolic association compensate for the essential simplicity of that action.

Here are just some of the paired images running through *The Farthest Shore*. The magician who has defied death is nicknamed Cob, a dialect word for spider. He weaves shadows and hides at their center waiting for prey. He causes knowledge and power to run "by little strings like spiderwebs" out of the eyes and mouths of those who listen to him.[30] But Ged, too, is a weaver, a maker of patterns. His web is his art, like that of the tiny spider he watches early in the story: "between two tall grass blades in the clearing a spider had spun a web, a circle delicately suspended. The silver threads caught the sunlight" (p. 14).

Cob calls himself Lord, and then King. He covets power and honor. Those who wish to follow him must pay homage. But it is Arren who fulfills the prophecy and becomes King of Earthsea, by acclaim rather than by coercion and out of duty instead of lust for power.

Cob is blind. When Ged and Arren finally stand before him at the dry river, they see that his eyes are empty sockets. Ged, though, is one who sees more clearly and more deeply than most. His eyes are "bright and fierce" like those of the sparrowhawk he is nicknamed for (p. 4). The boat in which he and Arren set sail on their quest is called the Lookfar.

Cob scorns natural things. He stands alone, not wishing to communicate with any other creature, like an Orpheus in reverse. In his presence even the wise and formidable dragons lose the gift of speech. But Ged has struggled to learn the tongue of dragons: it is the basis of his art. Throughout the book he is always pausing to contemplate the look of a tree, the feel of a rock, the taste of water. All things speak to him.

When Cob undoes death, he opens a gap between life and death. This gap is visible in the twilit world as a black hole in a rock wall at the head of a dry riverbed. Even in the dry land, we are told, one can feel a greater dryness flowing out of the hole. The imagery associated with it is harsher even than that used for the empty throne in Atuan: "that dry, dark springhead, the mouth of dust, the place where a dead soul, crawling into earth and darkness, was born again dead. . . . Through it was neither light nor dark, neither life nor death. It was nothing. It was a way that led nowhere" (p. 207).

But there are other springs in Earthsea that represent rightness as the dry spring represents wrongness. The first image in the book shows which way the flow should go, from shadow into light, from self-renunciation and death into life in a continually renewed circle: "In the Court of the Fountain the sun of March shone through young leaves of ash and elm, and water leapt and fell through shadow and clear light" (p. 3). If we have not made the symbolic association—and it is not at all obvious at that point—it is reinforced and expanded in the vision of the Fountains of Shelieth, as recounted by one of the Masters of Roke:

> The pools and basins and the waterfalls, the silver-curtained dripping caves where ferns grow in banks of moss, the rippled sands, the leaping up of the waters and the running of them, the outwelling of deep springs from earth, the mystery and sweetness of the source, the spring. . . . (p. 160)

These waters, which represent a cluster of ideas that we might more scientifically term entropy, reproduction, natural cycling, or continuous creation, are threatened by Cob's fountain of dryness. When it begins to flow, they begin to ebb. The balance is restored only when Ged and Arren make the decision that the world's life outweighs the inevitability of their own deaths.

These paired, opposing, ultimately reconciled images closely resemble the intense paradoxes of metaphysical poetry. *The Farthest Shore* is, like many visionary poems, an inward, spiritual journey. It is no accident that many of its images echo those of a poem like Theodore Roethke's "In a Dark Time": from "In a dark time, the eye begins to see, / I meet my shadow in the deepening shade" to "A man goes far to find out what he is—/ Death of the self in a long, tearless night, / All natural shapes blazing unnatural light. /"[31] Using character, setting, and event, rather than meter and metaphor, Le Guin illustrates the same kind of experience that Roethke outlines in his poem. In this last volume, Earthsea becomes a potent inner, as well as a convincing outer, landscape.

The Farthest Shore does not completely abandon the morphology of the folktale. There is an adversary, there are helpers (dragons again, and a madman), and Arren gains a kingdom in the end. Neither did Tolkien abandon the fairy tale structure in his great fantasy, but he, in a sense, reimagined it: each function and each movement is called into play by the demands of his moral drama. In this way he earned his happy ending, as traditional tales never did, or needed to. Le Guin goes further still. She strips the fairy tale pattern to its fundamental upward curve, making it a single compelling movement toward balance, integration, understanding—all of her cardinal virtues.

One way Le Guin earns her harrowing but triumphant ending is by creating a hero who truly represents the values she intends to uphold. In *A Wizard of Earthsea*, Ged is a proud, hot-tempered boy. His stature is human, not heroic, so that he can be our entry into the fantasy world. In *The Tombs of Atuan*, the role of mediator is taken by Tenar, and in her eyes Ged appears dazzling, almost godlike. In *The Farthest Shore*, we again have a mediating observer, the boy Arren, but our view of Ged is considerably more complex. We see Ged at the height of his power and wisdom as Archmage of Roke. The bold virility he showed as a young man in *The Tombs* is toned down, but he retains an unmistakable authority. We also see him as a quiet, sometimes weary, middle-aged man. Arren finds his companion's patience frustrating and puzzles over his failure to display the powers he must possess. But by not acting where it is not necessary to act, Ged makes clear the value of action. The climactic moment when he closes the gaping hole among the rocks becomes more than the struggle of one magician against another, or the undoing of a great mistake, though it is also those things. It is an act profoundly creative and alarmingly brave, as if Ged has just conceived the universe, with all its beauty and terror, and said: Let this exist, at my expense.

Anyone who has read much of Le Guin's fiction recognizes Ged immediately. He is a brother to Genly Ai in *The Left Hand of Darkness*, George Orr in *The Lathe of Heaven*, Shevek in *The Dispossessed*, Odo, Rocannon, Falk, and all the rest of her heroic breed. These characters are

unconquering explorers, anarchists who bring order, imperturbable cata-
lysts of revolution, fallible and creative people enough like us to be likable
and different enough to be admirable. There are not many contemporary
writers who even attempt heroes, though there are villains and victims
aplenty, because of the burden a hero must carry. I said before that fantasy
is most effective when it touches on modern problems. The hero of a
fantasy represents the author's response to those problems, and so his
character is the test of the meaningful order proposed within the imagined
world. The kind of quiet integrity Le Guin has developed in her heroes fits
like a keystone into her pattern of magic and meaning.

What kinds of meanings are expressed in the stories of Earthsea? What
questions are asked—and answered—by Ged's adventures? The questions
are big, familiar ones. Who am I? in the first book. What is evil? in the
second, and, alongside it, What is love? In the third book: What is death,
and What does my life mean in relation to it? These questions are unanswer-
able in that there are so many answers to them that we can accept none as
final or wholly satisfactory. But a work of fiction, especially a work of
fantasy, can posit trial answers and, by eliminating certain of the confusions of actual existence, construct a world in which those answers seem
complete, like a simulation game for philosophy. Then it is the reader's job
to compare the simplified world with the world he knows and judge how
accurately the abstraction represents reality.

The answer to the question, Who am I? is: I am Ged. Speaker,
observer, maker of patterns, unleasher of evil, binder of evil—that is, man,
in Earthsea at any rate. Because both question and answer are couched in
story form they become personal and concrete. It is a matter of life and
death to Ged to know what he is. And because the story is a fantasy we
actually see the elements that make up Ged as they start to grow and
connect with one another. One part is the witch-aunt who mumbles spells
to call goats or influence the weather. Another part is the girl who wants to
know about shape-changing and summoning the dead. Another is the
Zen-like master whose teaching is his own way of life. Another is the wily,
fierce dragon, so much a part of nature that magic is its native tongue. Yet
another is the fragile, graceful sailboat *Lookfar*, with eyes painted on its
prow. And the fountain at Roke. And the small trusting otak on Ged's
shoulder. And the falcon in whose shape he flees from Terrenon. And most
of all the shadow, like a shapeless black beast, that he tames with his own
name.

The answers in Le Guin's fantasy are coherent and cumulative. Once
Ged knows who he is, he is able to explore the world around him and to sort
it out into light, dark, loved, unloved, good, and evil. That is the adventure
in *The Tombs of Atuan*: to accept the whole of existence and yet to align

oneself with the better part of it. Again the issue is concretely symbolized: empty throne, dark labyrinth, prisoners starved to death, on the one hand; rune-covered ring, glowing wizard's staff, Tenar bringing water to unconscious Ged, on the other.

Armed with that knowledge of good and evil, knowing that both are human responses to the natural order, Ged is prepared in *The Farthest Shore* to make his own ultimate response. He pledges himself to maintaining the Balance, which is a metaphysical rendering of a concept more familiar to Americans from science. We know it as ecology—the sense that all things are related in a closed, finite system. It is a concept rather alien to most of Western philosophy: to our linear or progressive idea of history, to our notion of manifest destiny, to our image of an unbounded God, and to our man-centered system of values. The ecological concept has come to us primarily from scientific observation, and thus in a colorless and mechanistic form, but there are other cultural systems to which ecological theory would come as verification of a whole way of looking at and living in the world. Zen Buddhism offers one approach to an ecological viewpoint in its interlocking yin and yang, light and dark. Native American religion, based on circles of time and space, offers another. Primitive magic, which treats the universe as a living, powerful entity, offers a third. In *The Farthest Shore*, those world views are joined with a scientific understanding of natural cycles and interrelationships to produce a new literary myth, or myth–imitation if you prefer. The book is an attempt to express the emotional side of an intellectual truth, and, conversely, to validate a set of old beliefs with the stamp of scientific approval.

Le Guin does not just talk about Balance; she has Ged pledge his life to it. The old myths were not only pictures of the universe, but guides for living as well. Any successful world view must also provide for personal fulfillment. We can see the pleasure Ged takes in understanding the Balance and watching it at work, but at the end of the story, when he shouts the spell that may kill him but will heal the world, he achieves more than satisfaction. It is a moment of absolute commitment, beyond joy or sorrow, a moment of knowing without doubt the worth of his own life.

I have compared Le Guin's waste land to T. S. Eliot's, and her manipulation of symbolic action to that of Theodore Roethke. I might also compare her Americanization of Oriental philosophy to Gary Snyder's Zen-inspired poetry, and her way of drawing strength from the idea of death to Walt Whitman's. It is in poetry that we are used to finding such ideas tested against the immediacies of sensation and emotion. Le Guin's fantasies do, indeed, operate on a level of meaning that almost demands to be called poetic. Without falling into a mannered kind of prose poetry, she matches the orphic, prophetic quality distinctive to much of the best

American poetry. She establishes patterns of metaphor and paradox that lead, of their own accord, to new insights into significant experience. And she is pursuing the same lines of inquiry that occupy most modern American poets.

But fantasy is not poetry, rather an independent road to the same goal of finding timeless truths underlying the confusions of contemporary life. It has the advantage over poetry of being accessible, of taking the reader step by step into its heart of meaning, whereas poetry, especially modern poetry, presents a tight knot of significance that turns many readers away in bafflement. A work of fantasy can be read in conjunction with a difficult poem in such a way that one can assign at least tentative values to the most obscure poetic references. *The Farthest Shore*, for instance, may be read as a gloss on Roethke's "In a Dark Time," and without exhausting the meaning of either work, one's understanding of both is enriched. Le Guin's visualization of the land of death can lend perspective to Eliot's land of hollow men. Her characterization of Ged may reinforce Snyder's evocation of an earth-centered way of life. And she can gloss her own poetry. The epigraph to *A Wizard of Earthsea* is an Earthsean poem, according to the text the oldest poem in Earthsea, called *The Creation of Éa*:

> Only in silence the word,
> only in dark the light,
> only in dying life:
> bright the hawk's flight
> on the empty sky.[32]

All that happens in the three volumes refers to this poem, and, one feels, all the history of Earthsea since creation must also refer to it.

I cannot leave the subject of meaning in Earthsea without mentioning one more piece of poetry so close in theme and imagery that it might have served as epigraph in place of the passage from *The Creation of Éa,* which it resembles as a painting resembles an ink drawing of the same subject. It is the end of Wallace Stevens' "Sunday Morning," and readers of the Earthsea trilogy will recognize the vision it expresses:

> We live in an old chaos of the sun,
> Or old dependency of night and day,
> Or island solitude, unsponsored, free,
> Of that wide water, inescapable.
> Deer walk upon our mountains, and the quail
> Whistle about us their spontaneous cries;
> Sweet berries ripen in the wilderness;
> And, in the isolation of the sky,
> At evening, casual flocks of pigeons make

Ambiguous undulations as they sink,
Downward to darkness, on extended wings.[33]

I cite all this poetry partly in an attempt to place Le Guin's work within an American tradition. American poetry has long ceased to be concerned with its own Americanness, in the way Emerson and Longfellow—and even Joseph Rodman Drake—were concerned with it. The American landscape and way of life have been shaped into poetry so many times and in so many ways that they may be more or less assumed: the poet simply writes from his own experience and the cultural background comes across without effort, even when, as in T. S. Eliot's poems, other traditions are drawn in.

American fantasy, on the other hand, has never been secure enough in its cultural base to be eclectic—until now. The stories of Earthsea depend on Tolkienian technique, Pacific geography, Oriental philosophy, and tribal institutions, but there is no question of their Americanness. Underneath its borrowings and adaptations, the Earthsea trilogy is, as we might expect, another instance of the American archetypal story: the high, lonely wilderness quest of an Ishmael or Leatherstocking. Nor is it surprising that Le Guin includes in her fantasy world no angels or demons, only men, in various guises, and nature. We are still in our literature a land without antecedents or intermediaries.

The whole tradition of the marvelous in this country stands behind the work of Le Guin and other contemporary fantasists, though very little of it may show up in the final product as homage or direct influence. America today is not primarily an oral culture but a literate one; thus the stock of imaginative impossibilities that has built up in our literature is now of more weight in determining our interests and habits of thought than the barrenness of our supernatural oral literature. Washington Irving told one fairy tale that enchanted a tiny section of the Catskills. Hawthorne led us to wonder whether there might not be a magical interpretation of some of the events in our past, and opened up European fairylands to our children. L. Frank Baum told the fundamental wonder tale about America itself, a tale of opportunity that up to his time had been mistaken for sober fact. Baum also showed how to turn an American character into an enchanted being: make him part of the furniture, like a scarecrow or a sawhorse.

Once all those steps had been taken, they could be taken for granted. The next group of writers increased the scope of an already established American Other World or reexamined it with increasing sophistication. Burroughs claimed all the unknown territories on earth and in space for the frustrated businessman. Lovecraft showed that even the most familiar scenes could reveal unsettling secrets. Cabell proved that imaginary countries could harbor real wit, ribaldry, and philosophy. Bradbury showed how important it was to retain a child's sense of wonder—it is what saves us from the despair that plays funeral music at three o'clock in the morning. Edward Eager imposed on magic the child's sense of fair play and fun. Thurber turned words into ideas and ideas into people and places. His resource was the whole English language.

A writer of fantasy today may choose any or all of the techniques pioneered by his predecessors. Le Guin creates few colorful characters à la Baum, but she does much with words made concrete. Sometimes she exploits the strangeness hidden in the familiar, as Lovecraft does, and other times she makes the reader feel at home in the exotic. She treats the marvelous with childlike sobriety and with the critical eye of an adult. She does not try to match Cabell's wit, but she surpasses his philosophy.

A fantasist may make use of any memorable character, scene, or incident from an earlier work, so long as he really understands the borrowed item and has a new use for it in his own story. Baum stole a pumpkin-head from Hawthorne, and Zelazny lifted a Steel General from Baum. It is difficult to find such borrowings in Le Guin because she assimilates them so completely, but there is a flavor of Howard Pyle, a hint of Andre Norton, a touch of Bradbury. Her nameless malevolent forces disguised as gods remind one of Lovecraft or perhaps of his primary source, Lord Dunsany. It does not matter which, because any source once absorbed into the American stream is also fair game. The world of Earthsea may be an echo of *Mardi*, or it may indicate independent rediscovery of a potent metaphor. All of this means that the would-be fantasist has a really sizable pool of materials to choose from. The situation is as different as possible from that of the early nineteenth century, when the first faltering steps toward American fantasy were being taken. And this body of available material functions in another way to ease the path of the contemporary writer. Each item of description, each character, each insight into the nature of magic as a metaphor for human experience provides a model for new creations. If Frank Stockton successfully domesticates an English griffin, then by analogous methods Ursula Le Guin ought to be able to import Chinese dragons. It is still, of course, a matter of understanding every fantastic detail and communicating one's understanding well enough to inspire confident secondary belief in the reader. One must be a good writer with a genuine feeling for the marvelous. But if one meets the entrance requirements, there is a diverse and experienced faculty waiting to point the way toward consistent, rich, and rewarding fantasy in an American vein.

From the standpoint of the author, then, the American fantasy tradition makes possible the creation of fantasy worlds of a high order indeed, as witnessed by the stories of Earthsea. It also counterbalances the valuable but intimidating example of English high fantasy, especially that of Tolkien. Simply to know that there are other ways of dealing with the marvelous helps in avoiding slavish imitation. But what does it mean to the reader and to the critic of American civilization? How do they gain by becoming aware of what is admittedly a divergent current in American literature?

The reader is given a framework in which to set certain problematic works. Cabell, for instance, has always seemed to be a strange literary sport. Historians figuratively shrug their shoulders and say, Well, coming out of the decadent South, after all. . . . But if one can see certain traces of Pyle, certain similarities to Burroughs, then we must see Cabell as a member of a hitherto undescribed breed. The same process established American romance as something more than a rash of quirky novels.

Too, the reader gains a new perspective on all the fields adjoining fantasy, especially romance and science fiction. Both of those genres rely on a fantastic base overlaid with alternative rationalistic interpretations. Both feed into fantasy proper—as in the case of Le Guin, who learned the craft of fantasy by writing science romances—and both are fed by it.

The academically inclined reader might also take pleasure in watching the themes and motifs that typify American fantasy grow and alter from writer to writer. The fragmentary legends, jokes, and songs gathered by our early folklorist–authors gradually expand and link together to form an estimable body of lore, no longer folklore but still in a sense communal, with a flavor distinct enough to absorb batch after batch of imported ingredients. It is like a fruitcake that ends up more fruit than cake, but still takes its character from the cupful of batter with which you began.

For the student of American culture, the fantasy tradition outlines a profound shift in the national outlook. We began as a nation hostile to fantasy for three reasons. First, fantasy is fictional, and our Puritan forebears considered any deviation from sanctioned "truth" to be a wicked deception—unless, of course, they believed the fictions, in which case they became witchcraft, subject to burning. Second, we embraced the Enlightenment as part of our new national identity. An inherited pastime like the fairy tale could hardly hold its own against the initial excitement of scientific and political experiment. Third, and probably most importantly, our attention as a nation is directed primarily toward material things: new scenery, new artifacts, new wealth. We have been slow to acknowledge the effect of these external things on our minds, or to investigate their relationships as symbols.

Unquestionably all three of these objections to fantasy are still current: they would explain the hostility with which many readers view the entire genre, a violent antipathy which precludes recognition of the virtues or flaws of any individual work. But such people no longer hold absolute sway; indeed, among younger readers at least, they seem to be a rather small minority. To the extent that we have accepted the marvelous at last, we have given up the certainties of dogma, reason, and material possession in favor of the shifting, complex truths of symbolic fiction.

This means a certain dimming of the American dream. We turn for consolation, not to America as it is, or even as it might become, but to places that never were. Instead of congratulating ourselves on our gains, we look longingly at values we think we have lost: the simplicity, harmony, and beauty of the archetypal green world that underlies all fairylands. But obviously fantasy is not responsible for our disillusionment, nor is it the only sign. Eliot, Fitzgerald, Hemingway, Faulkner—all the major mainstream writers of this century show equal dissatisfaction with contemporary life. But fantasy, growing out of the fundamentally optimistic fairy tale, represents a uniquely positive response to disaffection. The fantasist responds to destructiveness by building, to disorder by imagining order, and to despair by calling forth wonder.

The American fantasy tradition is important because fantasy is conservative. It holds ancient beliefs and insights safe within a shell of seeming inconsequence. Its roots go back beyond writing and beyond recall, but it also continues to alter as our lives change. American fantasy retells the oldest stories in new and pertinent forms and examines our national experience in a timeless context. The fantasies that are undoubtedly being written today, if they can successfully learn from Le Guin as she learned from Tolkien, without being overwhelmed, will arise from as yet unguessable troublings within American life. And they will convert those irritations—not simply cover them over with coats of pearl but completely reshape them—into meaningful narratives new in insight and richly traditional in form and matter.

Notes

1. LOCATING FANTASY

1. W. R. Irwin, *The Game of the Impossible: A Rhetoric of Fantasy* (Urbana, Ill.: University of Illinois Press, 1976), p. 4.

2. J. R. R. Tolkien, "On Fairy-Stories," in *Tree and Leaf* (Boston: Houghton Mifflin Company, 1965), p. 55.

3. C. S. Lewis, *An Experiment in Criticism* (Cambridge: Cambridge University Press, 1961), p. 56.

4. Tolkien, p. 37.

5. E. M. Forster, *Aspects of the Novel* (New York: Harcourt, Brace & World, Inc., 1927), p. 108.

6. C. N. Manlove, *Modern Fantasy: Five Studies* (Cambridge: Cambridge University Press, 1975), p. 7. Manlove includes in his definition a qualification that the work must evoke wonder, which seems to me to be insisting that all fantasy be good fantasy.

7. Tzvetan Todorov, *The Fantastic: A Structural Approach to a Literary Genre*, trans. Richard Howard (Cleveland: Case Western Reserve University Press, 1973), p. 25.

8. Eric R. Rabkin, *The Fantastic in Literature* (Princeton, N. J.: Princeton University Press, 1976), p. 37.

9. Linda Dégh, *Folktales and Society: Story-Telling in a Hungarian Peasant Community*, trans. Emily M. Schossberger (Bloomington, Ind.: Indiana University Press, 1969), p. 63.

10. Ibid., p. 63.

11. Ibid., p. 87.

12. Ibid., p. 81.

13. Bruno Bettelheim, *The Uses of Enchantment: The Meaning and Importance of Fairy Tales* (New York: Vintage Books, 1977), p. 309.

14. Marianna Thalmann, *The Romantic Fairytale*, trans. Mary B. Corcoran (Ann Arbor: The University of Michigan Press, 1964).

15. Max Lüthi, *Once Upon a Time: On the Nature of Fairy Tales*, trans. Lee Chadeayne and Paul Gottwald (Bloomington, Ind.: Indiana University Press, 1976), pp. 84-85.

187

16. Robert Kirk, *The Secret Common-Wealth*, ed. Stewart Sanderson (Cambridge: D. S. Brewer Ltd., 1975), pp. 50-51.

17. Thomas Keightley, *The Fairy Mythology*, rev. ed. (London: H. G. Bohn, 1850), pp. 289, 413.

18. George MacDonald, "The Fantastic Imagination," in *The Gifts of the Child Christ*, ed. Glenn Edward Sadler (Grand Rapids, Mich.: William B. Eerdmans Publishing Company, 1973), 1:23-24.

19. Philip Henderson, *William Morris: His Life, Work, and Friends* (New York: McGraw-Hill Book Company, 1967), p. 8.

20. William Morris, *The House of the Wolfings* (Boston: Roberts Brothers, 1890), p. 7.

21. C. S. Lewis, "De Descriptione Temporum," in *Selected Literary Essays*, ed. Walter Hooper (Cambridge: Cambridge University Press, 1969), p. 14.

22. C. S. Lewis, "Preface" to George MacDonald, *George MacDonald: An Anthology*, ed. C. S. Lewis (New York: The MacMillan Company, 1960), p. 20.

23. C. S. Lewis, "On Stories," in *Of Other Worlds*, ed. Walter Hooper (New York: Harcourt, Brace & World, Inc., 1966), pp. 35-36.

24. C. S. Lewis, *Perelandra* (New York: Avon Publications, Inc., 1944), p. 30.

25. C. S. Lewis, *An Experiment in Criticism*, pp. 57-73.

26. Edmund Wilson, "Oo, Those Awful Orcs!" *Nation* 182 (14 April 1956):312-13; Manlove, *Modern Fantasy*.

27. Tolkien, pp. 68-69.

28. Humphrey Carpenter, *Tolkien: A Biography* (Boston: Houghton Mifflin Company, 1977), pp. 64 ff.

29. J. R. R. Tolkien, *The Lord of the Rings*, rev. ed. (Boston: Houghton Mifflin Company, 1965), 1:33.

30. Lüthi, p. 47.

31. Vladimir Propp, *Morphology of the Folktale*, trans. Laurence Scott, 2d ed., rev. and ed. Louis A. Wagner (Austin, Tex.: University of Texas Press, 1968).

2. Fantasy and the Folk Tradition

1. John Greenleaf Whittier, *The Supernaturalism of New England*, ed. Edward Wagenknecht (1847; reprint ed., Norman Okla.: The University of Oklahoma Press, 1969), p. 60.

2. Katharine Briggs, "Faults Condemned by the Fairies," in *An Encyclopedia of Fairies* (New York: Pantheon Books, 1976), pp. 167-68.

3. Tristram P. Coffin, *The British Traditional Ballad in North America*, rev. ed. (Austin, Tex.: University of Texas Press, 1977), p. 3.

4. M. J. C. Hodgart, *The Ballads* (New York: W. W. Norton & Company, Inc., 1962), p. 116.

5. Albert B. Friedman, *The Ballad Revival* (Chicago: University of Chicago Press, 1961), p. 8.

6. J. R. R. Tolkien, "On Fairy-Stories," in *Tree and Leaf* (Boston: Houghton Mifflin Company, 1965), p. 5.

7. Francis James Child, *The English and Scottish Popular Ballads* (Boston and New York: Houghton Mifflin and Company, 1898), 1:5.

8. Lowry Charles Wimberly, *Folklore in the English and Scottish Ballads* (Chicago: The University of Chicago Press, 1928).

9. Coffin, pp. 49-50.

10. Bertrand Harris Bronson, *The Traditional Tunes of the Child Ballads* (Princeton: Princeton University Press, 1959), 1:351.

11. Malcolm Laws, *Native American Balladry* (Philadelphia: The American Folklore Society, 1964), p. 2.

12. Ibid., p. 56.

13. "Tying Knots in the Devil's Tail," also known as "The Sierry Petes," has entered into tradition, but it was written by Gail I. Gardner in 1917, according to Katie Lee, *Ten Thousand Goddam Cattle* (Flagstaff, Ariz.: Northland Press, 1976), p. 222. Its unusual flirtation with the supernatural may be explained by the relatively late date of composition and by its semiliterary origin.

14. Katharine M. Briggs and Ruth L. Tongue, eds., *Folktales of England* (Chicago: The University of Chicago Press, 1965).

15. Ernest W. Baughman, *Type and Motif Index of the Folktales of England and North America*, Indiana University Folklore Series no. 20 (The Hague: Mouton & Co., 1966), p. viii.

16. Richard Chase, *The Jack Tales* (Boston: Houghton Mifflin Company, 1943), p. 3.

17. Vance Randolph, *Who Blowed Up the Church House?* (New York: Columbia University Press, 1952), p. 140.

18. Constance Rourke, *American Humor: A Study of the National Character* (1931; reprint ed., New York: Harcourt Brace Jovanovich, Inc., 1959).

19. Richard M. Dorson, *America in Legend* (New York: Pantheon Books, 1973), p. 170.

20. Briggs, *An Encyclopedia of Fairies.*

21. Richard M. Dorson, *American Folklore and the Historian* (Chicago: The University of Chicago Press, 1971), p. 36.

22. Briggs, *An Encyclopedia of Fairies*, p. 6, told in full on pages 29-30, but with the final line altered to "Aye, Johnny lad, we're flitting, ye see."

23. Dorson, *America in Legend*, pp. 1-9.

24. Whittier, p. 27.

25. James Russell Lowell, "Witchcraft," in *The Works of James Russell Lowell* (1868; reprint ed., Boston and New York: Houghton Mifflin Company, 1913), vol. 2, *Literary Essays*, pp. 313-17.

26. Walt Whitman, *Leaves of Grass* (New York: The Modern Library, 1950), p. 450.

27. Linda Dégh, "The 'Belief Legend' in Modern Society: Form, Function, and Relationship to Other Genres," in *American Folk Legend*, ed. Wayland D. Hand (Berkeley and Los Angeles: University of California Press, 1971), p. 55.

28. Richard M. Dorson, "How Shall We Rewrite Charles M. Skinner Today," in *American Folk Legend*, ed. Hand, p. 69.

29. Charles Montgomery Skinner, *Myths and Legends of Our Own Land*, 2 vols. (Philadelphia: J. B. Lippincott Company, 1896), 1:55-56.

30. Samuel Adams Drake, *A Book of New England Legends and Folklore*, 2d rev. ed. (Boston: Little, Brown, and Company, 1910), p. 461.

31. Joseph Rodman Drake, *The Culprit Fay, and Other Poems* (New York: George Dearborn, Publisher, 1835), p. 12.

32. John Milton Harney, *Crystalina; A Fairy Tale* (New York: George F. Hopkins, 1816).

33. William Gibson, *A Vision of Faery Land, and Other Poems* (Boston and Cambridge: James Munroe and Company, 1853).

34. S. G. Goodrich, *Fairy Land, and Other Sketches for Youth* (Boston: James Murve and Co., 1844), pp. 48-55.

35. Emily Dickinson, *The Complete Poems of Emily Dickinson*, ed. Thomas H. Johnson (Boston: Little, Brown and Company, 1960), pp. 242-43, 619.

36. William Austin, "Peter Rugg, the Missing Man," in *A Book of New England Legends and Folklore*, ed. Samuel Adams Drake, pp. 90-105.

37. Daniel Hoffman, *Form and Fable in American Fiction* (New York: Oxford University Press, 1961), p. 85 n. See also Philip Young, "The Story of the Missing

Man," in *Directions in Literary Criticism*, ed. Stanley Weintraub and Philip Young (University Park, Penn.: The Pennsylvania State University Press, 1973), pp. 143–59.

38. Washington Irving, "Rip Van Winkle," in *Irving's Works*, Geoffrey Crayon Edition, vol. 2, *The Sketch Book* (New York: G. P. Putnam's Sons, 1880), p. 74.

39. See Briggs, *An Encyclopedia of Fairies*, p. 62, s.v. "Captives in Fairyland."

40. Washington Irving, "The Catskill Mountains," in *The Home Book of the Picturesque* (Gainesville, Fla.: Scholars' Facsimiles & Reprints, 1967), p. 72.

3. BELIEF, LEGEND, AND ROMANCE

1. Samuel Taylor Coleridge, *Biographia Literaria*, ed. George Watson (New York: Everyman's Library, 1967), p. 168.

2. Maud Bodkin, *Archetypal Patterns in Poetry* (1934; reprint ed., London: Oxford University Press, 1963), pp. 26–89.

3. Eleanor Cameron, *The Green and Burning Tree* (Boston: Little, Brown and Co., 1969), p. 44.

4. J. R. R. Tolkien, "On Fairy-Stories," in *Tree and Leaf* (Boston: Houghton Mifflin Company, 1965), p. 37.

5. C. S. Lewis, *An Experiment in Criticism* (Cambridge: Cambridge University Press, 1961), p. 57.

6. C. S. Lewis, *Letters of C. S. Lewis*, ed. W. H. Lewis (New York: Harcourt, Brace & World, Inc., 1966), p. 203. Lewis may be commenting here on David Lindsay's *A Voyage to Arcturus* (1920), which attempts to describe new sexes and colors but never manages to bring them to life. They remain abstract and unimaginable, like mathematical speculations on the higher dimensions. Incidentally, Edgar Allan Poe made use of the same point in praising Thomas Moore's "Alciphron" over Joseph Rodman Drake's "The Culprit Fay" ("Alciphron: A Poem," *The Complete Works of Edgar Allan Poe*, ed. James A. Harrison [New York: Thomas Y. Crowell & Company, 1902], 10:63). Poe, however, seems to regret this limitation upon the imagination and calls for an "ideality," a new moral conception, which transcends the mere juxtaposition of old elements. Lewis intimates that if the borrowed details are handled with sufficient conviction, ideality will take care of itself.

7. Washington Irving, "Rip Van Winkle," in *Irving's Works*, Geoffrey Crayon Edition, vol. 2, *The Sketch Book* (New York: G. P. Putnam's Sons, 1880), p. 74.

8. Tolkien, p. 14.

9. Washington Irving, "Adventure of the German Student," in *Irving's Works*, Geoffrey Crayon Edition, vol. 4, *Tales of a Traveller* (New York: G. P. Putnam's Sons, 1888), p. 74.

10. Edgar Allan Poe, "The Fall of the House of Usher," in *Collected Works of Edgar Allan Poe*, ed. Thomas Ollive Mabbott, vol. 2, *Tales and Sketches, 1831-1842* (Cambridge, Mass.: Harvard University Press, 1978), p. 397.

11. Poe, "Ulalume," in *Collected Works*, vol. 1, *Poems* (Cambridge, Mass.: Harvard University Press, 1969), p. 416.

12. Poe, "Dream-Land," *Poems*, p. 344.

13. Poe, "Fairy-Land," *Poems*, p. 140.

14. Nathaniel Hawthorne, *The Centenary Edition of the Works of Nathaniel Hawthorne*, ed. William Charvat et al., vol. 4, *The Marble Faun* (Columbus, Oh.: Ohio State University Press, 1968), p. 3.

15. R. W. B. Lewis, *The American Adam* (Chicago: The University of Chicago Press, 1955), p. 124.

16. Hawthorne, *The Centenary Edition*, vol. 3, *The Blithedale Romance* (Columbus, Oh.: Ohio State University Press, 1964), pp. 1-2.

17. Hawthorne, *The Centenary Edition*, vol. 2, *The House of the Seven Gables* (Columbus, Oh.: Ohio State University Press, 1965), p. 1.

18. Hawthorne, *The Marble Faun*, p. 3.

19. Hawthorne, "Feathertop, A Moralized Legend," in *The Centenary Edition*, vol. 10, *Mosses from an Old Manse* (Columbus, Oh.: Ohio State University Press, 1974), p. 223.

20. "Dickon" is undoubtedly a variation on "Dickens," a joking name for the Devil.

21. Ernest W. Baughman, *Type and Motif Index of the Folktales of England and North America* (The Hague: Mouton & Co., 1966).

22. Max Lüthi, *Once Upon a Time*, trans. Lee Chadeayne and Paul Gottwald (Bloomington, Ind.: Indiana University Press, 1976), p. 84.

23. Constance Rourke, *American Humor* (1931; reprint ed., New York: Harcourt Brace Jovanovich, Inc., 1959), pp. 188-89.

24. Hawthorne, "The Custom-House," in *The Centenary Edition*, vol. 1, *The Scarlet Letter* (Columbus, Oh.: Ohio State University Press, 1962), p. 32.

25. Northrop Frye, *Anatomy of Criticism* (Princeton, N.J.: Princeton University Press, 1957), p. 37.

26. C. S. Lewis, *An Experiment in Criticism*, p. 55.

27. Jay Leyda, *The Melville Log* (New York: Harcourt, Brace and Company, 1951), 1:274.

28. Herman Melville, *The Works of Herman Melville*, standard ed., vols. 3 and 4, *Mardi* (1849; reprint ed., London: Constable and Company Ltd., 1922), p. 398.

29. Leyda, 1:347.

30. Ibid.

31. Daniel Hoffman, *Form and Fable in American Fiction* (New York: Oxford University Press, 1961), pp. 234 ff.

32. Samuel Clemens, "Political Economy," in *The Complete Short Stories of Mark Twain*, ed. Charles Neider (Garden City, N. Y.: Doubleday & Company, Inc., 1957), pp. 59-64.

33. Melville, "The Lightning-Rod Man," in *The Works of Herman Melville*, vol. 10, *The Piazza Tales* (London: Constable and Company Ltd., 1923), pp. 179-80.

34. Leyda, 2:515.

35. Ibid., 2:565.

36. Melville, *The Works of Herman Melville*, vol. 12, *The Confidence-Man* (London: Constable and Company Ltd., 1923), p. 243.

37. Hoffman, pp. 33-82.

4. FANTASY FOR AMERICAN CHILDREN

1. Nathaniel Hawthorne, "Preface" to *A Wonder Book*, in *The Centenary Edition of the Works of Nathaniel Hawthorne*, ed. William Charvat et al., vol. 7, *A Wonder Book* and *Tanglewood Tales* (Columbus, Oh.: Ohio State University Press, 1972), pp. 3-4.

2. T. W. Higginson, "An Evening with Mrs. Hawthorne," *Atlantic Monthly* 28 (October 1871):432-33, quoted in Calvin E. Schorer, "The Juvenile Literature of Nathaniel Hawthorne" (Ph. D. diss., University of Chicago, 1948), p. 16.

3. All these works are discussed in Alice M. Jordan, *From Rollo to Tom Sawyer* (Boston: The Horn Book Inc., 1948), pp. 3-7.

4. Roy Harvey Pearce, "Historical Introduction: True Stories, A Wonder Book, Tanglewood Tales," in Hawthorne, *The Centenary Edition*, vol. 6, *True Stories from History and Biography*, p. 288.

5. Jordan, pp. 7-8.

6. Samuel G. Goodrich, *Recollections of a Lifetime*, 2 vols. (New York: Miller, Orton and Mulligan, 1857), 1:166.

7. Ibid., 2:320.

8. Hawthorne, "Tanglewood Porch," in *A Wonder Book*, pp. 5–6.

9. Hawthorne, "The Gorgon's Head," in *A Wonder Book*, p. 26.

10. Hawthorne, "The Golden Touch," in *A Wonder Book*, p. 48.

11. C. B. Burkhardt, *Fairy Tales and Legends of Many Nations* (New York: Baker and Scribner, 1848).

12. Lydia M. Child, ed., *Rainbows for Children* (New York: C. S. Francis & Co., 1848). Alice M. Jordan suggests that the author, Mrs. Child's anonymous friend, was a Mrs. Tappan (Jordan, p. 54).

13. Child, "Preface," *Rainbows for Children*, p. 8.

14. Anon., *Stories: Fairy Land* (Boston: Brown Bazin & Co., 1855).

15. Jane Austin, *Fairy Dreams; or, Wanderings in Elf-Land* (Boston: J. E. Tilton and Company, 1859).

16. "Three Friends" (H. H. Weston, C. Clark, and L. Gibbons), *The Fairy Egg* (Boston: Fields, Osgood, & Co., 1870).

17. T. F. Crane, "Italian Fairy Tales," *St. Nicholas* 6 (November 1878–November 1879):101.

18. Julian Hawthorne, "Rumpty-Dudget's Tower," *St. Nicholas* 6 (November 1878–November 1879). Reprinted in *The St. Nicholas Anthology*, ed. Henry Steele Commager (New York: Random House, Inc., 1948), pp. 276–90. I use the pagination in the anthology.

19. Maurice Bassan, *Hawthorne's Son* (Colombus, Oh.: Ohio State University Press, 1970), p. 131.

20. Charles Carryll, *Davy and the Goblin* (Boston: Ticknor and Company, 1886).

21. Virginia Baker, *Prince Carotte: and Other Chronicles* (Boston: Press of Rockwell and Churchill, 1881).

22. Frank R. Stockton, *Ting-a-Ling Tales* (New York: Charles Scribner's Sons, 1882).

23. Martin I. J. Griffin, *Frank R. Stockton* (Philadelphia: University of Pennsylvania Press, 1939), p. 11. Quoted from Mrs. F. R. Stockton, "A Memorial Sketch of Mr. Stockton," in Frank R. Stockton, *The Shenandoah Edition of the Novels and Stories of Frank R. Stockton*, vol. 23, *A Bicycle of Cathay* (New York, 1899–1904), p. 192.

24. Griffin, p. 11.

25. Both stories are found in Frank R. Stockton, *The Novels and Stories of Frank R. Stockton*, vol. 17, *Stories III* (New York: Charles Scribner's Sons, 1900).

26. Griffin, p. 73.

27. Elizabeth Nesbitt, *Howard Pyle*, a Walck Monograph (New York: Henry Z. Walck, Incorporated, 1966), p. 24.

28. Ibid., p. 11.

29. Howard Pyle, *Pepper & Salt* (New York: Harper and Brothers, 1885).

30. Howard Pyle, *The Garden behind the Moon* (New York: Charles Scribner's Sons, 1895), p. 1.

31. Nesbitt, p. 48.

32. James Kirke Paulding, *A Christmas Gift from Fairyland* (New York: D. Appleton & Co., 1838).

33. James Kirke Paulding, *The Book of St. Nicholas* (New York: Harper & Brothers, 1836).

34. Henry Schoolcraft, *The Indian Fairy Book* (New York: Mason Brothers, 1856).

35. Christopher Pearse Cranch, *The Last of the Huggermuggers* (Boston: Phillips, Sampson and Company, 1856); and *Kobboltozo* (Boston: Phillips, Sampson and Company, 1857).

36. "Hammawhaxo" and "Stitchkin" are occupational puns, and "Kobboltozo" is derived from the German *kobold*, a kind of bad-tempered gnome.

37. May Wentworth, *Fairy Tales from Gold Lands*, The Golden Gate Series (San Francisco: A. Roman & Company, Publishers, 1867).

38. Edward Eggleston, "Queer Stories," originally published in a separate volume in 1871, the plates for which burned in the Chicago fire. Reprinted in *The Schoolmaster's Stories* (Boston: Henry L. Shepard & Co., 1874).

39. Virginia W. Johnson, *The Catskill Fairies* (New York: Harper & Brothers, Publishers, 1876).

40. Laura E. Richards, *Toto's Merry Winter* (Boston: Roberts Brothers, 1877); and Lily F. Wesselhoeft, *The Fairy-Folk of Blue Hill* (Boston: Joseph Knight Company, 1895). Richards' book is a sequel to *The Joyous Story of Toto*.

41. Samuel L. Clemens, *A Connecticut Yankee in King Arthur's Court*, Harper & Brothers ed. (New York: P. F. Collier & Son Company, 1889).

5. Oz

1. Frank Joslyn Baum and Russell P. MacFall, *To Please A Child* (Chicago: Reilly & Lee Co., 1961), pp. 112–13.

2. Ibid., p. 113. Michael Patrick Hearn, in his introduction to *The Annotated Wizard of Oz* (New York: Clarkson N. Potter, Inc., 1973), p. 28, dismisses the story, saying that publisher George M. Hill accepted the book with no reservations except about the time of release. If so, Hill showed more acuity than one would expect: the book was an undoubted novelty and therefore a gamble.

3. Maud Gage Baum, in a letter quoted by Martin Gardner in "The Royal Historian of Oz," *The Wizard of Oz and Who He Was*, by Gardner and Russel B. Nye (East Lansing, Mich.: Michigan State University Press, 1957), p. 25.

4. Edward Wagenknecht, " 'Utopia Americana' A Generation Afterwards," *The American Book Collector* 13 (December 1962):13.

5. Raylin Moore, in her monograph, *Wonderful Wizard Marvelous Land* (Bowling Green, Oh.: Bowling Green University Press, 1974), p. 29, cites a British reviewer in recent years who felt compelled to explain to her readers the plot of *The Wizard*—and got it wrong.

6. All quotations from *The Wizard of Oz* are taken from *The Annotated Wizard of Oz*, ed. Michael Patrick Hearn. Hearn's text is taken from the original George M. Hill edition of 1900, actually titled *The Wonderful Wizard of Oz*. His introduction and annotations summarize most of the critical and biographical work done on Baum to date, and the reproductions of text and illustrations are of uniformly high quality.

7. L. Frank Baum, *The Road to Oz* (1909; reprint ed., Chicago: Rand McNally & Co., n.d.), p. 43.

8. Henry Nash Smith, *Virgin Land: The American West as Symbol and Myth* (Cambridge, Mass.: Harvard University Press, 1950), pp. 174–83.

9. Hearn, *The Annotated Wizard*, p. 106.

10. Henry Littlefield, "The Wizard of Oz: Parable on Populism," *American Quarterly* 16 (Spring 1964):47–58.

11. Selma Lanes, *Down the Rabbit Hole* (1971; reprint ed., New York: Atheneum, 1976), p. 111.

12. Fred Erisman, "L. Frank Baum and the Progressive Dilemma," *American Quarterly* 20 (Fall 1968):616–23.

13. Cited in Daniel Aaron, *Men of Good Hope: A Story of American Progressives* (New York: Oxford University Press, 1961), pp. 135–36.

14. L. Frank Baum, *Mother Goose in Prose* (1897; reprint ed., Indianapolis, Ind.: The Bobbs-Merrill Company, 1905).

15. L. Frank Baum, *A New Wonderland* (New York: R. H. Russell, 1900) was revised and retitled *The Surprising Adventures of the Magical Monarch of Mo and His People* in 1903 (Indianapolis: The Bobbs-Merrill Company; reprint ed., New York: Dover Publications, Inc., 1968).

16. L. Frank Baum, *Queen Zixi of Ix; or the Story of the Magic Cloak* (New York: Century Co., 1905).

17. L. Frank Baum, "Modern Fairy Tales," *The Advance* (19 August 1909), quoted in Hearn, *The Annotated Wizard*, p. 91.

18. Ibid.

19. The road to Ántonia's house is lined with sunflowers and described as "a gold ribbon across the prairie"—another yellow brick road? Willa Cather, *My Ántonia* (Boston and New York: Houghton Mifflin Company, 1946), p. 19.

20. L. Frank Baum, *The Land of Oz* (1904; reprint ed., Chicago: Rand McNally & Co., n.d.), p. 14.

21. Marius Bewley, "The Land of Oz: America's Great Good Place," *The New York Review of Books* (3 December 1964), reprinted in his *Masks and Mirrors* (New York: Atheneum, 1970), p. 259–60.

22. From an inscription to his sister, quoted by Gardner and Nye, p. 42 n. More of the passage bears quoting here: "...aside from my evident inability to do anything 'great,' I have learned to regard fame as a will-o-the-wisp which, when caught, is not worth the possession; but to please a child is a sweet and lovely thing that warms one's heart and brings its own reward...."

23. Roger Sale, "L. Frank Baum and Oz," *The Hudson Review* 25 (Winter 1972–73):591.

6. Fantasy and Escape

1. Eva Katharine Gibson, *Zauberlinda the Wise Witch* (Chicago and Lansing: Robt. Smith Printing Co., 1901).

2. Quoted in Irwin Porges, *Edgar Rice Burroughs: The Man Who Created Tarzan* (Provo, Utah: Brigham Young University Press, 1975), p. 284. I detect a bit of condescension in the phrase "fairy tale man," which is certainly not justified by the relative literary skills of the two men.

3. Some time before Burroughs sent his imagination across the heavens to Mars, he wrote a curious little story for his family. It was a Westernized fairy tale, reminiscent of *The Wizard of Oz* and *Zauberlinda*, which he called "Minidoka 937th Earl of One Mile Series M. An Historical Fairy Tale." A summary of it may be found in Porges, pp. 712–15. The tale does not indicate any particular strengths of Burroughs as a writer of fairy tales: Burroughs stuck his true vein in *A Princess of Mars*.

4. Edgar Rice Burroughs, *A Princess of Mars* (1912; reprint ed., New York: Ballantine Books, 1963), p. 20.

5. "His response to my manifestation of affection was remarkable to a degree; he stretched his great mouth to its full width, baring the entire expanse of his upper rows of tusks and wrinkling his snout until his great eyes were almost hidden by the folds of flesh. If you have ever seen a collie smile you may have some idea of Woola's facial distortion" (Burroughs, *Princess*, p. 51).

6. For a discussion of the subgenre and its history, see Thomas D. Clareson, "Lost Lands, Lost Races: A Pagan Princess of their Very Own," in *Many Futures, Many Worlds*, ed. Thomas D. Clareson (Kent, Oh.: The Kent State University Press, 1977), pp. 117–39.

7. "Editor's Note" to "Under the Moons of Mars," the original, periodical version of *A Princess of Mars*, entire page reproduced in Porges, p. 122.

8. Hans Joachim Alpers, "Loincloth, Double Ax, and Magic: 'Heroic Fantasy' and Related Genres," trans. Robert Plank, *Science-Fiction Studies* 14 (March 1978):19–32.

9. George P. Elliott, "Getting Away from the Chickens," *The Hudson Review* 12 (Autumn 1959): 392.

10. James Branch Cabell, *Straws and Prayer-Books: Dizain des Diversions* (New York: Robert M. McBride & Company, 1924), p. 52. There is considerable disagreement as to which editions of Cabell's books are best suited to scholarly use, the early ones expressing original intentions or the later, reconsidered "authorized" versions. I have solved the problem by using what was available to me.

11. This is the essential argument, as I read it, of Cabell's *Beyond Life: Dizain des Demiurges* (New York: Robert M. McBride & Company, 1919).

12. Quoted in Arvin Wells, *Jesting Moses: A Study in Cabellian Comedy* (Gainesville, Fla.: University of Florida Press, 1962), p. 3.

13. H. L. Mencken, *James Branch Cabell* (1917). Reprinted in *James Branch Cabell: Three Essays* (Port Washington, N. Y.: Kennikat Press, 1967), p. 14.

14. Carl Van Doren, *James Branch Cabell* (1932). Reprinted in *James Branch Cabell: Three Essays*), p. 19.

15. Cabell, *Straws and Prayer-Books*, p. 290.

16. Ibid., p. 293.

17. Quoted in Desmond Tarrant, *James Branch Cabell: The Dream and the Reality* (Norman, Okla.: University of Oklahoma Press, 1967), p. 26.

18. James Branch Cabell et al., *Between Friends: Letters of James Branch Cabell and Others*, ed. Padraic Colum and Margaret Freeman Cabell (New York: Harcourt, Brace & World, Inc., 1962), p. 244.

19. Cabell quotes this phrase with some pique in a letter to Burton Rascoe, Cabell, *The Letters of James Branch Cabell*, ed. Edward Wagenknecht (Norman, Okla.: University of Oklahoma Press, 1975), p. 72.

20. Published in New York by Frederick A. Stokes & Co., later revised and retitled *Domnei: A Comedy of Woman Worship* (New York: Robert M. McBride & Company, 1924).

21. In a letter to Vincent Starrett, *Letters*, p. 199.

22. There is a discussion of the geography of Poictesme in Tarrant, pp. 44–46.

23. James Branch Cabell, *The Cream of the Jest* (New York: The Modern Library, 1917), p. 39.

24. James Branch Cabell, *Jurgen: A Comedy of Justice*, Kalki ed. (New York: Robert M. McBride & Company, 1927), p. 42 and elsewhere.

25. In a letter to Burton Rascoe, Cabell, *Between Friends*, pp. 126–28.

26. Mencken, *James Branch Cabell*, p. 12.

27. Ernest Hemingway, *The Sun Also Rises* (1926; reprint ed., New York: Bantam Books, 1949), p. 94.

28. Paul Brewster, "*Jurgen* and *Figures and Earth* and the Russian Skaski," *American Literature* 13 (January 1942):308–10.

29. Ibid., p. 305, n. 2.

30. L. Sprague de Camp, *Lovecraft: A Biography* (Garden City, N. Y.: Doubleday & Company, Inc., 1975), pp. 4–6, 20–23.

31. Published in 1927 in an amateur journal called *The Recluse*. Of many reprints, that of Dover Publications, Inc. (New York: 1973) is most readily available.

32. Cabell, *Beyond Life*, p. 266.

33. De Camp, p. 63.

34. Barton Levi St. Armand, *The Roots of Horror in the Fiction of H. P. Lovecraft* (Elizabethtown, N. Y.: Dragon Press, 1977), p. 3.

35. These stories are collected in *At the Mountains of Madness: and Other Novels*, selected by August Derleth (Sauk City, Wisc.: Arkham House, Publishers, 1964).

36. H. P. Lovecraft, "Celephais," in *Dagon: and Other Macabre Tales*, selected by August Derleth (Sauk City, Wisc.: Arkham House, Publishers, 1965), p. 65.

37. H. P. Lovecraft, "The Silver Key," in *At the Mountains of Madness*, pp. 386–97. Lovecraft's conception of the dream world had changed somewhat when he wrote this story, but the point remains.

38. De Camp, p. 138.

39. From a letter to V. Finlay, quoted in de Camp, pp. 30–31.

40. St. Armand, pp. 59–77. St. Armand gives credit to Keith Waldrop for pointing out the importance of "viscosity" in horror fiction in his dissertation "Aesthetic Uses of Obscenity in Literature" (University of Michigan, 1964).

41. Philip A. Shreffler, *The H. P. Lovecraft Companion* (Westport, Conn.: Greenwood Press, 1977), points out two motifs in Lovecraft's "The Shunned House" which are derived from Charles M. Skinner's *Myths and Legends of Our Own Land*, 2 vols. (Philadelphia: J. P. Lippincott Company, 1896).

7. THE BAUM TRADITION

1. Gore Vidal, for example, credits his addiction to reading to *The Emerald City of Oz*, in his essay "The Wizard of 'The Wizard,' " *The New York Review of Books* 24 (29 September 1977):10.

2. Ray Bradbury, *Dark Carnival* (Sauk City, Wisc.: Arkham House, Publishers, 1948). This collection was expanded and reissued as *The October Country* (New York: Alfred A. Knopf, 1955).

3. Ray Bradbury, "The Emissary," in *The October Country*, p. 112.

4. Ray Bradbury, *The Martian Chronicles* (Garden City, N. Y.: Doubleday & Company, Inc., 1958).

5. Ray Bradbury, "Introduction" to Irwin Porges, *Edgar Rice Burroughs* (Provo, Utah: Brigham Young University Press, 1975), p. xviii.

6. Ray Bradbury, "The Exiles," in *The Illustrated Man* (Garden City, N. Y.: Doubleday & Company, Inc., 1951), p. 145.

7. Ray Bradbury, "Preface" to Raylin Moore, *Wonderful Wizard Marvelous Land* (Bowling Green, Oh.: Bowling Green University Popular Press, 1974), p. xiii.

8. Ray Bradbury, *Dandelion Wine* (Garden City, N. Y.: Doubleday & Company, Inc., 1957).

9. Ray Bradbury, "Something Wicked This Way Comes (1962; reprint ed., New York: Bantam Books, Inc., 1963).

10. One might compare this facet of Green Town with the embattled house of Englishman William Hope Hodgson's Lovecraftian *House on the Borderland* (Sauk City, Wisc.: Arkham House, Publishers, 1946).

11. Joseph Campbell, *The Hero with a Thousand Faces*, Bolingen Series 17 (Princeton, N. J.: Princeton University Press, 1949), p. 261.

12. Charles G. Finney, *The Circus of Dr. Lao* (1935; reprint ed., New York: Bantam Books, Inc., 1964).

13. Peter S. Beagle, *The Last Unicorn* (New York: Ballantine Books, 1968).

14. Edward Eager, *Seven-Day Magic* (New York: Harcourt, Brace & World, Inc., 1962), p. 11.

15. Edward Eager, "A Father's Minority Report," *The Horn Book Magazine* 24 (March–April 1948):107.

16. Edward Eager, *Half Magic* (New York: Harcourt, Brace & World, Inc., 1954), pp. 3–4.

17. Sir James George Frazer, *The New Golden Bough*, rev. and ed. Theodor H. Gaster (New York: The New American Library, Inc., 1959), p. 35.

18. C. S. Lewis, *An Experiment in Criticism* (Cambridge: Cambridge University Press, 1961), p. 55.

19. James Thurber, "The Secret Life of James Thurber," in *The Thurber Carnival* (New York: Harper & Brothers, 1945), p. 33.

20. Ibid., p. 34.

21. James Thurber, "The Black Magic of Barney Haller," in *The Thurber Carnival*, p. 137.

22. James Thurber, "The Admiral on the Wheel," in *The Thurber Carnival*, p. 91.

23. Ibid., p. 90.

24. Richard C. Tobias, *The Art of James Thurber* (Athens, Oh.: Ohio University Press, 1969), p. 84.

25. James Thurber, "The Wizard of Chit[t]enango," *The New Republic* 81 (12 December 1934):141.

26. James Thurber, *The White Deer* (New York: Harcourt, Brace & World, Inc., 1945), pp. 3–4.

27. James Thurber, *The 13 Clocks* (New York: Simon and Schuster, 1950), p. 50.

28. Charles S. Holmes, *The Clocks of Columbus* (New York: Atheneum, 1972), p. 231.

29. This ability may be connected with his extraordinary facility, despite a lack of technique, with the cartoon form. In "A New Natural History," in *Alarms and Diversions* (New York: Harper & Brothers, Publishers, 1957), pp. 123–42, Thurber drew plants and animals suggested by such words as "quandary," "thesaurus," and "Johnny-come-lately." They are immediately recognizable.

30. Burton Bernstein, *Thurber* (New York: Dodd, Mead & Company, 1975), pp. 66, 404.

31. From a letter to Dr. Russel Voorhees, 3 March 1951, in Bernstein, p. 405.

32. For a fuller interpretation of the meanings in Thurber's fantasies, see Tobias, *The Art of James Thurber*, chapter 7.

33. Thurber, *The 13 Clocks*, pp. 11–12.

8. AFTER TOLKIEN

1. A good example is Douglass Parker's article "Hwaet We Holbytla," in the *Hudson Review* 9 (1956–57):598–609. Parker gives Tolkien credit for illustrating the artistic potential of the genre.

2. Roger Sale, *Modern Heroism: Essays on D. H. Lawrence, William Empson, & J. R. R. Tolkien* (Berkeley: University of California Press, 1973), p. 239.

3. Terry Brooks, *The Sword of Shannara* (New York: Ballantine Books, 1977). Brooks' book was a best seller, which indicates a need for educating the American public on the difference between real fantasy and ersatz.

4. Sale, *Modern Heroism*, pp. 233–34.

5. Lloyd Alexander, *The Book of Three* (New York: Holt, Rinehart and Winston, 1964).

6. Lloyd Alexander, *Taran Wanderer* (New York: Holt, Rinehart and Winston, 1967).

7. Lloyd Alexander, *The High King* (New York: Holt, Rinehart and Winston, 1968).

8. Andre Norton, *Judgment on Janus* (New York: Harcourt, Brace & World, Inc., 1963).

9. Andre Norton, *The Jargoon Pard* (New York: Atheneum, 1974).

10. Peter Beagle, "Tolkien's Magic Ring," Preface to *The Tolkien Reader* (New York: Ballantine Books, 1966).

11. Peter Beagle, *A Fine and Private Place* (New York: Dell Publishing Company, 1963).

12. Peter Beagle, *The Last Unicorn* (New York: Ballantine Books, 1968), p. 3.

13. The three volumes of the trilogy are entitled *Lord Foul's Bane, The Illearth War*, and *The Power That Preserves* (New York: Holt, Rinehart and Winston, 1977).

14. Roger Zelazny, *Nine Princes in Amber* (1970; reprint ed., New York: Avon Books, 1972), p. 5. The lineage of the tough-guy hero predates Bogart, of course. He may be found in the detective novels of Dashiel Hammett and Raymond Chandler, and those two writers probably found him in Hemingway. In science fiction, he has been used most consistently by Robert Heinlein.

15. Ursula K. Le Guin, *From Elfland to Poughkeepsie* (Portland, Ore.: Pendragon Press, 1973), pp. 19–20.

16. Ibid., p. 20.

17. Ursula K. Le Guin, *The Wind's Twelve Quarters* (New York: Harper & Row, Publishers, 1975).

18. Ursula K. Le Guin, *Rocannon's World* (New York: Ace Books, 1966).

19. Robert Scholes, *Structural Fabulation* (Notre Dame: University of Notre Dame Press, 1975), p. 39. In addition to his discussion of the genre as a whole, this includes Scholes' perceptive essay on Le Guin, originally published in *The Hollins Critic* 11 (April 1974) under the title "The Good Witch of the West." There is no escaping Baum's influence.

20. Ursula K. Le Guin, *The Left Hand of Darkness* (New York: Ace Books, 1969; reprint ed., with new introduction by the author, 1976), p. 233.

21. Samuel Delaney, *The Jewel-Hinged Jaw: Notes on the Language of Science Fiction* (New York: Berkeley Publishing Corporation, 1977), pp. 218–83.

22. Ursula K. Le Guin, "Dreams Must Explain Themselves," *Algol* 21 (November 1973):8.

23. T. A. Shippey studies Le Guin's views on language and magic in "The Magic Art and the Evolution of Words: Ursula Le Guin's *Earthsea Trilogy*," *Mosaic* 10, no. 2 (Winter 1976–77):147–63.

24. Le Guin, "Dreams Must Explain Themselves," p. 12.

25. Again, see Shippey, pp. 150–58.

26. T. S. Eliot, *The Complete Poems and Plays: 1909–1950* (New York: Harcourt, Brace & World, Inc., 1962), p. 57. Le Guin says that a more immediate influence than Eliot was Rainer Maria Rilke, in his final Duino Elegy (personal correspondence, 19 April 1979).

27. Ursula K. Le Guin, *The Tombs of Atuan* (New York: Atheneum, 1971), p. 54.

28. Ernest W. Baughman, in *Type and Motif Index of the Folktales of England and North America*, Indiana University Folklore Series no. 20 (The Hague: Mouton & Co., 1966), p. 280, lists one variant of the "Sorcerer's Apprentice" story in which a group of Harvard students raise a devil. The president of the university (back when Harvard presidents were expected to be spiritual leaders) returns from a journey, finds out what has happened, and lays the devil. This story essentially makes Harvard into a school for wizards much like Le Guin's. This motif is G297 in Stith Thompson's revised *Motif Index of Folk-Literature* (Bloomington, Ind.: Indiana University Press, 1955–58).

29. There is a common tale type called "The Magician and his Pupil" (no. 325 in the 1928 Aarne-Thompson *Types of the Folk-Tale*) which could easily incorporate the "Sorcerer's Apprentice" motif in its structure, though in a different manner from Le Guin's.

30. Ursula K. Le Guin, *The Farthest Shore* (New York: Atheneum, 1972), pp. 94–95.

31. Theodore Roethke, *The Collected Poems of Theodore Roethke* (Garden City, N. Y.: Doubleday and Company, Inc., 1966), p. 239. My article "Two Explorers of the Dark," *Extrapolations* (forthcoming) is an extended reading of *The Farthest Shore*, using the Roethke poem to spotlight Le Guin's symbolic method.

32. Ursula K. Le Guin, *A Wizard of Earthsea* (Berkeley, Cal.: Parnassus Press, 1968), p. 7.

33. Wallace Stevens, *The Palm at the End of the Mind*, ed. Holly Stevens (1971; reprint ed., New York: Vintage Books, 1972), p. 8.

Bibliography

GENERAL WORKS ON FANTASY AND ROMANCE

Applebee, Arthur N. *The Child's Concept of Story: Ages Two to Seventeen.* Chicago: The University of Chicago Press, 1978.

Bettelheim, Bruno. *The Uses of Enchantment: The Meaning and Importance of Fairy Tales.* New York: Random House, Inc., 1976.

Cameron, Eleanor. *The Green and Burning Tree.* Boston: Little, Brown and Co., 1969.

de Camp, L. Sprague. *Literary Swordsmen and Sorcerers: The Makers of Heroic Fantasy.* Sauk City, Wisc.: Arkham House, Publishers, 1976.

Carpenter, Humphrey. *Tolkien: A Biography.* Boston: Houghton Mifflin Company, 1977.

Carter, Lin. *Imaginary Worlds.* New York: Ballantine Books, 1973.

Chase, Richard Volney. *The American Novel and Its Tradition.* Garden City, N. Y.: Doubleday & Company, Inc., 1957.

Chesterton, G. K. *Tremendous Trifles.* 1909. Reprint. New York: Dodd, Mead and Company, 1922.

Clareson, Thomas D., ed. *Many Futures, Many Worlds: Theme and Form in Science Fiction.* Ohio: The Kent State University Press, 1977.

Cook, Elizabeth. *The Ordinary and the Fabulous: An Introduction to Myths, Legends, and Fairy Tales for Teachers and Storytellers.* Cambridge: Cambridge University Press, 1969.

Cornwell, Charles Landrum. "From Self to the Shire: Studies in Victorian Fantasy." Ph.D. dissertation, University of Virginia, 1972.

Cott, Jonathan, ed. *Beyond the Looking Glass: Extraordinary Works of Fairy Tale and Fantasy.* New York: The Stonehill Publishing Company, 1973.

Crouch, Marcus. *Treasure Seekers and Borrowers: Children's Books in Britain 1900-1960.* London: The Library Association, 1962.

Delany, Samuel. *The Jewel-Hinged Jaw: Notes on the Language of Science Fiction.* New York: Berkley Publishing Corporation, 1977.

Forster, E. M. *Aspects of the Novel.* New York: Harcourt, Brace & World, Inc., 1927.

Fredericks, S. C. "Problems of Fantasy." *Science-Fiction Studies* 14 (March 1978): 33–44.

Frye, Northrop. *Anatomy of Criticism: Four Essays*. Princeton, N. J.: Princeton University Press, 1957.

———. *The Secular Scripture: A Study of the Structure of Romance*. Cambridge, Mass.: Harvard University Press, 1976.

Green, Roger Lancelyn. *Tellers of Tales*. London: Edmund Ward Ltd., 1965.

Hoffman, Daniel. *Form and Fable in American Fiction*. New York: Oxford University Press, 1961.

Hunter, Mollie. "One World." *The Horn Book Magazine* 51 (December 1975):557–63; 52 (February 1976):32–38.

Irwin, W. R. *The Game of the Impossible: A Rhetoric of Fantasy*. Urbuna, Ill.: University of Illinois Press, 1976.

Le Guin, Ursula K. *From Elfand to Poughkeepsie*. Portland, Ore.: Pendragon Press, 1973.

———. *The Language of the Night*. Edited by Susan Wood. New York: G. P. Putnam's Sons, 1979.

Lewis, C. S. *An Experiment in Criticism*. Cambridge: Cambridge University Press, 1961.

———. *Of Other Worlds*. Edited by Walter Hooper. New York: Harcourt, Brace & World, Inc., 1966.

———. *Selected Literary Essays*. Edited by Walter Hooper. Cambridge: Cambridge University Press, 1969.

Lochhead, Marion. *The Renaissance of Wonder in Children's Literature*. Edinburgh: Canongate Publishing Limited, 1977.

Lovecraft, H. P. *Supernatural Horror in Literature*. 1927. Reprint. New York: Dover Publications, Inc., 1973.

MacDonald, George. *The Gifts of the Child Christ: Fairy Tales and Stories for The Childlike*. Edited by Glenn Edward Sadler. 2 Vols. Grands Rapids, Mich.: William B. Eerdmans Publishing Company, 1973.

Manlove, C. N. *Modern Fantasy: Five Studies*. Cambridge: Cambridge University Press, 1975.

Mobley, Jane. "Magic Is Alive: A Study of Contemporary Fantasy Fiction." Ph.D. dissertation, University of Kansas, 1974.

———. "Toward a Definition of Fantasy Fiction." *Extrapolation* 15 (1973–74): 117–28.

Mosaic 10, no. 2 (Winter 1976–77). Special issue on "Faerie, Fantasy, & Pseudo-Mediaevalia in Twentieth-Century Literature."

Penzoldt, Peter. *The Supernatural in Fiction*. 1952. Reprint. New York: Humanities Press, 1965.

Porte, Joel. *The Romance in America: Studies in Cooper, Poe, Hawthorne, Melville, and James*. Middletown, Conn.: Wesleyan University Press, 1969.

Prickett, Stephen. *Victorian Fantasy*. Bloomington and London: Indiana University Press, 1979.

Rabkin, Eric S. *The Fantastic in Literature*. Princeton, N. J.: Princeton University Press, 1976.

Reeve, Clara. *The Progress of Romance*. 1785. Reprint. New York: The Facsimile Text Society, 1930.

Ross, Eugene Garland, Jr. "The American Novel of Fantasy." Ph.D. dissertation, University of Virginia, 1949.

Sale, Roger. *Fairy Tales and After: From Snow White to E. B. White*. Cambridge: Harvard University Press, 1978.

———. *Modern Heroism: Essays on D. H. Lawrence, William Empson, & J. R. R. Tolkien*. Berkeley and Los Angeles: University of California Press, 1973.

Sanders, Joseph Lee. "Fantasy in the Twentieth Century British Novel." Ph.D. dissertation, Indiana University, 1972.

Scarborough, Dorothy. *The Supernatural in Modern English Fiction.* New York: G. P. Putnam's Sons, 1917.

Scholes, Robert. *Structural Fabulation: An Essay on Fiction of the Future.* Notre Dame: University of Notre Dame Press, 1975.

———, and Kellogg, Robert. *The Nature of Narrative.* New York: Oxford University Press, 1966.

Thalmann, Marianne. *The Romantic Fairy Tale: Seeds of Surrealism.* Translated by Mary B. Corcoran. Ann Arbor: The University of Michigan Press, 1964.

Todorov, Tzvetan. *The Fantastic: A Structural Approach to a Literary Genre.* Translated by Richard Howard. Cleveland: Case Western Reserve University Press, 1973.

Tolkien, J. R. R. *Tree and Leaf.* Boston: Houghton Mifflin Company, 1965.

Wolfe, Gary K. "Symbolic Fantasy." *Genre* 8 (September 1975):194–209.

WORKS ON SUPERNATURAL LORE AND AMERICAN FOLKLORE

Aarne, Antti, and Thompson, Stith. *The Types of the Folk-Tale.* 2d revision. Helsinki: Suomalainen Tiedeakatemia, 1961.

Baughman, Ernest W. *Type and Motif Index of the Folktales of England and North America.* Indiana University Folklore Series, no. 20. The Hague: Mouton & Co., 1961.

Briggs, Katharine. *An Encyclopedia of Fairies: Hobgoblins, Brownies, Bogies, and Other Supernatural Creatures.* New York: Pantheon Books, 1976.

———. *The Fairies in English Tradition and Literature.* Chicago: The University of Chicago Press, 1967.

———, and Tongue, Ruth L., eds. *Folktales of England.* Chicago: The University of Chicago Press, 1965.

Campbell, Marie. *Tales from the Cloud Walking Country.* Bloomington, Ind.: Indiana University Press, 1958.

Chase, Richard. *The Jack Tales.* Boston: Houghton Mifflin Company, 1943.

Child, Francis James. *The English and Scottish Popular Ballads.* 5 vols. Boston and New York: Houghton, Mifflin and Company, 1898.

Coffin, Tristram P. *The British Traditional Ballad in North America.* Rev. ed. Austin: University of Texas Press, 1977.

Dégh, Linda. *Folktales and Society: Story-Telling in a Hungarian Peasant Community.* Translated by Emily M. Schossberger. Bloomington, Ind.: Indiana University Press, 1969.

Dorson, Richard M. *America in Legend: Folklore from the Colonial Period to the Present.* New York: Pantheon Books, 1973.

———. *American Folklore and the Historian.* Chicago: The University of Chicago Press, 1971.

———. *Jonathan Draws the Long Bow.* Cambridge, Mass.: Harvard University Press, 1946.

Drake, Samuel Adams. *A Book of New England Legends and Folklore, In Prose and Poetry.* 1883. Reprint. Boston: Little,.Brown and Company, 1910.

———. *The Myths and Fables of To-Day.* Boston: Lee and Shepard, 1900.

Drake, Samuel G. *Annals of Witchcraft in New England: and Elsewhere in the United States, From their First Settlement.* 1869. Reprint. New York: Benjamin Blom, Inc., 1967.

Hand, Wayland D., ed. *American Folk Legend: A Symposium.* Berkeley and Los Angeles: University of California Press, 1971.

Hoffman, Daniel. *Paul Bunyan: Last of the Frontier Demigods.* New York: Temple University Publications, 1952.

Keightley, Thomas. *The Fairy Mythology.* Rev. ed. London: H. G. Bohn, 1850.
Kirk, Robert. *The Secret Common-Wealth.* Edited by Stewart Sanderson. Cambridge: D. S. Brewer Ltd., 1975.
Laws, G. Malcolm, Jr. *Native American Balladry.* Philadelphia: The American Folklore Society, 1964.
Lüthi, Max. *Once Upon a Time: On the Nature of Fairy Tales.* Translated by Lee Chadeayne and Paul Gottwald. Bloomington, Ind.: Indiana University Press, 1976.
Propp, Vladimir. *Morphology of the Folktale.* Translated by Laurence Scott. 2d ed. Revised and edited by Louis A. Wagner. Austin: University of Texas Press, 1968.
Randolph, Vance. *Ozark Magic and Folklore.* 1947. Reprint. New York: Dover Publications, Inc., 1964.
––––––. *Who Blowed Up the Church House? and Other Ozark Folk Tales.* New York: Columbia University Press, 1952.
Roberts, Leonard. *Old Greasybeard: Tales from the Cumberland Gap.* Detroit, Mich.: Folklore Associates, Inc., 1969.
Rourke, Constance. *American Humor: A Study of the National Character.* 1931. Reprint. New York: Harcourt Brace Jovanovich, Inc., 1959.
Skinner, Charles Montgomery. *Myths and Legends of Our Own Land.* 2 vols. Philadelphia: J. B. Lippincott Company, 1896.
Thompson, Stith. *The Folktale.* New York: Holt, Rinehart and Winston, 1946.
––––––. *Motif-Index of Folk-Literature.* Rev. ed. 6 vols. Bloomington, Ind.: Indiana University Press, 1955–58.
Whittier, John Greenleaf. *The Supernaturalism of New England.* Edited by Edward Wagenknecht. Norman, Ok.: University of Oklahoma Press, 1969.
Wimberley, Lowry Charles. *Folklore in the English and Scottish Ballads.* Chicago: The University of Chicago Press, 1928.

SECONDARY WORKS ON AMERICAN FANTASISTS

The American Book Collector 13 (December 1962). Special issue on Oz.
Baum, Frank Joslyn, and MacFall, Russell P. *To Please a Child: A Biography of L. Frank Baum, Royal Historian of Oz.* Chicago: Reilly & Lee Co., 1961.
The Baum Bugle. 1957–date.
Cabell, James Branch. *Beyond Life: Dizain des Demiurges.* New York: Robert M. McBride & Company, 1919.
––––––. *Straws and Prayer-Books: Dizain des Diversions.* New York: Robert M. McBride & Company, 1924.
The Cabellian. 1968–72.
de Camp, L. Sprague. *Lovecraft: A Biography.* Garden City, N.Y.: Doubleday & Company, Inc., 1975.
Egoff, Sheila, Stubbs, G. T., and Ashley, L. F., eds. *Only Connect: Readings on Children's Literature.* New York: Oxford University Press, 1969.
Erisman, Fred Raymond. "There Was a Child Went Forth: A Study of *St. Nicholas Magazine* and Selected Children's Authors, 1890–1915." Ph.D. dissertation, University of Minnesota, 1966.
Gardner, Martin, and Nye, Russel B. *The Wizard of Oz & Who He Was.* East Lansing, Mich.: Michigan State University Press, 1957.
Griffin, Martin I. *J. Frank R. Stockton: A Critical Biography.* Philadelphia: University of Pennsylvania Press, 1939.
Holmes, Charles S. *The Clocks of Columbus: The Literary Career of James Thurber.* New York: Atheneum, 1972.
Jordan, Alice M. *From Rollo to Tom Sawyer: and Other Papers.* Boston: The Horn Book Inc., 1948.

Lanes, Selma. *Down the Rabbit Hole: Adventures and Misadventures in the Realm of Children's Literature.* 1971. Reprint. New York: Atheneum, 1976.

Leyda, Jay. *The Melville Log: A Documentary Life of Herman Melville 1819-1891.* 2 vols. New York: Harcourt, Brace and Company, 1951.

Littlefield, Henry M. "The Wizard of Oz: Parable on Populism." *American Quarterly* 16 (Spring 1964):47-58.

Lupoff, Richard. *Edgar Rice Burroughs: Master of Adventure.* New York: Canaveral Press, 1965.

Mencken, H. L., Van Doren, Carl, and Walpole, Hugh. *James Branch Cabell: Three Essays.* Port Washington, N. Y.: Kennikat Press, 1967.

Moore, Raylyn. *Wonderful Wizard Marvelous Land.* Bowling Green, Ohio: Bowling Green University Popular Press, 1974.

Nesbitt, Elizabeth. *Howard Pyle.* A Walck Monograph. New York: Henry Z. Walck, Incorporated, 1966.

Porges, Irwin. *Edgar Rice Burroughs: The Man Who Created Tarzan.* Provo, Utah: Brigham Young University Press, 1975.

Redden, Sister Mary Maurita. *The Gothic Fiction in the American Magazines.* Washington, D. C.: The Catholic University of America Press, 1939.

St. Armand, Barton Levi. *The Roots of Horror in the Fiction of H. P. Lovecraft.* Elizabethtown, N. Y.: Dragon Press, 1977.

Shreffler, Philip A. *The H. P. Lovecraft Companion.* Westport, Conn.: Greenwood Press, 1977.

Tarrant, Desmond. *James Branch Cabell: The Dream and the Reality.* Norman, Ok.: University of Oklahoma Press, 1967.

Tobias, Richard C. *The Art of James Thurber.* Athens, Ohio: Ohio University Press, 1969.

Wagenknecht, Edward. *As Far As Yesterday: Memories and Reflections.* Norman, Ok.: University of Oklahoma Press, 1968.

_____. *Utopia Americana.* University of Washington Chapbooks, no. 28. Seattle: University of Washington Bookstore, 1929.

Wells, Arvin. *Jesting Moses: A Study in Cabellian Comedy.* Gainesville: University of Florida Press, 1962.

AMERICAN TALES (AND OCCASIONAL POEMS) OF THE IMAGINATION

Akers, Dwight. *The King's Mule.* New York: The Junior Library Guild, and Minton, Balch & Company, 1933.

Alexander, Lloyd. *The Black Cauldron.* New York: Holt, Rinehart and Winston, 1965.

_____. *The Book of Three.* New York: Holt, Rinehart and Winston, 1964.

_____. *The Castle of Llyr.* New York: Holt, Rinehart and Winston, 1966.

_____. *The High King.* New York: Holt, Rinehart and Winston, 1968.

_____. *Taran Wanderer.* New York: Holt, Rinehart and Winston, 1967.

Austin, Jane G. *Fairy Dreams; or, Wanderings in Elf-Land.* Boston: J. E. Tilton and Company, 1859.

Babbitt, Natalie. *The Search for Delicious.* New York: Farrar, Straus and Giroux, 1969.

Bailey, Carolyn Sherwin. *Miss Hickory.* New York: The Viking Press, 1946.

Baker, Virginia. *Prince Carrotte: and Other Chronicles.* Boston: Press of Rockwell and Churchill, 1881.

Baum, L. Frank, *American Fairy Tales.* 1901. Reprint. New York: Dover Publications, Inc., 1979.

_____. *The Annotated Wizard of Oz.* Edited by Michael Patrick Hearn. New York: Clarkson N. Potter, Inc., 1973.

_____. *Babes in Birdland: A Nature Fairy Tale.* Chicago: The Reilly & Britton Co., 1911.

_____. *Dorothy and the Wizard In Oz.* Chicago: The Reilly & Lee Co., 1908.

_____. *Dot and Tot of Merryland.* Indianapolis: The Bobbs-Merrill Company, 1901.

_____. *The Emerald City of Oz.* Chicago: The Reilly & Lee Co., 1910.

_____. *The Enchanted Island of Yew: Whereon Prince Marvel Encountered the High Ki of Twi and Other Surprising People.* Chicago: M. A. Donohue & Company, 1903.

_____. *Glinda of Oz.* Chicago: The Reilly & Lee Co., 1920.

_____. *John Dough and the Cherub.* Chicago: The Reilly & Lee Co., 1906.

_____. *The Land of Oz.* Chicago: The Reilly & Lee Co., 1904.

_____. *The Life and Adventures of Santa Claus.* 1902. Reprint. New York: Dover Publications, Inc., 1976.

_____. *The Lost Princess of Oz.* Chicago: The Reilly & Lee Co., 1917.

_____. *The Magic of Oz.* Chicago: The Reilly & Lee Co., 1919.

_____. *The Magical Monarch of Mo.* Originally *A New Wonderland,* 1900. Revised and retitled, 1903. Reprint. New York: Dover Publications, Inc., 1968.

_____. *The Master Key: An Electrical Fairy Tale.* 1901. Reprint. Westport, Conn.: Hyperion Press, Inc., 1974.

_____. *Mother Goose in Prose.* 1897. Reprint. Indianapolis: The Bobbs-Merrill Company, 1905.

_____. *Ozma of Oz.* Chicago: The Reilly & Lee Co., 1907.

_____. *The Patchwork Girl of Oz.* Chicago: The Reilly & Lee Co., 1913.

_____. *Rinkitink in Oz.* Chicago: The Reilly & Lee Co., 1916.

_____. *The Road to Oz.* Chicago: The Reilly & Lee Co., 1909.

_____. *The Scarecrow of Oz.* Chicago: The Reilly & Lee Co., 1915.

_____. *The Sea Fairies.* Chicago: The Reilly & Lee Co., 1911.

_____. *Sky Island.* Chicago: The Reilly & Lee Co., 1912.

_____. *Tik-Tok of Oz.* Chicago: The Reilly & Lee Co., 1914.

_____. *The Tin Woodman of Oz.* Chicago: The Reilly & Lee Co., 1918.

Beagle, Peter. *A Fine and Private Place.* New York: Dell Publishing Company, 1963.

_____. *The Last Unicorn.* New York: The Viking Press, Inc., 1968.

Binns, Archie. *The Radio Imp.* Philadelphia: John C. Winston Company, 1950.

Blish, James. *There Shall Be No Darkness.* With Leiber, *Conjure Wife,* and Pratt, *The Blue Star,* in *Witches Three.* New York: Twayne Publishers, Inc., 1952.

Bond, Nancy. *A String in the Harp.* New York: Atheneum, 1977.

Boucher, Anthony. *The Compleat Werewolf.* New York: Simon and Schuster, 1969.

Bradbury, Ray. *Dandelion Wine.* Garden City, N. Y.: Doubleday & Company, Inc., 1957.

_____. *The Illustrated Man.* Garden City, N. Y.: Doubleday & Company, Inc., 1951.

_____. *The Martian Chronicles.* Garden City, N. Y.: Doubleday & Company, Inc., 1958.

_____. *The October Country.* New York: Alfred A. Knopf, 1970.

_____. *Something Wicked This Way Comes.* New York: Simon & Schuster, Inc., 1962.

Burkhardt, C. B. *Fairy Tales and Legends of Many Nations.* New York: Baker and Scribner, 1849.

Burroughs, Edgar Rice. *The Gods of Mars.* 1912. Reprint. New York: Ballantine Books, 1963.

———. *A Princess of Mars.* 1912. Reprint. New York: Ballantine Books, 1963.

———. *The Warlord of Mars.* 1913–14. Reprint. New York: Ballantine Books, 1963.

Cabell, James Branch. *The Cream of the Jest: A Comedy of Evasions.* New York: The Modern Library, 1917.

———. *Figures of Earth: A Comedy of Appearances.* 1921. Reprint. New York: Robert M. McBride & Company, 1926.

———. *The High Place: A Comedy of Disenchantment.* New York: Robert M. McBride & Company, 1923.

———. *Jurgen: A Comedy of Justice.* 1919. Reprint in The Kalki Edition. New York: Robert M. McBride & Company, 1927.

———. *The Silver Stallion: A Comedy of Redemption.* The Kalki Edition. New York: Robert M. McBride & Company, 1926.

———. *Something about Eve: A Comedy of Fig-leaves.* New York: Robert M. McBride & Company, 1927.

———. *The Soul of Melicent.* New York: Frederick A. Stokes & Co., 1913. Revised and retitled *Domnei: A Comedy of Woman-Worship.* New York: Robert M. McBride & Company, 1920.

———. *The Witch-Woman.* New York: Farrar, Straus & Co., 1948.

Cameron, Eleanor. *The Court of the Stone Children.* New York: E. P. Dutton & Co., Inc., 1973.

———. *The Wonderful Flight to the Mushroom Planet.* Boston: Little, Brown and Company, 1954.

de Camp, L. Sprague. *The Tritonian Ring.* New York: Twayne Publishers, Inc., 1953.

Carryll, Charles E. *Davy and the Goblin, or, What Followed Reading "Alice's Adventures in Wonderland."* Boston: Ticknor and Company, 1886.

Child, L. Maria, ed. *Rainbows for Children.* New York: C. S. Francis & Co., 1848.

Clemens, Samuel. *The Complete Short Stories of Mark Twain.* Edited by Charles Neider. Garden City, N. Y.: Doubleday & Company, Inc., 1957.

———. *A Connecticut Yankee in King Arthur's Court.* Harper & Brothers ed. New York: P. F. Collier & Son Company, 1889.

Commager, Henry Steele, ed. *The St. Nicholas Anthology.* New York: Random House, Inc., 1948.

Cranch, Christopher Pearse. *Kobboltozo: A Sequel to the Last of the Hugger-muggers.* Boston: Phillips, Sampson and Company, 1857.

———. *The Last of the Huggermuggers, A Giant Story.* Boston: Phillips, Sampson, and Company, 1856.

Curran, Ronald, ed. *Witches, Wraiths & Warlocks: Supernatural Tales of the American Renaissance.* Greenwich, Conn.: Fawcett Publications, Inc., 1971.

Curry, Jane Louise. *The Birdstones.* New York: Atheneum, 1977.

Donaldson, Stephen R. *The Chronicles of Thomas Covenant the Unbeliever.* 3 vols. New York: Holt, Rinehart and Winston, 1977.

Drake, Joseph Rodman. *The Culprit Fay, and Other Poems.* New York: George Dearborn, Publisher, 1835.

Eager, Edward. *Half Magic.* New York: Harcourt, Brace & Company, Inc., 1954.

———. *Knight's Castle.* New York: Harcourt, Brace & World, Inc., 1956.

———. *Magic by the Lake.* New York: Harcourt, Brace & Company, Inc., 1957.

———. *Magic or Not.* New York: Harcourt, Brace & World, Inc., 1959.

———. *Seven-Day Magic.* New York: Harcourt, Brace & World, Inc., 1962.

———. *The Time Garden.* New York: Harcourt, Brace & World, Inc., 1958.

———. *The Well Wishers.* New York: Harcourt, Brace & World, Inc., 1960.

Eggleston, Edward. *The Schoolmaster's Stories, for Boys and Girls.* Boston: Henry L. Shepard & Co., 1874.

Enright, Elizabeth. *Tatsinda.* New York: Harcourt, Brace & World, Inc., 1963.

Farmer, C. M. *The Fairy of the Stream, and Other Poems.* Richmond, Va.: Harrold & Murray, 1847.

Fenton, Edward. *The Nine Questions.* Garden City, N. Y.: Doubleday & Company, Inc., 1959.

_____. *Once Upon a Saturday.* Garden City, N. Y.: Doubleday & Company, Inc., 1958.

Finney, Charles G. *The Circus of Dr. Lao.* 1935. Reprint. New York: Bantam Books, Inc., 1964.

Gibson, Eva Katharine. *Zauberlinda the Wise Witch.* Chicago: Robt. Smith Printing Co., 1901.

Gibson, William. *A Vision of Faeryland, and Other Poems.* Boston and Cambridge: James Munroe and Company, 1853.

Goodrich, S. G. *Fairy Land, and Other Sketches for Youth.* Boston: James Murve and Co., 1844.

Grabo, Carl. *The Cat in Grandfather's House.* New York: Laidlaw Bros., Inc., 1929.

Harney, John Milton. *Crystalina; A Fairy Tale.* New York: George F. Hopkins, 1816.

Hawthorne, Nathaniel. *The Centenary Edition of the Works of Nathaniel Hawthorne.* 13 vols. Edited by William Charvat, Roy Harvey Pearce, Claude M. Simpson, et al. Columbus, Ohio: Ohio State University Press, 1962–77.

Heinlein, Robert. *Three by Heinlein.* Including *The Puppet Masters, Waldo,* and *Magic, Inc.* Garden City, N. Y.: Doubleday & Company, Inc., 1965.

_____. *The Unpleasant Profession of Jonathan Hoag.* Hicksville, N. Y.: Gnome Press, Inc., 1959.

Irving, Washington. *Irving's Works.* Geoffrey Crayon Edition. 27 vols. New York: G. P. Putnam's Sons, 1880–.

_____. *Tales of a Traveller.* Vol. 4, The Author's Revised Edition. New York: G. P. Putnam's Sons, 1888.

Jackson, Shirley. *The Sundial.* 1958. Reprint. New York: Ace Books, Inc., n.d.

Jarrell, Randall. *The Animal Family.* New York: Pantheon Books, 1965.

Johnson, Virginia W. *The Catskill Fairies.* New York: Harper & Brothers, Publishers, 1876.

Juster, Norton. *The Phantom Tollbooth.* New York: Random House, 1961.

Kendall, Carol. *The Gammage Cup.* New York: Harcourt, Brace & World, Inc., 1959.

Kuttner, Henry. *The Best of Henry Kuttner, Vol. I.* London: Mayflower Books, 1965.

Le Guin, Ursula K. *City of Illusions.* New York: Harper & Row, Publishers, 1967.

_____. *The Dispossessed.* New York: Harper & Row, Publishers, 1974.

_____. *The Farthest Shore.* New York: Atheneum, 1972.

_____. *The Lathe of Heaven.* New York: Charles Scribner's Sons, 1971.

_____. *The Left Hand of Darkness.* New York: Ace Books, 1969. Reprint with new introduction by the author, 1976.

_____. *Planet of Exile.* New York: Ace Books, 1966.

_____. *Rocannon's World.* New York: Ace Books, 1966.

_____. *The Tombs of Atuan.* New York: Atheneum, 1971.

_____. *The Wind's Twelve Quarters.* New York: Harper & Row, Publishers, Inc., 1975.

_____. *A Wizard of Earthsea.* Berkeley, Cal.: Parnassus Press, 1968.

_____. "The Word for World Is Forest." In *Again, Dangerous Visions,* edited by Harlan Ellison. Garden City, N. Y.: Doubleday & Company., Inc., 1972. Reprint. New York: Berkley Publishing Corp., 1976.

Leiber, Fritz. *Conjure Wife*. With Blish, *There Shall Be No Darkness*, and Pratt, *The Blue Star*, in *Witches Three*. New York: Twayne Publishers, Inc., 1952.

L'Engle, Madeleine. *A Swiftly Tilting Planet*. New York: Farrar, Straus and Giroux, 1978.

———. *A Wind in the Door*. London: Methuen & Co., Ltd., 1975.

———. *A Wrinkle in Time*. New York: Farrar, Straus and Giroux, 1962.

Lovecraft, H. P. *At the Mountains of Madness: and Other Novels*. Selected by August Derleth. Sauk City, Wisc.: Arkham House, Publishers, 1964.

———. *Dagon: and Other Macabre Tales*. Selected by August Derleth. Sauk City, Wisc.: Arkham House, Publishers, 1965.

McHargue, Georgess. *Stoneflight*. New York: The Viking Press, 1975.

McKillip, Patricia A. *Harpist in the Wind*. New York: Atheneum, 1979.

———. *Heir of Sea and Fire*. New York: Atheneum, 1977.

———. *The Riddle Master of Hed*. New York: Atheneum, 1976.

Melville, Herman. *The Works of Herman Melville*. Standard ed. 16 vols. London: Constable and Company Ltd., 1922–24.

Merritt, Abraham. *The Face in the Abyss*. 1931. Reprint. New York: The Macmillan Company, 1961.

Nathan, Robert. *Portrait of Jennie*. New York: Alfred A. Knopf, Inc., 1940.

Norton, Andre (Alice Mary). *Witch World*. New York: Ace Books, 1963.

Ormondroyd, Edward. *Time at the Top*. Berkeley, Cal.: Parnassus Press, 1963.

Paulding, James Kirke. *The Book of Saint Nicholas*. New York: Harper & Brothers, 1836.

———. *A Christmas Gift from Fairyland*. New York: D. Appleton & Co., 1838.

Poe, Edgar Allan. *Collected Works of Edgar Allan Poe*. Edited by Thomas Ollive Mabbott. Cambridge, Mass.: Harvard University Press, 1969–.

Pratt, Fletcher. *The Blue Star*. With Blish, *There Shall Be No Darkness*, and Leiber, *Conjure Wife*, in *Witches Three*. New York: Twayne Publishers, Inc., 1952.

———. *The Incomplete Enchanter*. New York: Henry Holt & Company, Inc., 1941.

———, and de Camp, L. Sprague. *Land of Unreason*. New York: Henry Holt & Company, Inc., 1942.

Pyle, Howard. *The Garden behind the Moon: A Real Story of the Moon Angel*. New York: Charles Scribner's Sons, 1895.

———. *Pepper & Salt, or Seasoning for Young Folk*. New York: Harper and Brothers, 1885.

———. *The Wonder Clock: or Four and Twenty Marvellous Tales, Being One for Each Hour of the Day*. 1887. Reprint. New York: Harper & Row, Publishers, 1915.

Richards, Laura. *Toto's Merry Winter*. Boston: Roberts Brothers, 1877.

Selden, George. *The Genie of Sutton Place*. New York: Farrar, Straus and Giroux, 1973.

Smith, Thorne, *Topper*. New York: Robert M. McBride and Company, 1926.

Stockton, Frank R. *Stories III. The Novels and Stories of Frank R. Stockton*. New York: Charles Scribner's Sons, 1900.

———. *Ting-a-Ling Tales*. 1870. Reprint. New York: Charles Scribner's Sons, 1882.

Sturgeon, Theodore (Edward Hamilton Waldo). *E Pluribus Unicorn*. New York: Abelard-Schuman, Ltd., 1953.

Thurber, James. *Alarms and Diversions*. New York: Harper & Brothers, Publishers, 1957.

———. *Lanterns and Lances*. New York: Harper & Brothers, Publishers, 1961.

———. *Men, Women and Dogs*. 1943. Reprint. New York: Dodd, Mead & Company, 1975.

_____. *The 13 Clocks*. New York: Simon and Schuster, 1950.

_____. *The Thurber Carnival*. New York: Harper & Brothers, 1945.

_____. *The White Deer*. New York: Harcourt, Brace and World, Inc., 1945.

Varley, John. *Titan*. New York: Berkley Publishing Corp., 1979.

Wentworth, May. *Fairy Tales from Gold Lands*. The Golden Gate Series. San Francisco: A. Roman & Company, Publishers, 1867.

Wesselhoeft, Lily F. *The Fairy-Folk of Blue Hill*. Boston: Joseph Knight Company, 1895.

Weston, H. H., Clark, C., and Gibbons, L. *The Fairy Egg: and What It Held*. Boston: Fields, Osgood, & Co., 1870.

White, E. B. *Charlotte's Web*. New York: Harper & Row, Publishers, 1952.

_____. *Stuart Little*. New York: Harper & Row, Publishers, 1945.

_____. *The Trumpet of the Swan*. New York: Harper & Row, Publishers, 1970.

Zelazny, Roger. *The Courts of Chaos*. Garden City, N. Y.: Doubleday and Company, Inc., 1978.

_____. *The Guns of Avalon*. Garden City, N. Y.: Doubleday and Company, Inc., 1972.

_____. *The Hand of Oberon*. Garden City, N. Y.: Doubleday and Company, Inc., 1976.

_____. *Nine Princes in Amber*. Garden City, N. Y.: Doubleday and Company, Inc., 1970.

_____. *Sign of the Unicorn*. Garden City, N. Y.: Doubleday and Company, Inc., 1975.

Index

Alexander, Lloyd, 156-57
Allegory, 43, 127-28
Austin, Jane, 65
Austin, William: "Peter Rugg, the Missing Man," 29, 55

Bailey, Carolyn Sherwin, 152
Baker, Virginia, 68
Ballads, 17-21, 33; British, 17-19; American, 19-21. *See also* Folklore, supernatural
Baughman, Ernest W., 21, 46
Baum, L. Frank, 82-110, 133-34, 136, 141-42, 145-47, 149, 160, 168, 183-84; American geography transformed in, 85-90; "Aunt Jane's nieces" stories, 88; and Carroll, 95-96, 98; *Dorothy and the Wizard in Oz*, 94; early works of, 93; *The Emerald City of Oz*, 85, 95, 103, 149; exploration theme in, 87, 97; fairy tale morphology in, 91-95; and folklore, 91, 94-95; *Glinda of Oz*, 95, 99; *The Land of Oz*, 94, 99, 101; *The Magic of Oz*, 103; magical characters in, 99-104; meaning in, 102, 104-107; *A New Wonderland*, 93; *Ozma of Oz*, 94; *The Patchwork Girl of Oz*, 103, 107; and Populism, 86-87; *Queen Zixi of Ix*, 93-94, *Rinkitink in Oz*, 95; *The Road to Oz*, 85, 87, 94, 107; *The Scarecrow of Oz*, 94; *Tik-Tok of Oz*, 95; utopianism of, 85; *The Wizard of Oz*, 83-96, 98-100
Beagle, Peter, 139, 158-59; *A Fine and Private Place*, 158; *The Last Unicorn*, 139, 158-59; and Tolkien, 158-59
Bellamy, Edward, 59, 88
Bettelheim, Bruno, 5
Binns, Archie, 152
Bloch, Robert, 152
Bodkin, Maud, 34
Boucher, Anthony, 152
Bradbury, Ray, 133-41, 172, 177, 184; and Baum, 136; and Burroughs, 135-36; *Dandelion Wine*, 136-37, 140; "The Exiles," 136; and Lovecraft, 135; *The Martian Chronicles*, 135; and Melville, 138-39; *Something Wicked This Way Comes*, 136-40
Bradley, Marion Zimmer, 163
Briggs, Katharine, 22-23

Brooks, Terry, 155
Bunyan, Paul, 22
Burkhardt, C. B., 63-64
Burroughs, Edgar Rice, 110-19, 122, 128-29, 133, 135-36, 172, 183; and Baum, 110; *The Gods of Mars*, 116; heroic fantasy in, 113-16; *A Princess of Mars*, 111-16; *Tarzan of the Apes*, 111; *The Warlord of Mars*, 116

Cabell, James Branch, 110, 118-29, 183-85; allegory in, 127-28; *The Cream of the Jest*, 122-23; critical reception of, 120; *Jurgen*, 120, 122-28; and Pyle, 121-22; *Something about Eve*, 122; *The Soul of Melicent*, 122; sources of, 120-21, 123, 126; *Straws and Prayer Books*, 120-21
Cameron, Eleanor, 34, 152-53
de Camp, L. Sprague, 152
Carroll, Lewis, 67, 95-96, 98, 149
Carryll, Charles, 67-68, 96
Child, Lydia M., 63-64
Children's literature, American, 59-83, 107, 109, 134-35, 141-44, 152-53
Clemens, Samuel, 55, 79-81, 97, 110, 149
Coffin, Tristram, 17
Coleridge, Samuel Taylor, 33-34
Cranch, Christopher, 76-80, 110; *Kobboltozo*, 76, *The Last of the Huggermuggers*, 76-77
Crane, T. F., 65

Dégh, Linda, 4, 20, 26
Donaldson, Stephen, 158-60
Dorson, Richard, 23-25, 27
Drake, Joseph Rodman: "The Culprit Fay," 28-29, 75, 104, 183
Drake, Samuel Adams, 28
Dunsany, Lord Edward, 129-30, 135, 184

Eager, Edward, 134, 141-44, 184; and Baum, 141-42; *Half Magic*, 141-44; *Knight's Castle*, 144; *Magic by the Lake*, 144; and Nesbit, 141-44; rules of magic in, 143; *Seven-Day Magic*, 141-42; *The Time Garden*, 144
Eggleston, Edward, 78-79, 86
Eliot, T. S., 170, 181-83

210